The Student Guide to Freire's *Pedagogy of the Oppressed*

Also available from Bloomsbury

Education for Critical Consciousness, Paulo Freire
Paulo Freire, Daniel Schugurensky
Paulo Freire's Intellectual Roots, edited by Robert Lake and Tricia Kress
Paulo Freire's Philosophy of Education, Jones Irwin
Pedagogy of Hope, Paulo Freire
Pedagogy of the Heart, Paulo Freire
Pedagogy of the Oppressed, 50th Anniversary Edition, Paulo Freire

The Student Guide to Freire's
Pedagogy of the Oppressed

Antonia Darder

BLOOMSBURY ACADEMIC
LONDON • NEW YORK • OXFORD • NEW DELHI • SYDNEY

BLOOMSBURY ACADEMIC
Bloomsbury Publishing Plc
50 Bedford Square, London, WC1B 3DP, UK
1385 Broadway, New York, NY 10018, USA
29 Earlsfort Terrace, Dublin 2, Ireland

BLOOMSBURY, BLOOMSBURY ACADEMIC and the Diana logo are trademarks of
Bloomsbury Publishing Plc

First published in Great Britain 2018
This edition published 2024

A catalogue record for this book is available from the British Library.

A catalog record for this book is available from the Library of Congress.

ISBN: HB: 978-1-3501-9005-4
PB: 978-1-3501-9006-1
ePDF: 978-1-3501-9002-3
eBook: 978-1-3501-9003-0

Typeset by Deanta Global Publishing Services, Chennai, India
Printed and bound in Great Britain

To find out more about our authors and books visit www.bloomsbury.com and
sign up for our newsletters.

This book is dedicated to the memory of Paulo Freire, whose work continues to inspire new generations of revolutionaries committed to a more just and loving world.

Contents

Figures

Preface

I believe, or rather I am convinced, that we have never needed radical positions, in the sense of the radicalness I advocate in Pedagogy of the Oppressed, as we need them today.

—Paulo Freire (2002)

As the world emerges from the pandemic crisis of the last three years, everywhere populations must contend with the growing authoritarian climate of neoliberal fascism.[1] Revolutionary educators around the globe have faced agonizing difficulties in their efforts to preserve Paulo Freire's dream for a more just and loving world. In Freire's own beloved Brazil, the country's former right-wing reactionary government, led by Jair Bolsonaro, sought to "rid references to LGBTQ and feminist theory, along with famed socialist educator, Paulo Freire," according to Brazilian news sources.[2] Yet, in the face of this political arrogance and the neoliberal logic of greed and profit that informed these outlandish attacks, educators worldwide gathered in a variety of virtual forums to celebrate and commemorate Paulo Freire's 100th birthday. The huge success of these conferences and symposiums, in the midst of a debilitating pandemic, helped to illustrate that, despite efforts to extinguish his legacy, Paulo Freire's ideas continue to flourish through innovative readings of his works and the reinventions of his ideas. So much so that more than fifty years after the first publishing of *Pedagogy of the Oppressed*, Walter Kohan (2021) reminds us that Freire is needed *more than ever*.

In pondering his history and contributions, what is important to acknowledge here is that Paulo Freire must be better understood as an early

---

[1] See: https://camri.ac.uk/blog/Articles/henry-a-giroux-and-the-culture-of-neoliberal-fascism/.
[2] See: https://www.telesurenglish.net/news/Bolsonaro-To-Erase-Paulo-Freire-and-Feminism-From-Textbooks-20190212-0018.html.

epistemologist of the South[3] (Santos, 2007). That is to say, his epistemological sensibilities emerge directly from his contestation of what Quijano (2000) calls the *coloniality of power* inherent in Brazilian society of the early twentieth century. Brazil was then and continues to be a country rooted in a political economy that thrives, more often than not, on the poverty of the majority of its people. Freire witnessed, over his life, a moral disregard for the casualties that capitalism left behind, despite the widespread presence of government and church institutions in Latin America and other parts of the world, which often turned a deaf ear and blind eye to human suffering. In the 1960s, the decade in which *Pedagogy of the Oppressed* was conceived, Brazil, as a nation, was heavily embroiled in a contentious politics historically linked to its "damaging legacy of Portuguese colonialism, and . . . its own complex internal politics" (Irwin, 2012, p. 2). In response, Freire's epistemological interventions can be understood in sync with the anti-colonial preoccupations of Latin American philosophers on the left as well as revolutionary writers such as Frantz Fanon, Albert Memmi, Aime Cesaire, Julius Nyerere, and Amilcar Cabral. In an unapologetic acknowledgment of the brutality of human oppression, Freire's *Pedagogy of the Oppressed* sought to intentionally shift the focus away from a dehumanizing and debilitating epistemology of knowledge construction toward a liberating and humanizing one. In this way, Freire's approach was imbued with an early decolonizing sensibility that directly connected material conditions of oppression to the brutal forces of cultural invasion imposed on the oppressed in Brazil and other parts of the world.

However, beyond these philosophical concerns, what often is left unacknowledged is the recognition of Freire's distinct cultural origins, which are fully situated within both an early-twentieth-century colonizing context of Latin America and an early Southern epistemological formation, which defies what Boaventura de Sousa Santos (2007) terms an *abyssal divide* characteristic of Eurocentric epistemicides and blatant forms of cognitive injustice (Paraskeva, 2011). Of this abyssal divide, Santos (2007) writes, "What most fundamentally characterizes abyssal thinking is thus the impossibility

---

[3] To avoid any confusion, the use of "South" here refers to the Global South or the Southern hemisphere.

of the co-presence of the two sides of the line. To the extent that it prevails, this side of the line only prevails by exhausting the field of relevant reality. Beyond it, there is only nonexistence, invisibility, non-dialectical absence" (p. 1). As such, hard analytical boundaries prevail between how "this or that" is defined and regulated, collapsing the dialectics of human existence. Within such restrictions, there is often an inability to grasp epistemologically the *paradoxical rationality* of the decolonizing mind—an approach that is in opposition to the narrow Aristotelian logic[4] of the West and that "assumes that A and non-A *do not exclude* each other" (Fromm, 1956), in contrast to classical European logic.

It is useful to note here the multidimensionality characteristic of Freire's decolonizing epistemic approach. Kohan (2021) highlights this multidimensionality in what he refers to as Freire's five critical principles or *engines of thinking*—life, equality, love, errantry, and childhood. The *principle of life* is reflected in an educational philosophy and practice that opens us not only to being attentive to the meanings we give life but also to the possibilities of bringing a new force of life to our teaching, through adventurous and courageous encounters with disquieting questions. The *principle of equality* in Freire's work, epistemologically and politically, attributes equal value to all life. The *principle of love* refers to a vital political force of encounter that inspires solidarity and collective sensibilities in our engagement with others. Inspired by the notion of Freire as *wanderer traveling all his life to many places*, the fourth *principle of errantry* is conceived as a philosophical and practical place where we can wander freely in the process of intellectual formation. This opens the space to err, so mistakes are now embraced as necessary to the unfinishedness of life. And last, albeit perhaps unexpected, the *principle of childhood* refers to the place of beginnings and new transformational possibilities within us. It is this sense of childhood that speaks most to Freire's relationship to radical hope

---

[4] In *Art of Loving*, Fromm (1956) takes up this question of paradoxical thinking. "Aristotle explains his position very clearly in the following sentence: 'It is impossible for the same thing at the same time to belong and not to belong to the same thing and in the same respect; and whatever other distinctions we might add to meet dialectical objections, let them be added. This, then, is the most certain of all principles . . .' This axiom of Aristotelian logic has so deeply imbued our habits of thought that it is felt to be 'natural' and self-evident, while on the other hand the statement that X is A *and* not A seems to be nonsensical" (73).

and his concern with the epistemological curiosity that stirs us teachers and students toward new questions and to renew expectations of what might be. Reflecting on these principles, I'm reminded that Freire was not timid about beginning anew. In fact, *Pedagogy of the Oppressed* is the product of a powerful moment in his life when he had to begin anew. Moreover, as overlapping expressions of Freire's epistemic multidimensionality, these decolonizing principles are closely akin to a Southern epistemological knowing and being in the world.

Yet, Freire has often been critiqued precisely for what might be deemed his Southern epistemological reading and reinvention of Western revolutionary ideas—critiques, ironically, issued through narrow Western frameworks of scholars unable to suspend their belief in the existence of one correct, universal way to articulate truths, to which they alone are privileged with true clarity and insight. The challenges that Santos (2014) poses, in order to move beyond the abyssal divide, entails "two main procedures . . . ecologies of knowledges and intercultural translations."[5] About this intercultural translation, Santos (2014) writes,

> Because it is a work of mediation and negotiation, the world of translation requires that the participants in the translation process defamiliarize themselves to a certain extent vis-à-vis their respective cultural backgrounds. In the case of North/South translations, which tend to be also Western/ non-Western translation, the task of defamiliarization is particularly difficult because the imperial North has no memory of itself as other than imperial and, therefore, as unique and as universal. (p. 223)

It seems that such difficulties with intercultural translation constitute, at times, precisely the epistemological challenges inherent in reading *Pedagogy of the Oppressed*. Moreover, central here is the idea that "different types of knowledge are incomplete in different ways and that raising the consciousness of reciprocal

---

[5] About intercultural translation, Santos (2014) writes, "Because it is a work of mediation and negotiation, the world of translation requires that the participants in the translation process defamiliarize themselves to a certain extent vis-à-vis their respective cultural backgrounds. In the case of North/South translations, which tend to be also Western/non-Western translation, the task of defamiliarization is particularly difficult because the imperial North has no memory of itself as other than imperial and, therefore, as unique and a universal" (223).

incompleteness (rather than looking for completeness)" is a precondition for achieving cognitive justice (p. 212).

With *Pedagogy of the Oppressed*, Freire sought to unveil the oppressor/oppressed contradiction, unleash it of its ideological stranglehold, and counter the binary and closed system of Eurocentric rationality and the *epistemologies of blindness* (Santos, 2014) it produces. This is a phenomenon that, unwittingly or unwittingly, blunts the capacity of the Western mind to grasp decolonizing ideas forged through epistemologies of the South. As such, hard positivist boundaries prevail between how "this and that" are defined and regulated as absolute categories, collapsing the dialectics of human thought to power relations as well as denying the historicity and, thus, fragility and impermanence of all theoretical postulations. Within such restrictions, there is often an inability, generally unacknowledged, to grasp the paradoxical rationality of decolonizing epistemologies. It is for this reason that Freire embraces the unfinishedness of knowledge, in ways that openly engage the reciprocal incompleteness of the knowledge that teachers and students bring to the process of learning.

Over the years, various critiques of Freire's *Pedagogy of the Oppressed* have been made about a variety of questions and contradictions in his work (Ohliger, 1995). Many speak to sincere concerns and contradictions, of which, as with all critiques, some are valid, while others not so much. Critics have bemoaned the *romanticization* of Freire's discourse, the problematics of applying Freire's method, concluding that Freire, rather than being revolutionary, "acted as a liberal member of a Catholic intellectual elite" (Facundo, 1984). Others called out Freire's use of patriarchal language and his failure to engage questions of gender (Brady, 1984);[6] and still others judged *Pedagogy of the Oppressed* to be an "illogical and inconsistent" text (Foy, 1971) or filled with a contradictory discourse, lacking

---

[6] On several occasions, Paulo spoke about this issue and, in fact, did change the language in his later books. However, initially, he refused to make changes to *Pedagogy of the Oppressed*, in that he believed it was important to maintain the historicity of the text. That is to say, when he wrote the book, the language reflected his lack of awareness on this issue. In later writings, the change reflects the evolution of his thought. Freire insisted that we are historical beings and therefore our writings become a testimony to this reality, by reflecting our changes in consciousness over time. He considered this a significant pedagogical question and a human characteristic that reinforced humility and intellectual honesty.

systematic analysis (Leach, 1982). While yet others deemed Freire's writings as "petite bourgeois revolutionism," given his supposed vacillation between the "sectarianism" and "opportunism" derived of an idealism considered to be in direct conflict with orthodox Marxist readings of education, society, and social movement (Gibson, 1994). At other times, Freire's ideas have been considered to be "harmful not just to students but to the teachers entrusted with their Education" (Stern, 2009), which, incidentally, echoes the political views of the Tucson Unified School District in the state of Arizona that in 2012 banned *Pedagogy of Oppressed* from classroom use for two years (Cammarota and Romero, 2014). While other critics have challenged Freire's *speciesism* (Kahn, 2010) or privileging of human life in his articulations of freedom and empowerment,[7] reflected in the manner he articulates the relationship of humans to animals. In many instances, Freire actually made intentional efforts to rethink his language and perspective, shifts reflected in his writings over the course of his lifetime.

But more recently, critiques are being issued by the emerging school known as posthumanism. At the core, the tenets of posthumanism seek to dismantle the long-standing Enlightenment logic of humanism, perceived as encompassing Western Eurocentric notions of hierarchy, binaries, linearity, causation, and rationalism. Concepts of "humanity" or "humanization," so much a part of Paulo Freire's discourse, are critiqued as inadvertently reinscribing commonsense discourses of supremacy, patriarchy, and oppression—values in direct contradiction to Freire's expressed liberatory intent. Although historically employed to advance an egalitarian vision, posthumanist critics argue that humanism functions to obscure the complexity of lived experience, obstruct the enactment of an egalitarian worldview, and, as such, perpetuate long-standing forms of violence and imperialism (Braidotti, 2013). Here, we can only imagine Freire's response, which more than likely would have been to read and listen carefully to the criticism unfolding and perhaps offer alternative readings in ways that would welcome deeper reflection and dialogue. Central concerns

---

[7] Speciesism refers to a human-centric belief system, which views other living species on the planet as intrinsically inferior to human life. See *Critical Pedagogy, Ecoliteracy, and Planetary Crisis* by R. Kahn (2010) for and better understanding of this critique and some ways he proposes to extend Freire's work toward addressing the question of speciesism in our perspectives of education and its relationship to the well-being of all living beings.

would have been linked to the political consequence of such critiques as well their overarching impact on our thinking, actions, politics, and pedagogy. The dialogue would have been unquestionably thoughtful, engaging, and passionate.

However, anti-dialogical academic dismissals of Paulo Freire's pedagogical praxis are often rendered by way of wholesale denial of his personal self-vigilance, willingness to enter into self-criticism, and commitment to open dialogue—characteristics that remained central to his pedagogy and relationships, throughout his life. About the "blind spot" of many critics, hooks (1994) asserts, "in so much of Paulo's work there is a generous spirit, a quality of open-mindedness that I feel is often missing from the intellectual and academic arena in U.S. society, and feminist circles have not been an exception" (p. 152). As such, to divorce Paulo's words from their cultural, linguistic, and historical foundations, as well as the profound political tensions inherent in the colonizing limitations of his era, is to, wittingly or unwittingly, reinscribe the elitist Western epistemological gaze that Freire fought so persistently to derail in his scholarship, teaching, and everyday relationships. Similarly, another criticism of Freire, issued from those within and outside Brazil, is that he too easily conflates questions of education and politics. However, Irwin (2012) argues, "This accusation underestimates the complex and specific analysis which Freire gives of education and the pedagogical process" (p. 46).

As one would expect, Freire was well aware of the critiques and tensions that surrounded his theoretical ideas and pedagogical praxis; but as an emancipatory intellectual in the decolonizing tradition, he also firmly believed in the relational necessity of engaging conflicting dimensions across ontological and epistemological differences as well as to grapple with tensions rooted in the binary formations of the oppressor/oppressed contradiction. Thus, he persisted in speaking across a variety of philosophical perspectives within the totality of the intellectual field, conceiving this level of openness to ideas as a democratic imperative for scholars from oppressed populations who sought to unravel the impact of the coloniality of power on their thinking, politics, pedagogy, and way of life. This, unfortunately, is not necessarily appreciated or recognized among those decisively steeped in the compartmentalizing and blinding ethos of a reductionist philosophical tradition, where Freire's so-called "eclectic" or multidimensional advances are deemed an anathema.

Hence, in an examination of his intellectual journey, what stands out most clearly is that Freire was not a rigid or dogmatic thinker—in that his early lived history of surviving and maneuvering extremely difficult conditions of social and economic oppression perhaps prepared him to see the folly in such sectarian pretenses—intolerant pretenses generally associated with academic battles for dominance in the field. Freire, therefore, recognized such critiques, devoid of opportunities for dialogue, as anti-dialogical or cultural manifestations rooted in the authoritarian tradition of the colonizer, which still plagues university scholarship today. This points to scholarship that seldom emerges from the concrete social and material conditions of the people or from a spirit of solidarity, necessary for comprehending the significance of *Pedagogy of the Oppressed* to a politics of liberation. Further, Freire's epistemology cannot be understood through straight-line trajectories, detached of concrete historical events, economic conditions, personal relationships, pedagogical practices, or philosophical traditions from which he consistently grappled to make sense of human oppression and the role of education as either a force for domination or emancipation. Hence, Freire must be also understood as a post-disciplinary[8] thinker, who took up and engaged concepts multidimensionally from a variety of authors and disciplines, systematically mining their salience to revolutionary struggle. And, in so doing, it was "he who gave them [an] international resonance" (Martínez Gómez, 2015, p. 57)—so much so that almost thirty years after his death, Freire's contribution continues to spark the imagination of revolutionary educators around the globe.

---

[8] Post-disciplinary here draws on the writing of such scholars as Andrew Sayer (1999) and Bob Jessop and Ngai-Ling Sum (2001), who refer to an approach to teaching and research that extends knowledge construction beyond disciplinary boundaries, by following a coherent group of "ideas and connections wherever they lead instead of following them only as far as the border of [the] discipline" (Sayer 1999: 5). Traditionally, the process of knowledge construction has been held hostage by the arbitrary boundaries of disciplines (i.e., philosophy, history, political economy, anthropology, sociology, psychology), which result in the unfortunate compartmentalization and fracturing of knowledge, which often, wittingly or unwittingly, conceals the extent of power and control held by the dominant class and culture. As such, we can think of decolonizing epistemologies as a systematic foray outside the abyssal divide (Santos 2007) of disciplinary approaches within the Western-inspired university tradition.

Foreword

Donaldo Macedo

University of Massachusetts, Boston

False love, false humility, and feeble faith in others cannot create trust . . . to say one thing and do another—to take one's words lightly—cannot inspire trust. To glorify democracy and to silence the people is a farce; to discourse on humanism and to negate people is a lie.

—Paulo Freire
Pedagogy of the Oppressed

I could not think of a more suited scholar than Antonia Darder to write *The Student Guide to Paulo Freire's Pedagogy of the Oppressed*. Darder truly embodies the meaning of solidarity and the value of gratitude for mutual support in the collective cocreation of a political project that dares to imagine a world where people are less narcissistic, more just, less dehumanizing and more humane. She is well aware of the lies that undergird meritocracy as she is painfully cognizant that, while many educators critique neoliberalism's heightened individualism and its theology of the market, their actions, nevertheless, always take a detour through cost analysis measures which often sabotage the collective political project of becoming more fully human. That is, "the pursuit of full humanity, however, cannot be carried out in isolation or [individualistically], but only in the fellowship and solidarity,"[1]—a solidarity that should always be shaped and guided by generosity of the heart, collective responsibility, and gratitude— values that are almost always trumped by the current crass careerism predicated in *having more* instead of *being more human*.[2]

---

[1] Paulo Freire, *Pedagogy of the Oppressed* (London: Bloomsbury, 2012), 85.
[2] Ibid., 85–6.

Hence, Darder along with Henry Giroux, bell hooks, Linda Brodkey, Stanley Aronowitz, Lilia Bartolomé, and Peter McLaren are but a handful of activist-intellectuals who truly understand the "daunting task" of living the *Pedagogy of the Oppressed* to the extent that "[it] requires one to step into a vulnerable place and embrace a politically and culturally charged sensibility that can move beyond traditional conceptualizations of scholarship. This [humbling coherence which is predicated on an unyielding integrity] also demands that one dares to embody the spirit, passion, and commitment of Paulo Freire to make a world where it is possible to be more human, a world where it is possible to love,"[3] which is a *sine qua non* for the existence of dialogue that, in turn, requires "a profound love for the world and for people."[4] Thus, a pseudo-Freirean who remains shackled to a blind zeal for power and uses an anti-establishment critical discourse to disguise his or her need to dominate, "reveals the pathology of love: sadism in the dominator and masochism in the dominated."[5]

The challenge for the intellectual-activist is to have the courage to refuse "to dichotomize cognition from the emotion"[6]—a task that requires courage, coherence, and integrity—values that are evermore in short supply in a world where, according to President Trump, what matters is "to make a deal," irrespective of the human costs and the probable violation of ethics. Hence, many educators, including those who claim to be Freirean, sacrifice their integrity and coherence as they are spellbound by the careerist zeal of another promotion to a position of power even if it means emptying out the "authentic word . . . [which] . . . is deprived of its dimension of action, [and in which] reflection automatically suffers . . . and the word is changed into idle chatter, into verbalism, into an alienated and alienating 'blah.'"[7]

The fossilization of action by many pseudo-critical educators is usually contextually situated in textual critiques when the self-proclaimed Freireans

---

[3] Ibid., 89.
[4] Ibid.
[5] Ibid.
[6] Freire (1998), xviii.
[7] Freire, *Pedagogy of the Oppressed*, 87.

hollow out their critical anti-establishment discourse by paralyzing action so as to maintain their colonizing desires of reaping privileges from the very establishment that they denounce. Consequently, they reject any dialogue that includes theory, reducing their denouncement of the establishment to a fossilized dialogical method while chest-pounding to be a "man [or women] of action, one who draws his [her] lessons from experience."[8] This false dichotomy between theory and action not only reveals the distortion of the wanna-be-Freireans but, it simultaneously points to their failure to understand that all actions are informed by theory and authentic activists must know how to theorize their action. To do otherwise is to fall prey to an elitist academicism where theory and a discourse of critique are often disarticulated from action, rendering the denouncement of the unjust world to pure academic blah, blah, blah, "for denunciation is impossible without a commitment to transform, and there is no transformation without action."[9] In many respects, the pseudo-critical educator who rejects theory, acts like the "colonist [who] likes neither theory nor theorists. He who knows that he is in a bad ideological position boasts of being a man of action, one who draws his lessons from experience,"[10] one whose energy is razor focused on the community disarticulated from the very ideological and cultural factors that gave rise to the human misery that festers in that community in the first place and where subjugated people are relegated to sub-humanity.

As a profoundly organic intellectual, Antonia Darder keenly understands that "the act of love is a commitment to the [oppressed's] cause—the cause of liberation. And this commitment, because it is loving, is dialogical."[11] To the extent that it is dialogical, Darder's illuminating insights on Freire's ideals and philosophy of life make clear the unviability of a critical discourse that only denounces the social injustices at the level of text without a communion with the people who need to struggle and announce their freedom. Necessarily, an act of freedom invariably requires dialogue with the people on whose behalf the critical educator proclaims to fight as an anti-establishment expert against

[8] Albert Memmi, *The Colonizer and the Colonized* (Boston: Beacon Press, 1991), 26.
[9] Freire, *Pedagogy of the Oppressed*, 87.
[10] Memmi, *The Colonizer and the Colonized*, 26.
[11] Freire, *Pedagogy of the Oppressed*, 91.

the oppressive establishment. To do otherwise is to use a language of critique that denounces oppression at the level of text "as a pretext for manipulation."[12] That is, educators whose political project is always sacrificed at the altar of crass careerism and who speak for the people but are not with the people, are educators who fear the people and who visit the community as anthropological tourists to collect research data to support their critique of oppression. As anthropological tourists, they "might treat [the community] under study as though [they] are not participants in it. In [their] celebrated impartiality, [they] might approach this real world as if [they] were wearing 'gloves' and 'masks' in order to not contaminate or be contaminated by it."[13]

Like Freire, Darder never positions herself in the community as an anthropological tourist or as a savior who paternalistically sloganizes against oppression from the comfort and safety of the academy. Like Freire, Darder has never been seduced by the stifling middle-class smugness of the academy, which almost always coerces the working-class intellectual into forgetting dangerous childhood memories of economic hardship, violence, and dehumanization. Like Freire, Darder adheres to the necessary intellectual coherence in order to understand the critical difference between studying and writing about hunger and actually experiencing it. As Freire painfully recounts, "I didn't understand anything [in school] because of my hunger. I wasn't dumb. It wasn't lack of interest. My social condition didn't allow me to have an education."

Unlike domesticated educators and policy makers who hide hunger behind an abstract test score, Freire and Darder dare to name the violence implicated in the societal dismissal of the cruel and generalized poverty as "bad luck" or "lazy people attempting to mooch from taxpayers hard-earned money." According to Darder, Freire's "early experiences of poverty led him to discover the 'culture of silence' of the oppressed—whose response to the world, he would argue in *Pedagogy of the Oppressed*." I would go a step further and argue that *Pedagogy of the Oppressed* would not have been written had Freire not experienced the dehumanizing and humiliating experience of hunger in Morro da Saúde, a poor neighborhood in Jaboatão in the periphery of Recife,

---

[12] Ibid., 90.
[13] Paulo Freire, *The Politics of Education: Culture, Power, and Liberation* (South Hadley, MA: Bergin and Garvey, 1987), 132.

where I had the pleasure and honor of visiting Freire's humble house in June 2016, in the company of Darder and Freire's widow, Nita Freire. I agree with Darder that Freire's "early life experiences among impoverished rural and working people and in poor schools . . . [instilled] . . . in him a profound sense of love and compassion and an understanding for how difficult conditions of poverty subjected children from subaltern communities to a colonizing education, which further [increased] their disempowerment, domestication, and alienation."

Whereas Freire used his experiences of poverty to develop greater empathy with the people suffering from class oppression and all forms of social injustices, most educators and researchers go to great lengths to deny the existence of class in the United States, reproducing a pedagogy of lies which is normalized by "fake research" and legitimized by number crunching. That is, let us take the ideological trap in the field of reading and literacy that range from the reactionary call for scientifically based approaches to reading to the militaristic lock step marching orders of the dominant curriculum. While many educators courageously denounce the dehumanizing deskilling of both students and teachers who are coerced into rigid instructional methodologies, many liberal educators engage in an eternal dance of hypocrisy where, instead of denouncing the vicious attacks on poor children under the guise of science, they take refuge in a type of academic literacy research which is, at best, folk theory and, at worse, the reproduction of the very class warfare that is largely responsible for the inequalities that many well-intentioned liberals denounce at the level of discourse and from which they refuse to divest their privilege. Hence, one of Freire's major goals was the development of an emancipatory pedagogical process that is designed to teach students, through critical literacies, how to negotiate the world in thoughtful and just ways that expose and engage the relations between the oppressor and the oppressed.

For Freire, literacy as an act of *conscientization* has as its central educational objective to awaken in the oppressed the knowledge, creativity, and constant critical reflexive capacities necessary to demystify and understand the power relations responsible for their marginalization and, through this recognition, begin a project of liberation. Its commitment to critical reflection and transformative action makes *conscientization* central to critical literacy which requires, in turn, that the teacher perform the critical questioning inherent to *conscientization* in order to ensure that due consideration is given to important social, economic, and cultural contributors to social justice in teaching and learning.

Like Freire, Darder's insistence on integrity and intellectual coherence unmasks educators who study violence but fail to comprehend the difference between deploring violence and surviving it. Furthermore, integrity and intellectual coherence must also denounce academics' false benevolence of giving voice to the voiceless while simultaneously having their "tongue yanked"[14] by the academic discourse vigilantes who use high stakes testing and a banking model of "common core" to exclude non-middle-class (and often non-White students) from accessing quality education as an act of freedom.

In *The Student Guide to Freire's* Pedagogy of the Oppressed, Darder insightfully demonstrates that conviviality with economic deprivation teaches that poverty is not a disease but a social construction that uncritical and unreflexive teachers help construct. Darder challenges all educators to comprehend that poverty and human misery are not contagious but part of the architecture of class structure that most academics deny or denounce at the level of discourse but refuse to renounce through a pedagogy of lies as they continue to reap class privileges. In other words, most academics are, at various levels, engaged in the construction of human misery and poverty they correctly denounce in their critical discourse and wrongly reproduce through their burning colonial desires.

Darder brilliantly captures the essence of what it means to educate in Freire's denouncement of "the antidialogics of the banking method of education,"[15] which has gained ample terrain in the school reform movement that, while reforming, deforms. The overemphasis on methods has become a North American educational trade mark as argued by Lilia Bartolomé in her classic article, "Beyond the Methods Fetish: Toward a Humanizing Pedagogy"[16]—a humanizing pedagogy that electrifies Freire's perennial hope,

---

[14] Anzaldúa (1989).
[15] Freire, *Pedagogy of the Oppressed*, 91.
[16] Lilia I. Bartolomé, "Beyond the Methods Fetish: Toward a Humanizing Pedagogy," *Harvard Educational Review* 64, no. 2 (Summer, 1994): 173–94.

rooted in men's [and women's] incompletion, from which they move out in constant search—a search which can be carried out only in communion with others. Hopelessness is a form of silence, of denying the world and fleeing from it. The dehumanization resulting from an unjust order is not a cause for despair but for hope, leading to the incessant pursuit of the humanity denied by injustice ... As long as I fight, I am moved by hope; and if I fight with hope, then I can wait.[17]

---

[17] Freire, *Pedagogy of the Oppressed*, 91–2.

About This Book

I hope at least the following will endure: my trust in the people, and my faith in men and women, and in the creation of a world in which it will be easier to love.

—Paulo Freire[1]

Upon preparing the manuscript for the first edition, I noted that to write a student guide for a book like *Pedagogy of the Oppressed* by the late world-renowned Brazilian philosopher Paulo Freire is, indeed, a daunting task. This remains the case today, as I work to complete the second edition of this book, which has been well received by educators around the world. Translated in more than forty languages, the lasting appeal of the book has made Paulo Freire one of the most influential educational philosophers of the twentieth century. Hence, there is a certain respect and commitment required to return to this task—a task that requires one to step again into a vulnerable place and be willing to embrace a politically and culturally charged sensibility that obliges one to move beyond traditional philosophical conceptualizations. This also demands that one dare to embody the spirit, passion, and commitment of this brilliant, yet unassuming, educational philosopher, whose ideas came to represent "the response of a creative mind and sensitive conscience to the extraordinary misery and suffering of the oppressed around him" (Shaull, 1970, p. 10).

Pedagogy of the Oppressed, first published in Spanish in 1968 and then in English[2] in 1970, has transformed and deepened social justice educational discourses worldwide, by highlighting the significant role of education in the formation of citizens and the perpetuation of oppressive conditions within schools and societies. For more than five decades, the powerful message of *Pedagogy of the Oppressed* has been embraced by progressive educators

[1] See: P. Freire, *Pedagogy of the Oppressed* (30th Anniversary Edition) (New York: Continuum, 2005), 40.
[2] The book was translated into English by Myra Ramos.

and activists everywhere (as the last chapter of this book illustrates), while simultaneously being shunned, maligned, and banned by those whose perspectives support the hegemonic order of their times. Nevertheless, Freire's imaginative capacity to capture and articulate what might be understood as the *universalism of oppression*, particularly as enacted within the context of educational practice, spoke directly to the hearts and minds of oppressed people and their allies everywhere, whether they labored as teachers or social workers or nurses or ministers or artists or community activists.

Hence, this effort to create a student guide for the novice reader of *Pedagogy of the Oppressed* initially caused me to lose sleep and to rub my hands raw, seeking to find the way to speak to the complexities of Freire's political project, in language that is accessible and meaningful to students who now and in the coming decades will be assigned the book or simply pick it up serendipitously. No matter how one comes to *Pedagogy of the Oppressed,* from its inception, this book is meant for those sincerely committed to a better world. Never could Paulo Freire have imagined that his powerful insights into educational and societal oppression would continue to resonate so deeply with the struggles of so many, long after his death. How can one do justice to this astonishing feat? How can one simply tell the story of a book that was to become one of the most internationally read and cited texts in the social sciences (Green, 2023).

That said, it is important that seasoned readers of *Pedagogy of the Oppressed* also understand the purpose of this volume. It is to illuminate, as much as possible, the central thesis and critical concepts that Freire introduced in his memorable volume. In order to be true to this purpose, the focus of this book is only on *Pedagogy of the Oppressed*. Freire, however, went on to write many more books; and many Freirean scholars have labored persistently over the past forty years to elucidate and reveal further the strength and influence of Paulo's ideas and pedagogical insights. For those new to *Pedagogy of the Oppressed*, I hope this guide will provide emerging readers with ample philosophical support and encouragement to not only navigate more effectively the underlying intent and major themes but also engage more substantively the wisdom and challenge of this classical educational treatise. For educators who are using *Pedagogy of the Oppressed* as a text in their classrooms, this volume is meant to potentiate and enhance philosophical and pedagogical engagement with Freire's themes as well as to help more effectively navigate critical dialogues that the book is sure to generate in classrooms and communities where questions tied to our liberation from human oppression are central to teaching and learning.

However, it is important to remember that *The Student Guide to Freire's Pedagogy of the Oppressed* is not meant to substitute or supplant the reading of *Pedagogy of the Oppressed* as primary text but rather to serve as a faithful and loyal companion to readers who strive to overcome the many injustices that persist in education and society today. Underlying this volume is a radical sense of hope that its use will sustain the intellectual and political formation of students, enhancing their sensibility to the political and pedagogical possibilities for building democratic voice, participation, and solidarity in the struggle for our liberation from those social and material forces that betray our dignity and all respect for life.

More importantly, my approach to writing this book constitutes, as theologian Richard Shaull (1970) suggests, a form of *personal witness* to the power of Freire's praxis, as much as an *exciting adventure* into critical dialogue *with* and *across* Paulo's ideas—a process that has persisted, since I first read *Pedagogy of the Oppressed* in 1978. Since my first reading, I have engaged the book as a colonized subject of the United States, a working-class Puerto Rican woman who grew up in poverty. As such, my relationship with these ideas is intimate and embodied. The reader will note that at times my language in Chapter 3 reflects this inclusivity and identification with the oppressed. Similarly, the *notes from the field* in Chapter 5 provide a variety of personal accounts by educators around the world who have sought to both embody and reinvent Freire's ideas in their own particular contexts.

Finally, through both a critical and intimate dialogue with *the richness, depth, and complexity* of Paulo's thought, I hope this book will further your commitment to the arduous historical task that awaits us today, igniting deeper recognition of our significance as historical subjects, empowered political beings, and cultural citizens—particularly as we labor individually and collectively to end human suffering wherever encountered. In this way, we together can ensure that Paulo Freire's (1970) great hope will endure: "the creation of a world in which it will be easier to love" (p. 24) and where a new sense of dignity, compassion, and self-determination can fuel our revolutionary dreams.

Lived History

When people lack a critical understanding of their reality, apprehending it in fragments, which they do not perceive as interacting constituent elements of the whole, they cannot truly know that reality. To truly know it, they would have to reverse their starting point: they would need to have a total vision of the context in order subsequently to separate and isolate its constituent elements and by means of this analysis achieve a clearer perception of the whole.

—Paulo Freire (1970)

As one of the most influential educational philosophers of the twentieth century, Paulo Freire has been associated with literacy campaigns and popular education movements in Latin America.[1] In the United States, he is seen as one of the major intellectual inspirations for the foundation of critical pedagogy (Darder, Torres, and Baltodano 2017). And, although he is considered to be one of the most distinguished intellectual figures to emerge from Latin America, Freire's influence has spread far and wide and has continued to do so even after his untimely death in 1997. In the preface of the book, Paulo asserts, "Thought and study alone did not produce *Pedagogy of the Oppressed*; it is rooted in concrete situations." This epistemological proclamation provides us

---

[1] The term "popular culture" is a translation of *educação popular*. Both Portuguese and English versions are similar because of their Latin root. However, the meaning of *popular* is very different in Latin America. In this context, popular means something that is *for* and *from* the poor and dispossessed. In the Brazilian context, the popular educator is one who teaches the poor, especially those who are illiterate and unschooled. In addition, popular education, as conceived by Freire and others of his time, provides a pedagogical approach in which people not only become literate but also develop critical consciousness about their world and their particular place in that world. Hence, *popular education* is understood as community education that seeks the empowerment and well-being of the oppressed.

a hint into the significance of context to Freire's philosophy and the political sensibility that informs the book.

In the larger historical context, Freire's life must be understood within the sorted history of a massive country that occupies over half of the South American continent. From the inception of European colonization, the majority of Brazilians—indigenous people and Africans brought by force to work the lands—were violently subjected to the ravages of colonial subjugation and slavery. It is therefore impossible to fully comprehend Freire's *Pedagogy of the Oppressed* outside "the backdrop of the Brazilian history of exploitation and extermination, hunger and malnutrition" Bhattacharya (2011:173). These were obstinate conditions of oppression that persisted from the 1500s into the twentieth century. Freire experienced such conditions in his own life and would constantly reencounter them, through his literacy work in the northeastern region of Brazil—one of the poorest regions of the nation, where the violence of racism and poverty fully comingle.

The issue of context, moreover, is also understood here through a Freirean lens, which recognizes that it is impossible to understand human beings, including their philosophy and praxis, outside of the concrete historical, economic, and cultural conditions that shape their intellectual, emotional, physical, and spiritual sensibilities and, thus, their ongoing evolution as cultural citizen of the world. Hence, to more precisely grasp the fundamental ideas of *Pedagogy of the Oppressed* requires an understanding of the lived history from whence Freire's pedagogy emerged. This is also significant to understanding the man from Recife, himself, whose philosophical and political labor generated ideas intimately anchored to his everyday praxis in the rural countryside of his native Brazil, as well as his numerous international experiences. So, it is by way of understanding Paulo's lived history that we can achieve a clearer perception of the whole.

In keeping with this spirit, this chapter examines the manner in which Freire's lived history, first and foremost, informed his intellectual sensibilities and his political commitment to the emancipation of oppressed peasants in Brazil—a liberatory vision that extended beyond his native country. Paulo, indeed, encompassed a sincere and genuine concern for the suffering and oppression of subaltern populations worldwide. His persistent indignation for the unmerciful manner in which governments and the wealthy elite thwart the dignity of human beings is distinguishably palpable in *Pedagogy of the Oppressed* and the writings that would follow this groundbreaking testament to the oppressor's manufactured suffering of the poor.

An important dimension of Paulo Freire's pedagogy is found precisely in his recognition of how the power of lived histories in each individual impacts our reading of the world and influences the construction of knowledge, within and beyond the classroom (Darder 2015). Moreover, returning to one's lived history is also a vital means by which to continuing learning about one's place in the world. In *Letters to Cristina*, Freire (1996) notes:

> The more I return to my distant childhood, the more I realize there is always more worth knowing. I continue to learn from my childhood and difficult adolescence. I do not return to my early years as someone who is sentimentally moved by a ridiculous nostalgia or as someone who presents his not-so-easy childhood and adolescence as revolutionary credentials. (13)

Given the key role lived history plays in Freire's writing of *Pedagogy of the Oppressed*, beginning this book with a succinct examination of Paulo's life seems a useful place for students to commence their engagement of the book. By so doing, readers may gain insight into the evolution of Freire's philosophical sensibilities, his pedagogical practice, and the expression of his political voice, which for the last five decades has been a clarion call for liberation.

Early years

Paulo Relus Neves Freire, the youngest of four children, was born on September 19, 1921, to an economically comfortable working-class Catholic family in the port city of Recife, the capital of the state of Pernambuco. This northeastern region of Brazil was and continues to be one of the most impoverished in the country. When Paulo was only three years old, his father, an officer of the Pernambuco military police, was forced to retire prematurely due to a serious heart condition. This destabilized the family's economic condition, forcing them to move to Jaboatão dos Guararapes, a modest town outside of Recife.

Figure 1.1 Paulo at the age of one year and three years with his three siblings; Freire's siblings were Temístocles, Stela, and Armando.

Freire was a child during an extremely tumultuous political period in Brazil, where the rule of President Epitácio Lindolfo da Silva Pessoa, a man known for his blatant racism against Black Brazilians, was also marked by military revolts. This crisis generated by armed resistance through the 1920s eventually culminated in the Revolution of 1930, which resulted in a political coup that brought an end to the Old Republic. After a transitional period in which centralizing elements struggled with the old oligarchies for control, another coup in 1937 established the New State (Estado Novo) dictatorship, which ruled from 1937 to 1945. Hence, throughout his early life, Freire's family experienced political anxieties over the instability of the economy and politics of dictatorship within the Brazilian government.

The economy in Brazil suffered from a severe decline in world demand for coffee caused by the Great Depression and an excess capacity of production stemming from the 1920s. As a result, the price of coffee fell sharply and the country's trade deteriorated significantly. The world economic crisis of the time negatively affected the economic conditions of Freire's family, who fell into deeper poverty. The economic decline experienced by the family caused Freire to experience hunger and poverty at a young age. On October 31, 1934, his father died from a heart attack, leaving his mother with meager economic means.

About his father, Joaquim Temístocles Freire, Paulo recalled that he was always willing to talk with his family and that he treated his children with the sense of authority of the times. Nevertheless, he also exhibited human understanding for his children and the needs of others (Freire 1978). For example, "by taking a piece of wood and drawing words in the sand from the child's cultural universe, his father taught Paulo the alphabet even before the boy went to school. He then broke these words down into syllables and reunited them into new words" (Gerhardt 1993). Freire described his father as both "a spiritualist" and "a living example of the human qualities of generosity, solidarity, and humility, without any sacrifice to his dignity" (Freire 1994: 208). However, it was Paulo's mother, Edeltrudis Veves Freire, who he described as "Catholic, sweet, good, just," that he considered his primary spiritual influence. Freire (1996) remembered his parents as "a harmonious couple whose union did not lose them their individuality ... they respected each other's religious opinions. From them … I learned early on the value of dialogue" (25), which would become the cornerstone of his pedagogical approach.

In the years that followed his father's death, Freire, who was considered a mediocre student, struggled with school, preferring to spend most of his time playing with childhood friends from his neighborhood in Jaboatão dos Guararapes. With his mother left to fend for the family alone, Paulo's life was marked by poverty and hunger—conditions he firmly believed diminish a student's ability to learn. Drawing inspiration from the anticolonial theorist Frantz Fanon, Freire often referred to his childhood as one of "sharing the plight of the 'wretched of the earth' " (30). Undoubtedly, Freire's lived experience as a boy deeply influenced his life's work. About this time in his life, he wrote, "I didn't understand anything because of my hunger. I wasn't dumb. It wasn't lack of interest. My social condition didn't allow me to have an education. Experience showed me once again the relationship between social class and knowledge" (Gadotti 1994: 5). His early experiences of poverty, moreover, led

Figure 1.2 Paulo's mother, Edeltrudis Veves Freire, and father, Joaquin Temístocles Freire.

him to discover the "culture of silence" of the oppressed—whose responses to the world, he would argue in *Pedagogy of the Oppressed*, are products of economic, social, and political domination.

Freire credited his early experiences of living among very poor people and attending disadvantaged rural schools with instilling in him a profound sense of love, empathy, and compassion, as well as an understanding for how disabling conditions of poverty, reinforced by a colonizing system of education, subject subaltern students to debilitating conditions of disempowerment, domestication, and alienation. From this grounded sensibility, Freire was to construct an educational philosophy that fundamentally challenged oppression rooted in a colonizing model of schooling and class inequalities. Moreover, it was this sensibility that fueled Freire's ongoing commitment to struggle *at the side of the oppressed*, in order to transform the recalcitrant conditions of economic, pedagogical, and cultural injustice.

Despite the family's financial difficulties, Paulo's mother was determined her youngest child would be well educated. Toward this end, she convinced Aluizio Pessoa de Araujo, the principal of the Colégio Oswaldo Cruz (an elite private high school) to accept Paulo as a scholarship student. And so Freire returned to Recife for high school. He recalled that although it felt awkward attending this traditional, upper-class boys' high school and difficult to adapt to the new conditions, Paulo was considered "fairly intelligent" for an adolescent who had come from the impoverished outskirts of the city. In fact, while still attending high school, he became a grammar teacher at the school. And, although still a very young man, his humanistic sensibilities already steered him toward an emancipatory pedagogical approach centered on dialogue and a desire to understand his students' lives and their pedagogical needs.

Freire's work in Northeastern Brazil

At the age of twenty, Freire enrolled in law school at the University of Recife. However, the path was not easy and, on several occasions, his studies were interrupted, having to earn a living and contribute to the family's finances. While at the University of Recife, he majored in philosophy, focusing his studies on phenomenology and the psychology of language. It was also during this time that Freire commenced what would become more than two decades of intense literacy work in the northeastern region of Brazil—an experience that served as the lived foundation for his early writings. For a short time, he worked with the *Serviço Social da Indústria* (SESI) at the Regional Department of Education and Culture in the state of Pernambuco, a government agency created to utilize funds from a national coalition of factory owners to create social service programs to benefit the conditions of workers. It was also during this time that he began to conceptualize the practice of *cultural circles*.[2]

In 1944, Freire married fellow teacher Elza Maia Costa de Oliveira. The two worked together within the school and were briefly involved with the Catholic Action Movement, which they eventually left over differences with the church's conservative view, energy later redirected to their involvement in *Christian base communities*[3] (Roberts 2000). The couple had five children, Maria Madalena, Maria Cristina, Maria de Fátima, Joaquim, and Lutgardes—three who would become educators, in their own right. In his writings, Freire (1994) shared how Elza encouraged him in his systematic discussions of pedagogical questions, and until her death in 1986, Freire affirmed Elza's influence on his early vocational decisions, the elaboration of his literacy approach, and the pedagogical direction of his philosophical ideas. In many respects, this feature of his marital relationship bears witness to Paulo's astonishing warmth and capacity for engaging women horizontally, as equal collaborators and cocreators of knowledge. Later, this same magnanimous spirit would again be manifested, but in an even more mature and pronounced manner, in his relationship with Ana Maria Araújo Freire, his second wife.

---

[2] Cultural circles refer to a pedagogical process that provides the conditions for learners within classroom or communities to participate freely in naming their world and developing their voices, within a meaningful context of cultural respect and affirmation for their lived histories and everyday experiences. Freire would further develop the concept amid his work in Chile. More discussion will follow in Chapter 3.

[3] Christian Base communities are autonomous religious groups often associated with liberation theology. The meeting of Latin American Council of Bishops in 1968 in Medellin, Colombia, played a major role in popularizing them.

Upon graduation from law school in 1947, Freire completed all requirements and was admitted to the bar but decided against pursuing law after an epiphany he experienced with his first client. The young dentist had defaulted on a loan he had taken to purchase equipment and materials necessary to open his practice. Stirred by the irony and poignancy of the young dentist's situation—a poor man who not only did not have the resources to pay off the loan but was ready to lose everything in order to meet the debt—Freire decided to return to the Colégio Oswaldo Cruz, where he had completed his secondary degree three years earlier, to teach Portuguese. Simultaneously, however, Freire employed his legal skills as a trade union lawyer, assisting members to navigate legal matters.

Later in 1947, Freire was promoted as Director of the Division of Public Relations, Education, and Culture of the SESI. Working among illiterate impoverished communities, Freire embraced the radical Catholic ideas and values of a burgeoning social movement in the church that was spreading across Latin America. As point of reference, this was a time in Brazil when only those who were officially deemed literate could vote in presidential elections, a policy that raised grave concerns for Freire and others in the nation working to advance democratic life. Hence, it is not surprising that the historical necessity of the political moment would catapult Freire's focus toward the development of a revolutionary pedagogical approach, which simultaneously focused on ameliorating illiteracy, while also supporting workers from oppressed communities to enter collectively into the struggle for humanizing education and establishing a more just society.

Freire continued his work with SESI and served from 1954 to 1956 as superintendent of the organization. During these years, Freire's approach to literacy gradually drew the attention of the national office. During an effort in 1957 to appoint Freire as national director of the Division of Research and Planning, an interdepartmental letter praised Freire's "experience and knowledge," asserting that he would be invaluable to the division by "encouraging studies and the recruitment of individuals able to provide us with the effective means to formulate viable solutions pertaining to the pressing social issues in the current state of the nation" (Freire and Macedo 1998: 16).

Figure 1.3 Paulo Freire as a young man, *c.* 1940.

Figure 1.4 Paulo Freire speaking at a SESI meeting, *c.* 1950.

Of particular note, in 1958, was Freire's participation in the Second National Conference on Adult Education in Rio de Janeiro. He was a major contributor to the Pernambuco Regional Commission report, *Education of Adults and Marginal Populations: The Mocambos Problem.*[4] In his report, Freire advised that adult education in the mocambos had to be founded on "the consciousness of the existential knowledge of the personal and social reality of the people rather than in learning letters, words and sentences. Further, education for democracy could be achieved only if the literary process was not about or for learners but with learners and with their reality" (Clare 2006). Here it is worth noting that Freire's work in the mocambos, and elsewhere, was carried

---

[4]   A mocambo refers to a village community of runaway slaves in colonial Brazil (Clare 2006).

out with communities, whose illiteracy could be directly linked to a legacy of slavery and the brutal conditions of colonization that remained untouched by the modernization of Brazil (Prado 1969).

Throughout the following year, Freire continued to participate in the Movement for Popular Culture (MCP) in Recife that he cofounded and in the Cultural Extension Service (SEC) at the University of Recife. In the context of MCP, advocacy for the active exercise of democracy was at the heart of the organization's mission, in that the members were "moved by the desire to work with the popular classes and not above them ... [but] with them and for them" (Freire 1996: 110). The importance of his work with SEC, Freire noted, was the participation of universities in popular education, which the members believed "was the essence of a university's mission and did not undermine its rigor in teaching or research" (130).

Concurrently, Freire also worked systematically to delineate his literacy work with SESI in his dissertation, which he defended, amid some controversy,[5] at the University of Recife in 1959. Of this, Freire (1996) wrote:

> The Brazilian present has been enveloped by these colonial legacies: silence and the resistance to it—the search for a voice—and the rebelliousness that must become more critically revolutionary. This was the central theme of my academic thesis, "Education and Present-Day Brazil," which I defended in 1959 at the University of Recife ... I incorporated parts of this thesis in my first book, *Education as the Practice of Freedom.* My thesis reflected my experiences in SESI, which had significantly affected me. I combined my experiences at SESI with the critical reflection and extensive reading from a foundational bibliography. (87)

---

[5]   There seem to be some conflicting reports on this point. Gadotti (1994) notes that, given Freire's challenge of the status quo, he was considered a traitor among many university colleagues. Gerhardt (1993) claims Freire's dissertation did not receive the approval of the university committee, suggesting "the committee's decision was somewhat logical" (4), given Freire's claim that Brazil's universities had refused to make necessary reforms to move Brazilian society toward democracy (Gerhardt 1993: 4). Nevertheless, Clare (2006) notes, "Freire continued his work at the university and was appointed Professor of History and Philosophy of Education at the University of Recife's Faculty of Philosophy, Sciences and Letters the following year, teaching at the university from 1961 until he was ousted by the military coup in 1964—hence, the dissertation may not have been highly regarded by the committee, but was approved."

In 1961, Freire was appointed director of the Department of Cultural Extension of Recife University. In 1963, he had the first opportunity to conduct a larger application of his literacy approach, launching the "Bare feet can also learn to read" campaign in the state of Rio Grande de Notre, where 300 sugarcane workers in the interior village of Angicos were taught to read and write in 45 days. In response to the success of Freire's literacy efforts, President João Belchior Goulart and Minister of Education Paul de Tarso Santos invited Freire to rethink adult literacy programs on a national scale in an effort to forge a national literacy program. It is estimated that under Freire's direction, "20,000 cultural circles were programmed to be set up for 2,000,000 illiterate people" (Gadotti 1994: 15). However, despite this extraordinary opportunity to expand the reach of Freire's literacy work, Brazil was again embroiled in a turbulent moment in its history, where much uncertainty loomed over the political direction of the nation.

Within three months of its official initiation in January 21, 1964, the new military government shut down the National Literacy Program, in accordance with the coup d'état of March 31, 1964—an action supported and partly financed by the United States to protect its interest in Latin America (Lernoux 1980; William 2015). The Goulart government—whose reforms to socialize the profits of large corporations and landowners and to improve the well-being of all Brazilians, were deemed "a communist threat"—was overthrown and a military dictatorship was to rule the country for more than twenty years. At the time of the *Golpe de 64*, Freire had been working with the national program in Brasilia. Considered "an international subversive, a traitor to Christ and the Brazilian people" (Gadotti 1994: 34), Freire was accused of alleged "subversive activities," arrested twice, and imprisoned in Olinda and Recife for a total of seventy days. In one instance during his interrogation, Freire was asked, "Do you deny your method is similar to that of Stalin, Hitler, Peron, and Mussolini" (Cited in Schugurensky 2014: 23)?

Although Freire was not physically tortured during his incarceration, his imprisonment and subsequent exile had an enduring impact on his view of life and his philosophy, intensifying his heartfelt dedication to the struggle for liberation among the oppressed. About his response to the coup d'état and its impact on his political understanding of education, Freire (cited in Shor and Freire 1987) would later say:

> I began to understand the nature of limits on education when I experienced the shock of the coup d'état. After the coup, I was really born again with a new consciousness of politics, education, and transformation. You can see this in my first book, *Education for Critical Consciousness* … I don't make reference there to the politics of education. But, I was able to learn after that about history. All these things taught me how we needed a political practice in society … a permanent process for freedom, which would include an education that liberates. (32)

Years in exile

Forced into exile in 1964, Freire spent a short time in Bolivia, before arriving in Chile only days following the inauguration of President Eduardo Frei Montalvo. This was considered an enthusiastic and progressive moment in the country's history, where programs for the poor, including literacy efforts were supported. A new department was created that focused on adult education, independent from the Chilean Ministry of Education. Freire served as a UNESCO consultant for almost five years, working for the Christian Democratic Agrarian Reform Movement and the Food and Agriculture Organization of the United Nations. "Freire was able to extend his collaboration to the Ministry of Education and the people working in adult literacy, as to organize agrarian reform" (Grollios 2015). Freire's relationships and experiences with both liberation theologists and Marxists in Chile were to leave an indelible mark on his intellectual, pedagogical, and ideological formation (Holst 2006). Of this Freire wrote:

> The Chilean masses know very well that the fundamental contradiction human beings face is not between them and nature but that it takes place in the economic, political, and social spheres. Those are the things, I confess, that I learned in Chile. It is not that Chile made me a completely different man from the person I was before, but what it did exactly was to deepen in me a radicalization that was already in process. (Freire and Guimarães 1987: 127 trans. by Holst 2006)

Figure 1.5 Paulo Freire (left), with also exiled former mayor of Brasilia and minister of culture under João Belchior Goulart, Paulo de Tarso Santos, who was the first Brazilian to be granted asylum by the Chilean government.

Writing about Freire's time in Chile, James Holst (2006)[6] noted the often-ignored relationship between Freire's extensive hands-on literacy experiences and profound learning process in Chile and his articulation of what would become seminal ideas of his pedagogical project (i.e., banking education, problem-posing education, generative themes, culture of silence, conscientização, cultural action). Moreover, Freire often affirmed that it was in Chile where he "learned to learn." Key associations of that time included Marcela Gajardo, as well as Raul Veloso, whose theory of intentionality of consciousness became significant to Freire's own thinking (Austin 2003: 66). The changes Freire underwent were reflected in his writing. For example, in his first book, *Education as the Practice of Freedom*, which focused on his earlier efforts in Brazil, the text reflected a liberal democratic style and an emerging

---

[6] For an excellent discussion of Freire's years in Chile, see James Holst's (2006) incisive essay, "Paulo Freire in Chile, 1964–1969: Pedagogy of the Oppressed in Its Sociopolitical Economic Context" published in *Harvard Educational Review*. Also see Robert Austin's (2003) *The State, Literacy, and Popular Education in Chile*.

Brazilian national consciousness consistent with Freire's early views in Brazil (Mackie 1981). The tenor of his discourse, however, made a dramatic turn by the following year, when *Pedagogy of the Oppressed* was first published.[7, 8, 9]. Hence, it is safe to say that Chile profoundly nurtured his "politic shift to the Left," which unmistakably characterized the tenor of the book (Roberts 2000: 24).

Freire and his family remained in Chile until April 1969, when he was offered and accepted a temporary visiting post at Harvard University. The offer came at an opportune time, as there were suspicions that rising conservative politics had led to termination of his employment (Grollios 2015). In that same year, Freire assisted the governments of Peru and Nicaragua with literacy campaigns. In 1970, English and Spanish translations of *Pedagogy of the Oppressed* were released in a world that was still grasping for responses to the many issues and concerns raised by the social movements of the 1960s. Shortly after, the family moved to Geneva, Switzerland, where Freire was given a post with the World Council of Churches and established the Institute of Cultural Action. During this decade, Freire did literacy work in other parts of Latin America but also began work in Africa. First with the government of Julius Nyerere in Tanzania, then with revolutionary organizations in former Portuguese colonies of Angola (Movimento Popular Libertação de Angola) and Mozambique (Frente de Libertação de Moçambique), and more substantively in Guinea-Bissau, Cape Verde (Partido Africans para Independência da Guinea-Bissau e Cabo Verde), and Sao Tome and Principe, where literacy campaigns were strongly focused on the process of re-Africanization and nation building.

Paulo's efforts in Africa, however, were beleaguered by a variety of challenging conditions. The Apartheid government of South Africa banned *Pedagogy of the Oppressed*, while perpetrating every form of colonial abuse imaginable upon

---

[7] Myra Bergman Ramos provided the English translation of *Pedagogy of the Oppressed*.

[8] Consistent with the repression of Freire's ideas in Brazil and the circumstances of his live, *Pedagogy of the Oppressed*, written during his time in Chile, was first published in Spanish. The book was not to be published and circulated in Brazil until 1975, seven years after its first publication (Kirylo 2011).

[9] Morrow and Torres (2002) write, "Ironically, due to censorship in Brazil, his most important book—*Pedagogy of the Oppressed*—first appeared in Spanish and English in 1970 and did not appear in a Brazilian Portuguese edition until 1975. . . But by the early 1990s it had sold over half a million copies worldwide" (7).

Black South Africans. Moreover, problems with bureaucracies, the absence of adequate resources, the brutal impact of colonization, and inherent mistrust generated by these conditions stifled literacy efforts—issues often overlooked in criticisms of Freire's literacy efforts. Nevertheless, the difficulties Freire experienced at that time also generated significant realizations about the manner in which the colonizing language "blunted the radical potential … and the objective of literacy as a means to coming by a new consciousness, and stymied the capacity of people to 'read not only the word but also the world'" (Thomas 1996: 25). This experience, in particular, punctuated for Freire the complexity, multiplicity, contradictions, and "differentiated nature of social agency and conditions of struggle" (29). In Guinea-Bissau and Cape Verde, Freire worked briefly with revolutionary leader, Amilcar Cabral, who led the nationalist movement and war for independence, until he was assassinated in 1973.

Freire very much admired the spirit and brilliance of Cabral's ideas. Often the political sensibilities of the two men converged (Cortesão 2011). Both felt a deep sense of faith and respect for the culture and language of the people; and both wholeheartedly believed that popular education programs had to begin, first and foremost, within the concrete realities of people's lives. Both men also believed in the power of passion, intuition, and dreams that could usher in new possibilities into our lives and in the world. Through relationships such as these, Freire's revolutionary perspective was both deepened and complicated by his pedagogical experiences with a variety of movements in both Africa and Latin America.

Post-exile years

Freire's exile was lifted in 1979 and he returned to Brazil in1980, where he accepted posts to teach at the Pontifícia Universidade Católica de São Paulo and the Universidade de Campinas. Upon his return to Brazil, Freire joined the *Partido dos Trabalhadores* (Workers' Party) in Sao Paulo and headed up its adult literacy project for nearly six years. In 1988, when the party took control of São Paulo's municipality—the third largest city in the world—Freire was appointed Municipal Secretary of Education. While in office, Freire faced several political and pedagogical challenges, in that he inherited a broken educational system.

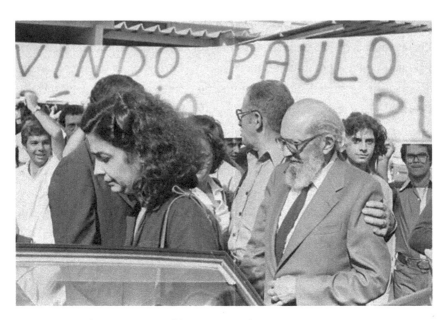

Figure 1.6 Paulo Freire returned home to Brazil in 1980.

Nevertheless, during his short tenure, Freire sought to implement literacy reforms consistent with his liberatory intent and to continue working with popular education movements, in the hopes of building alliances between civil society and the state (McLaren 2002). In 1991, in a short epilogue to *Pedagogy of the City*, Freire wrote "Manifesto to Those Who, by Leaving Stay," where he expressed both his satisfaction with the work done but also anguish in trying to contend with the vestiges of former conservative politics that still plagued the city's educational institutions.

From 1991 till his death, Freire continued his work in Brazil but was also invited often to conduct retreats and seminars, consult on projects, and lecture widely on his experiences, knowledge, and pedagogical ideas. True to his philosophy, Freire often reminded those who praised and adopted his ideas to not try to imitate his pedagogy, which was grounded in a particular historical and geographical context, but rather that we should seek ways to *reinvent* his ideas, so that our labor might truly be in sync with the actual conditions teachers are facing within their particular historical and geographic contexts.

In 1986, his wife Elza died, leaving Freire in tremendous grief. Many expressed much concerned for his well-being. Fortunately, and to much surprise, Paulo's grief was short-lived. While teaching a graduate seminar, he reconnected with an old family friend, Ana Maria (Nita) Araújo—who also happened to be the daughter of Aluizio Pessoa de Araújo, the principal of the Colégio Oswaldo Cruz in Recife, where Paulo had studied and taught. Paulo and Nita married in 1987. For the last ten years of his life, Freire shared with Nita a deep intimate bond, as lovers of life, political allies, and intellectual comrades. Paulo often said that Nita had saved him from the great abyss of his sorrow and that she was, for him, the unexpected culmination of radical love.

Over the last decade of his life, Freire persisted with literacy efforts in Brazil, but also traveled to different parts of the world as an ambassador of hope and a scholar on issues of education, adult literacy, and inequalities. His philosophical and pedagogical writings provided inspiration across a variety of disciplines. Paulo was honored with twenty *doctoris honoris causa* from universities around the globe.[10] In 1993, Paulo Freire was nominated for the Nobel Peace

Figure 1.7 Paulo with his second wife, Ana Maria Araújo Freire.

---

[10] In 1979, Freire was awarded an honorary doctorate from Claremont Graduate University. Coincidentally, it was at this ceremony that I received my doctoral degree in Philosophy of Education. I had the honor of being hooded by Paulo, my political inspiration and most notable intellectual mentor.

Prize, in recognition of his extraordinary contributions as a humanist and philosopher committed to social justice, economic democracy, and human rights. Freire served as the honorary president of the International Council for Adult Education, from 1985 until his death. Freire's conceptualization of education—as a serious political undertaking focused on the transformation of society—motivated the pedagogical efforts of revolutionary societies, as well as democratic organizations committed to a more just world. At the age of seventy-five, Freire suffered a massive heart attack and died on May 2, 1997, in São Paulo. Many of us around the world greatly mourned his death.

By way of this brief account of Paulo's lived history, we learn much about the powerful ways in which his experiences both shaped his intellectual and political growth and steadily deepened the development of his liberatory praxis. We can also gather from this recounting of Paulo's story the reasons why he was so adamant about honoring the importance of lived histories as meaningful aspects of our learning and as powerful forces in shaping our

Figure 1.8 Paulo Freire in India, circa 1980s.

Figure 1.9 Paulo Freire, circa 1990s.

lives. However, attention to only the context of lived experience is insufficient. Instead, as exemplified by Freire's own life, major philosophical influences from both relationships with people and texts constitute significant contextual material to motivate our actions, nourish our consciousness, and ultimately guide our evolution as loving and knowing political subjects, capable of ameliorating human suffering.

Intellectual History

My reading of revolutionary thinkers, specifically the nonoligarchic ones,
helped me a great deal while offering me scientific bases for supporting my
ethical and political beliefs.

—Paulo Freire (1996)

Over his lifetime, Freire drew on ideas of intellectuals from a variety of
traditions and diverse perspectives, in constructing a philosophy of education
that could speak to the massive inequalities he perceived, experienced,
and confronted during his lifetime. His relationships were also sources of
intellectual interrogation and sustenance. For example, Freire (1985) noted
that he was strongly influenced by Rui Barbosa, a lawyer and philosopher, and
Carneiro Ribeiro, a medical doctor. These Brazilian intellectuals transcended
the frontiers of their own disciplines, nurturing in Freire a profound respect for
the power of transdisciplinary thinking—a way of thinking that defied the one-
dimensionality of Western disciplinary approaches to the study of education
and other social phenomena. In examining Freire's intellectual history, this
transdisciplinary feature is evident in the authors he cited in *Pedagogy of the
Oppressed*, which will be the primary focus of this chapter.

The aim of this chapter is to provide students with a philosophical
foundation for understanding the unique interpretations Freire brings to his
analysis of schooling in *Pedagogy of the Oppressed*. Important to this effort
is the need to sustain the hermeneutic complexity generated by Freire's
consistent effort to combine philosophical, political, and pedagogical concerns
in the development of his praxis of liberation. Toward this end, this chapter
provides a succinct discussion of Freire's intellectual history in three parts,
pointing to the major intellectual traditions and philosophical thinkers whose

ideas shaped his interpretations; many of which he specifically utilized to substantiate scientifically the claims posited in *Pedagogy of the Oppressed*.

This strategy is rooted in a desire to remain in dialogue with the book itself, particularly with respect to how Freire employed the ideas of a variety of theological, existential, revolutionary, anticolonial, and critical social theorists, and educational philosophers who sought to critically interrogate cultural, social, cultural, economic, and political questions tied to the subjugation of subaltern populations. Moreover, these scholars and traditions reinforced Freire's profound commitment to an ethics of liberation and revolutionary strategies for cultural action in schools and communities. Here, the philosophical influences are presented in the quasi-chronological order in which they became part of Freire's intellectual history. The following discussion primarily focuses on those ideas within different traditions of specific thinkers, whose ideas appear[1] to have influenced Freire's arguments in *Pedagogy of the Oppressed*.[2]

Early Influences

Radical theological influences

Freire's Brazilian Catholic childhood, his involvement with the Catholic Action Movement and other Christian organizations, and his view of himself as *a man*

---

[1] The process of determining who would be discussed in this chapter was made primarily on the basis of those authors cited by Freire in *Pedagogy of the Oppressed*, as well as major thinkers of the traditions mentioned by Freire or about Freire in a variety of autobiographical and biographical writings about his intellectual influences. However, I acknowledge that in the absence of being able to directly corroborate with Paulo on this matter, there is the need to acknowledge a subjective aspect to this approach, which cannot be avoided and for which I take responsibility. Nevertheless, an effort has been made to rely on Freire's accounts and those who knew him closely. That said, there might be omissions, which I regret.

[2] Each of the traditions, philosophers, and writings presented in this section must be understood as hugely complex and deserving of far greater discussion. However, limitations in the scope of the book and its size prevent more in-depth discussion. It is, therefore, important that the new readers of *Pedagogy of the Oppressed* recognize that Freire's ideas are not one-dimensional and that they are informed by a wide variety of complex, often philosophically dense, and even seemingly contradictory traditions and values. If particular ideas here should peak greater interest, the reader should explore the rich literature that exists in each of the different intellectual influences discussed, as well as a variety of books and articles that engage specific aspects of each of the traditions and each thinker identified. Such a project will only serve to widen one's respect for the intellectual creativity and unwavering motivation of Freire's ideas to address both substantively and expansively questions of human oppression, along with the potential of education to serve as either a means for oppression or liberation.

of faith, cannot be underestimated (Kirylo and Boyd 2017; Madero SJ 2015). As a university student, Freire studied the ideas of the radical Catholic student movement and read the works of radical Catholic philosophers. For example, there is *Momentos dos Vivos*, where Cândido Mendes de Almeida (1966) coins the term "Catholic left" with a grounded sociological meaning that designates "the political positioning, until then unpublished in Brazil, of Catholic groups and intellectuals in favor of provoking a rupture in the socioeconomic structure that kept the country underdeveloped" (Oliveira 2007).[3] Mendez de Almeida challenges the fatalism reinforced by those in the church that mythologized the suffering and exploitation of the poor as God's will. There is also the work of Emmanuel Mounier (1970), who espoused a *personalist* philosophy where the ontological and epistemological process initiates within the dignity, status, and experience of the human being as undetermined and participatory subject (Kirylo and Boyd 2017). He respected the presence of intellectuals in the process of "necessary revolution" but argued they had to break with their bourgeois identity and abandon the culture of the elite. Mounier's ideas supported Freire's focus on "the humanization of man" in *Pedagogy of the Oppressed*; his notion of "class suicide" or political "conversion" to the side of the oppressed; his radically hopeful concept of history; and his belief in the capacity of human beings to transform their world (Elias 1994).

Radical Catholic thinkers

Others thinkers from this radical Catholic tradition include Jacques Maritain, who focused his work on economics and humanism; Gabriel Marcel (1949), whose "philosophy of existence" focused on the struggle of human beings to contend with the dehumanizing character of deeply materialist society; and Thomas Cardonnel, who championed the rights of the poor and helped to introduce the concept of "established disorder" in Brazil (Bruneau 1974: 181); along with the writings of other Catholic revolutionary movement authors who interpreted their writings, such as Alceu de Amoroso Lima, Henrique Lima Vaz and Herbert Jose de Souza among others (Gerhardt 1993: 3). The

---

[3] Cited in Wellington (2011).

social and political concerns raised by these philosophers were also aroused by the failure of the Brazilian government to establish an ethical and morally just social, political, and economic structure; the revolutionary events transpiring around the world in the 1960s; and, most important, a passionate belief among Catholic radicals in the collective possibility of overcoming the oppressive conditions people were facing in the country. In fact, "nowhere had change gone further in the Roman Catholic Church than in Brazil. Brazil has the most progressive Catholic episcopate in the Roman Church worldwide" (Mainwaring 1987: 2). Hence, the influence of these radical Catholic thinkers was at work in Freire's early philosophical and pedagogical work, although his articulations remained focused on the practice of literacy instruction with impoverished communities of the northeastern region of Brazil.

Following his exile and move to Chile, in 1964, Freire became more strongly influenced by his close association and engagement with the writings of liberation theologists, such Gustavo Gutiérrez, Leonardo Boff, Frei Betto, and Dom Hélder Câmara (Jeria 1986). It is useful to note that this is also the era of Vatican II (1962–1965), initiated by Pope John XIII and moved forward by Pope Paul VI—a time in which the church instituted significant changes in an effort to establish a closer ecumenical relationship with the people. These changes, however, were not readily embraced by all, constituting many tensions between more radical and conservative sectors of the Catholic Church, particularly in Latin America.[4]

Liberation theology

The roots of liberation theology in Latin America, a perspective in which Freire was not only well versed but also influenced (Kirylo and Boyd 2017; Reynolds 2013), focused on the importance of context, experience, reflection, action, and evaluative discernment in the interest of humanity and the well-

---

[4] The exclusion of women from the priesthood and thus, the leadership of the church also remained (and remains) a contentious question. In response, fifteen women were appointed as auditors in September 1964. Eventually twenty-three women were auditors at the Second Vatican Council, including ten women religious. The auditors had no official role in the deliberations, although they attended the meetings of subcommittees working on council documents, particularly texts that dealt with the laity (Allen Jr. 2012; Tobin 1986).

being of the entire community (Harnett SJ 2009; International Commission on the Apostolate of Jesuit Education 1993; Nowacek and Mountin 2012).[5] Moreover, these are accompanied by three central tenets: (1) praxis begins from *an option for the poor* as its ultimate motivation and inspiration; (2) acts of service (or social action) to address in concrete ways the present conditions of human suffering are highlighted; and (3) the question of liberation, which shuns the accumulation of wealth at the expense of the poor, underpins praxis (Libano 2017). At the heart of liberation theology then is a vision of spiritual life inextricably tied to material transformation. In his book *Theology of Liberation*, Gustavo Gutiérrez (1973) describes liberation theology as "a theological reflection born of the experience of shared efforts to abolish the current unjust situation and to build a different society, freer and more human[6] ... to give reason for our hope from within a commitment that seeks to become more radical, total, and efficacious" (ix).

With this in mind, liberation theology envisions a person's faith and spiritual commitment as the impetus for working toward the making of a better world (Gutiérrez 1973).[7] It therefore encompasses a moral commitment—not unlike what we find in Freire's writings—to be in solidarity with the poor or undergo a "conversion with the poor," as well as a willingness to undergo "the Easter experience" or transformative moment, where one "dies and is reborn" to

---

[5] Chubbuck and Lorentz (2006), explain that since the early 1970s, Jesuit education or Ignatian pedagogy has embraced a commitment to a "faith that does justice" (International Commission on the Apostolate of Jesuit Education 1993: 134), a commitment articulated by Fr. Pedro Arrupe in 1973 as education to prepare "men [and women] for others" who are "completely convinced that love of God which does not issue in justice for [humanity] is a farce" (Arrupe 1973: 32). To read more about the relationship of social justice, Ignatian pedagogy, and critical pedagogy, also see Chubbuck (2007).

[6] The issue of what is meant by "human" can surface in classroom discussions. Within the context of the church often "human" demarcate the distinction between Godlike and humanlike. Within secularized philosophical traditions, human nature is used to relate to that quality that is *distinctly* human (of women and men), a quality that separates the essence of humankind from other animals. Qualities that *we share* with animals are generally attributed to *aspects of our animal nature*. Critiques about anthropomorphism are linked to discourses that privilege human life over all other forms of living beings can also surface. Of concern is the manner in which anthropomorphism results in inappropriate behaviors or attitudes toward animals, such as trying to adopt an animal that lives undomesticated as a "pet" or misinterpreting the behaviors of these animals, along human terms.

[7] In *Cristianos y Marxista despues del Concilio* (cited by Freire), André Moine (1965) writes of some of the tensions, issues, and concerns at work as radical Catholics working in Christian-based communities found themselves at odds with Pope John's more conservative views. Often they were met by unfounded speculations that liberation theology might leave the needs of people unattended, in favor of misguided Marxist political fervor.

the struggle for a just world (Kirylo and Boyd 2017). Central to the politics of liberation theology was an internal critique of the church as sanctioning institutional violence (Gutiérrez 1973). Hence, Freire conceived his faith, as "a presence in history that does not preclude me from making history, but rather pushes me toward world transformation ... the fundamental importance of my faith [exists] in my struggle for overcoming oppressive reality and for building a less ugly society, one that is less evil and more humane" (Freire 1997: 103–104). Palpable in his words is the influence of liberation theology to his articulation of teacher-student qualities often perceived as spiritual in nature. Brazilian theologian, Leonard Boff (2011) has affirmed Freire's connection to liberation theology: "Paulo Freire is considered one of the founders of liberation theology. He was a Christian that lived his faith in a liberating way ... Paulo placed the poor and oppressed at the center of his method, which is important in the concept of preferential option for the poor, a trademark of liberation theology" (241).

The radical Catholic phenomenological influence of Pierre Teilhard de Chardon (1959) cannot be overlooked. Teilhard's writings advocated for an understanding of reality that would reinsert human beings into the existential struggle for their autonomy and freedom. Found here, is also the idea that the oppressed internalize the deficit views cast upon them by the oppressor and, thus, must undergo a struggle to regain their sense of autonomy and humanity. Teilhard embraced an evolution of humanity that he conceived as a dialectial union, which could simultaneously differentiate and personalize the subject. At the center of his revolutionary spirituality is the belief that the Divine and the world are not antagonists but rather exist in communion. Hence, human beings have a duty to challenge social inequalities in community and transform them in the interest of our evolution.

So, although Freire never formally linked his pedagogy to liberation theology or spiritual matters, the influence of his Latin American Catholic upbringing, his labor within a variety of radical Christian contexts, and his strong affiliation and affinity with revolutionary theologians, nevertheless, influenced and reinforced his views. More specifically, these included his perspective of humanity, transformation, the pedagogical indispensability of love, faith and hope, our capacity to *denounce* oppression and *announce* social justice, and his utopian belief (Madero SJ 2015) in the need to strive for a world where human indignities would cease.[8]

Other theological influences

Another important theological influence on Freire's praxis is Paul Tillich (1954), a Lutheran theologian who believed that theology had to be responsive to the *actual human situation*. For Tillich, as for Freire, we could not understand human existence outside the historical, social and political context that shaped the meaning of our lives (Suchocki 1985). Also pertinent to *Pedagogy of the Oppressed* is Tillich's notion of *kairos*—a key or promising moment for decision or action—that draws on the historical tenets of socialist thought to theorize a crucial liberatory moment, when social and material conditions of oppression could be overcome (Petruzzi 2001). Similarly, Tillich's critique of the ahistorical nature of rational science, which detaches human beings from knowledge and creates feigned neutrality and static knowing, echoes Freire's critique of banking education. And finally, Tillich argued that love, power, and justice constitute indispensable features of free human existence, an idea that resonates with Freire's *pedagogy of love* (Darder 2015).

Reinhold Niebuhr, an American theologian and ethicist, is another author cited in the *Pedagogy of the Oppressed*. Niebuhr's most important teaching centers on his notion of "common grace,"—a grace that he did not believe was dependent on Christian redemption. His was a staunch supporter of the working class and his political involvement was tied to socialist convictions influenced by Marxism, although he rejected the authoritarian communism of Joseph Stalin. In the late 1960s, Niebuhr maintained the United States was undergoing "the two main collective moral issues of our day—the civil rights movement that seeks democratic improvement for [the] black minority, and opposition to the terrible mistaken war in Vietnam." In 1963, King wrote an open letter from jail, stating: "As Reinhold Niebuhr has reminded us … freedom is never voluntarily given by the oppressor; it must be demanded by

---

[8] For an excellent discussion of faith, spirituality and Freirean thought, see *Paulo Freire: His Faith, Spirituality, and Theology* by James Kirylo and Drick Boyd (2017).

the oppressed."[9] In *Moral Man and Immoral Society: A Study in Ethics and Politics*, Niebuhr (1960) challenged the unjust structures of power and the violence of the powerful elite, who easily condemned "the violence of a strike by workers and [then] call upon the state in the same breath to use violence in putting down the strike" (130)—a view that also resonated with Freire.

Latin American philosophy

Latin American philosophy[10] of the twentieth century encompasses long-standing concerns with issues tied to indigenous rights, Latin American identity, coherent philosophical tradition, and feminist concerns within the context of deeply patriarchal relations of power. Debates across different historical epochs since the 1500s generally encompassed conservative ideologies of the elite who sought to protect pristine European influences and their governance over the masses, on one hand; and progressive and radical perspective that sought to challenge and break from the colonial legacy that stifled political participation, economic well-being, and the liberation of the oppressed.

For more than 500 years, the *coloniality of power* (Quijano 2000) has been fiercely enacted by way of oppressive epistemologies and economic imperatives in Latin America that rejected an *ethics of liberation*, negating "a rethinking of the totality of moral problems from the point of the view and the demand of 'responsibility' for the poor" (Dussel 2013: 142). Hence, of particular note here are fierce intellectual debates against Eurocentrism[11] that

---

[9]   Cited in Paulo Elie's (2007) essay, "A Man for All Reasons," published in *The Atlantic* November issue.

[10] This section draws on two very succinct but insightful articles. First Alexander Stehn's (2017) in "Latin American Philosophy," published in the *Internet of Encyclopedia of Philosophy*; and Jorge Garcia and Manuel Vargas's (2013) article, "Latin American Philosophy," published in the *Stanford Encyclopedia of Philosophy*. Both sources are well-respected peer-reviewed academic resources.

[11] *Eurocentrism*, according to Shohat and Stam (2014), refers to a mode of thought that engages in a variety of reinforcing intellectual forms. Briefly, five major aspects of this worldview include: (1) Europe is seen as the "motor" for progressive historical change; (2) attributes to the West an inherent progress toward democratic institutions; (3) elides non-European democratic traditions and obscures manipulation of Western democracy in subverting democracies abroad; (4) minimizes the West's oppressive practices; and (5) appropriates cultural and material production of non-Europeans, while denying both their achievements and their appropriation (see 2–3). Also see, J. M.

demarcated twentieth-century thought in Latin America—debates that surely also influenced Paulo's intellectual formation and development as an educator and philosopher in Brazil.

Backlash against the demeaning intellectual dominance of the West in the early 1900s led to foundational critiques of European positivism[12] and erecting a new Latin American material perspective that was culturally grounded in Latin American values and priorities, as well as could encompass the complexities of indigeneity within Latin American identity. Authors like Argentine philosophers of liberation, Enrique Dussel, Arturo Andrés Roig, and Horacio Cerutti-Guldberg; Marxist scholars, Adolfo Sánchez Vázquez in Mexico and Caio Prado Junior in Brazil; Darcy Ribeiro, the Brazilian anthropologist; Alvaro Vieira Pinto,[13] the Brazilian philosopher (also exiled in 1964) who writes on philosophy of science, and others offered new possibilities for the rethinking of Latin American identity, consciousness, and political context. Through their efforts, Latin American thought has undergone various stages in its evolution, as a variety of thinkers and historical events have motivated different ways of understanding and negotiating Latin American political and economic landscapes. What was to become exceedingly clear in the decades to follow was that philosophy could not be detached from geopolitics (Mignolo 2007).

The Mexican Revolution of 1910, for example, provided Latin American thinkers a more expansive geo-historical vision of the New World, in which the people could emancipate their lands and recover culturally, politically,

---

Balut's (1993) the *Colonizer's Model of the World* for an incisive discussion of Eurocentrism and its role in the colonizing worldview of the West.

[12] Briefly, six major features of *positivism* include: (1) the logic of inquiry is *universal* across all disciplines; (2) the goal of inquiry is to *explain and predict* conditions of social phenomenon; (3) research should be *empirically observable*, using *inductive logic* to make claims that can be tested; (4) inquiry should be *neutral*, objective, and value-free avoiding any form of personal bias; (5) inquiry should be detached or *decontextualized* from cultural or political morals, values, or beliefs; and (6) phenomenon in the world has an *independent existence* or "essence" which remains constant and is observable. Positivism is generally associated with the Enlightenment defined in note 25.

[13] Alvaro Vieira Pinto's writings on consciousness and intentionality are important to Freire's efforts to link education with co-intentionality and the development of social consciousness. Moreover, Pinto's (1960) expansion on Jasper's notion of limit situations is key to Freire's sense of hope; in that, limit-situations become for Pinto not "the impassable boundaries where possibilities end but the real boundaries where possibilities begin" (284). Moreover, Pinto posits a living sense of historical consciousness, where the present always contains the past and the future.

economically, and spiritually from a long saga of colonial violence. Régis Debray (1967) wrote of political struggles in Latin America and the need for "the worker and peasant masses" (18) to free themselves in the present from the contradictions of the past, through becoming conscious of the social and material conditions that stifled their liberation. Similarly, political scientist, Francisco Weiffert (1967) engaged key questions of revolutionary politics, class-consciousness, and the state. As struggles waged in China, Chairman Mao Tse-Tung's (1964) *Little Red Book* would inspire calls to actions; and the Cuban revolution would similarly serve as an impetus for flourishing movements for liberation, as the writings of Fidel Castro, Ernesto (Che) Guevara,[14] and other revolutionaries, inspired by the Cuban philosopher and poet, Jose Martí, reignited revolutionary dreams. So too, Freire's ideas found resonance in Martí's writings (Alvarado 2007).

Jose Martí

Jose Martí was one of the earliest critics of positivism in Latin America (Martí 2009). In contrast to European positivists or materialists, who blamed the problems of Latin America on the genetic inferiority of the races, Martí looked historically to the colonizing politics of cultural and economic domination around the world and its persistent impact on subaltern populations. In response, Martí, a staunch critic of US imperialism, beckoned Latin American intellectuals to develop their own ideas, rooted in the actual social, political, religious, and economic issues facing Latin American populations. Martí espoused a deeply inclusive Latin American identity, where all had the right to participate in forging a genuinely liberated Latin America. Although, Martí died during Cuba's war to gain independence from Spain, his writing called for liberating Latin America from the imperialistic impulses of both Europe and the United States.

---

[14] In *Pedagogy of the Oppressed*, Freire makes note to Che Guevara's (1969) memorable words regarding love and revolution, which echo his own: "Let me say, with the risk of appearing ridiculous, that the true revolutionary is guided by strong feelings of love. It is impossible to think of an authentic revolutionary without this quality" (398). Also see, Peter McLaren's (2000) *Che Guevara, Paulo Freire, and the Pedagogy of Revolution* for an interesting and creative comingling of Che Guevara and Paulo Freire's ideas as foundation for a revolutionary praxis of education.

José Carlos Mariátegui

An important thinker during the "rebellious" period of Latin American thought was the Peruvian scholar, José Carlos Mariátegui (1971), who through his writings offered a vision for Latin America that could transform the destructive social and economic impact of European conquest. Considered one of the most important Marxist thinkers in the history of Latin America thought, Mariátegui called for a socialist solution and asserted the key role of both aesthetics and spirituality to the communal struggle of the oppressed in creating a new, more egalitarian society. Works by Mariátegui and others of his era gave way to a distinctive Latin American school of thought that Francisco Miró Quesada called the *forjadores* (constructors), who are credited with developing a genuinely Latin American philosophy that in the 1940s critically moved the field toward the establishment of a philosophical perspective notably considered *Latin Americanism*. This generation and the next, who built on the writings of Mariátegui, as well as Jose Vascancellos and Leopoldo Zea, also read the works of Spanish philosophers such as Miguel de Unamuno and José Ortega y Gasset.

Spaniard philosophers

The Spanish educator and philosopher, Miguel de Unamuno, is considered an early existentialist whose work engaged the tensions and contradiction that exists between intellect and emotion, as well as faith and reason. At the heart of his ideas, Unamuno grappled with the meaning and limits of consciousness and ongoing conflicts and contradictions that make up the whole of human existence. Unamuno's writings, like Freire, are characterized by a deeply personal and passionate longing to know, even beyond death. A central theme in his writings reflects an underlying desire to preserve one's personal integrity in the face of social conformity, fanaticism, and hypocrisy. Unamuno's novels and plays intensely depict characters agonizing with conflicting human impulses. Unamuno also wrote a book titled *Amor y Pedagogía* (*Love and Pedagogy*), a concept reflected in *Pedagogy of the Oppressed* and Freire's later works (Darder 2015).

The Spanish philosopher and writer, José Ortega y Gasset's *philosophy of life* reflects aspects of pragmatism and realist phenomenology, which give rise to an early form of existentialism and dialectical historicism. For Ortega y Gasset, philosophers have an obligation to unveil beliefs, in order to challenge false notions and promote new ways of understanding the world. Despite an underlying individualism consistent with many philosophers of his time, Ortega y Gasset believed this is best accomplished through engaging the world openly and overcoming the limitations of idealism (where reality is centered around the ego) and a realism that presides *outside* the person. The only underlying true reality for Ortega y Gasset is *one's life*—the life of each individual. His core axiom, *Yo soy yo y mi circunstancia* (*I am me and my circumstance*), challenged the limitations of Descartes axiom, "I think therefore I am"; in that Ortega y Gasset asserts human beings are inextricably linked to the materiality of our world. As such, life is constantly stirred by the tensions and relationship between necessity and freedom, as well as the impact of our decisions upon our fate—a fate for which we often do not accept responsibility to transform. Moreover, Ortega y Gasset also argued for "historical reason," in that neither individuals nor societies exist or can be known outside of history.

Inseparability of coloniality and political economy

The historical inseparability of coloniality and the political economy of European conquest—later manifested through capitalist formations of European modernity[15]—have remained at the heart of the anticolonial imperative of Latin American thought. *Pedagogy of the Oppressed* must then be understood, first and foremost, as a translated Latin American text; where Freire's grappling with the colonial tensions and contradictions of the Latin American condition, the influences of his university formation in the 1940s, and later his experience

---

[15] Jorge Larraín (2000) in *Identity and Modernity in Latin America*, explains,

> For Marx, what was the basis of modernity was the emergence of capitalism and the revolutionary bourgeoisie, which led to an unprecedented expansion of productive forces and to the creation of the world market. Durkheim tackled modernity from a different angle by following the ideas of Saint-Simon about the industrial system. Although the starting point is the same as Marx, feudal society, Durkheim emphasizes far less the rising of the bourgeoisie as a new revolutionary class and very seldom refers to capitalism as the new mode of production implemented by it. The fundamental impulse to modernity is rather industrialism accompanied by the new scientific forces. In the work of Max Weber modernity is closely associated with the processes of rationalization and disenchantment of the world. (13)

as educator and philosopher in Brazil and Chile, became impetus for his humanizing praxis. Moreover, his evolving intellectual engagement with the devastating impact of what Latin American thinkers would come to refer to as the *colonial matrix of power* (Mignolo 2007; Patzi-Paco 2004; Quijano 2000) served as a significant foundation for Freire's revolutionary articulations of such concepts as *cultural invasion* and *banking education* as social phenomenon entrenched in the cruel interplay of economic, political, and ideological control (Tlostanova and Mignolo 2009), within both schools and society.

Existentialism

Freire followed the work of a group of Brazilian intellectuals who gathered at the *Instituto Superior de Estudos Brasilieros* (ISEB) in Rio de Janeiro. The institute was established in 1955 by the Ministry of Education and Culture to create an autonomous space for conducting studies that could contribute to a critical analysis of the Brazilian reality and encourage and promote national development (Abreu 1975). The institute was disbanded following the *Golpe de 64*. Members of the institute were influenced by the writings of existentialists, such as Søren Kierkegaard, Karl Mannheim, Karl Jaspers, Martin Buber, Immanuel Levinas, and Paul Sartre; along with phenomenologists like Edmund Husserl and Martin Heidegger, these authors were read among members of the ISEB and, in turn, influenced Freire's philosophy. So much so that repeated references to "existential situation" and "existential experience," for example, are found throughout *Pedagogy of the Oppressed*.

Existentialism refers to a broad and loosely defined intellectual movement of the twentieth century, which emerged from a deep sense of despair following the Great Depression and the Second World War. The nature of this despair has been chronicled by existentialist philosophers well into the 1970s and persists today, through the deep-rooted Western belief that the individual should have the freedom to choose his or her preferred moral belief system and lifestyle. Existentialists do not necessarily embrace a particular political or moral belief system, in that they may adhere to religious moralism, agnostic relativism, or moral atheism. Among existentialists, for example, can be found Kierkegaard, a religious philosopher, Nietzsche, an anti-Christian, as well as Sartre and

Camus, who were atheists. What unites them is their focus on human existence and their interest in the manner in which human beings often seek to transform their essence or nature over a lifetime. Existentialism has also been associated with several important movements, including phenomenology (which Freire studied as a university student), nihilism, and later postmodernism (which Freire marginally engaged, then later abandoned).

At the heart of existentialist philosophy is concern with understanding the self and the meaning of life through engaging questions tied to free will, choice, and personal responsibility. Inherent to this analysis is the quest of individuals to find out who and what they are by way of the choices they make in the world, generally based upon their lived experiences, beliefs, and worldviews. Similarly, personal choice is thought to emerge uniquely, without necessity of an objective form of truth. As such, once a choice is made, the individual must be held responsible for that choice, without the necessity of exerting public laws, societal rules, or cultural traditions upon individuals.

Another area of consensus among existentialists is that—in the face of inescapable suffering, losses, and defeats over time and an absence of perfection or full power and control over our existence—human life is neither ever *finished* nor fully satisfying. Yet, despite the tenuous quality of human existence, life is still viewed as meaningful by existentialists, since it is the actual search and journey for true self and true personal meaning that most determines one's sense of being. In direct contrast, it is when an individual, government, or cultural group exerts their power and imposes or demands arbitrary beliefs, values, or rules that the human being is *dehumanized* and reduced to an object. Existentialism then stresses that the individual's judgment should be the determining factor for what a person believes, rather than any religious or secular social order.

Søren Kierkegaard

The Danish philosopher Søren Kierkegaard (1949),[16] often at odds with the established institution of the church, believed that individual choice and risk is

---

[16] See: *The Essential* Kierkegaard (2000) edited by H. V. Hong and E. H. Hong and published by Princeton University Press.

a fundamental necessity in deciding life's ultimate meaning. For Kierkegaard, subjectivity signified the infinite depth of human beings and, therefore, could not be seen as the opposite of rational objectivity, but rather as something beyond. Subjectivity, here, refers not merely to the human feelings or emotions, but rather the way a person (the subject) relates to things in terms of his or her own existence. As such, subjectivity is understood always in relationship to objectivity, given that our understanding is always finite and, thus, can never fully grasp who or what we are as human subjects. Hence, the full extent of being a human being can only be captured by way of *lived experience*; never from the outside by way of objective definitions or scientific theories of human nature.

Karl Theodor Jaspers

Karl Theodor Jaspers (1953) was a German psychiatrist and philosopher. Among his best known contributions is his idea of the existence of *an axial period*, referring to a period in human history when the great intellectual, philosophical, and religious systems and traditions around the world came to shape human societies and cultural systems emerged. Jaspers theorized that around 800 BCE to 200 BCE there was a shift—or a turn, as if on an axis— away from more exclusively localized concerns and toward an aspiration of *transcendence*. This to say, that a shift occurred which motivated humankind to speculate about the fate of humanity, the relationship of humans to the cosmos, and the notion of *the good* in human beings (Taylor 2012).

Although Jaspers theory has been problematized for its attempt to universalize cognitive development and inconsistencies (Smith 2015), Jaspers's underlying intent sought to unify our understanding of complex human processes related to the radical demythologization of truth—achieved through *critical reflection* on mythological authority and common sense practices— in an effort to substantiate human solidarity as historical possibility. Also underlying Jaspers ontological quest is the ethical principle as a reflexive means by which human existence can transcend the dualism of the object/ subject split and, instead, embrace a consciousness where the person, as *both* object and subject, are brought into totality, emancipating one's humanity. Moreover, Jaspers argued, "There is no road leading backward .... We can no longer veil reality from ourselves by renouncing self-consciousness without simultaneously excluding ourselves from the historical course of human existence" (Jaspers 2010:143).

Another Jasperian concept important to the reading of *Pedagogy of the Oppressed* is his notion of *limits situation*—"Limit situations are moments, usually accompanied by experiences of dread, guilt or acute anxiety, in which the human mind confronts the restrictions and pathological narrowness of its existing forms, and allows itself to abandon the securities of its limitedness, and so to enter [a] new realm of self-consciousness" (Thornhill 2022). Limit situations signal undefined moments of human existence, generated by tensions and contradictions, which unveil the limits of one's consciousness or social conditions and, thus, compels human beings to transcend the situation. For Jaspers (1954), human beings are always more than what we think ourselves to be. We are never complete "but is a process ... endowed with possibilities through the freedom [we] possess to make of [ourselves] what [we] will by the activities on which [we] decide" (161). Yet, it cannot be ignored that Jaspers also warned of *ultimate situations*, inescapable realities that cannot be changed or surmounted (Jaspers 1954) and through which human beings, nevertheless, construct meaning.

French Existentialists[17]

Jean-Paul Sartre (1946), one of the most recognizable French existentialist philosophers, sought to engage those basic existential experiences that could reveal our fundamental human condition in relation to others and the world. Similar to other existentialists, Sartre embraced the notion "existence precedes essence." Inherent to this view, all existing things in the material universe only have meaning through consciousness, in that it is through consciousness that we create meaning. Therefore, there is no predefined essence to humanity and so human beings must decide the meaning of existence for themselves. As this infers, Sartre was concerned, in particular, with questions of freedom

---

[17] Although Freire does not mention the French philosopher Emmanuel Levinas in *Pedagogy of the Oppressed*, it seems likely that he would have read Levinas. In fact, given the logical connection here, there are scholars who have engaged their works simultaneously (Benade 2015; Gomez 2009; Joldersma 2001).

and responsibility. He argued that it is through our willingness to accept responsibility for our freedom, as well as the suffering that may come with it, that we become authentic human beings. Hence, it is, indeed, our actions that then make us who we are and these are determined not by predetermined destiny or the will of a God but by the choices and actions of human beings in the world.

Simone de Beauvoir, one of two women intellectuals cited in *Pedagogy of the Oppressed*, is best known as a French existentialist feminist for her literary and philosophical works—such as *The Second Sex*, originally published in 1949—which have been linked to the second-wave of feminism,[18] despite Beauvoir's expressed concerns with the failures of the first wave of the Women's Movement to liberate women. Beauvoir insisted that women could not be truly liberated until the system of patriarchal society itself was overthrown. Moreover, Beauvoir details "the inadequacies of biological, Freudian, and Engelsian historical materialist accounts of gender difference" (Mussett and Wilkerson 2012: 98) and that these theories had to be either modified or replaced "by an existential-phenomenologist approach, rooted in past and present lived experience, and leading to freely chosen reorientation of future societies in the direction of equality" (98). In her essay "The Ethics of Ambiguity," Beauvoir (1947) tackles the existential question of absolute freedom and the constraints of circumstance that stifle freedom. In *La Pensee de Droite, Aujourd'hui* (*The Political Thought of the Right, Today*), Beauvoir (1955) argues that the fundamental interests of the political right lie in "changing the consciousness of the oppressed, not the situation which oppress them" (34).

---

[18] The Feminist movement is often delineated by three waves of feminism. First wave: 1830s—early 1900s, where women fought for the right to vote, as well as equal contract and property rights. Second wave: 1960s–1980s, is an important period in which feminist debates were broadened in order to struggle for gender equity across the society; and Third wave, 1980s to present, often considered a time of *micropolitics* in the struggle for gender equity, where feminist perspective became more particularistic with respect to issues of racism, sexuality, ecofeminism, and so on. There are some, however, that argue we are actually now in the Fourth wave of feminism; a time in which feminist are working to contend with and move past what has been seen as the lack of focus and "divisiveness" of the third wave. Whatever the case, it is important to note that within each of this waves of feminisms there have been tensions and contradictions often linked to ideologies and epistemologies that exist somewhere across the spectrum from radical to ultraconservative debates. For more see: *An Introduction to Feminism* (Finlayson 2016) and *Feminism: A Very Short Introduction* (Walters 2006).

Mikel Dufrenne is another of the French philosophers whose work is recognized within the existential tradition.[19] In *Pedagogy of the Oppressed*, Freire makes particular reference to Dufrenne's (1968) *Pour L'Homme*, where the author speaks to the anguish caused by what seems to be a stubborn historical intractability toward the undoing of our humanity. In his work, he engages the need to restore human subjectivity to our construction of knowledge, given that it is our inalienable right—a right that is consistently compromised by systems of oppression. Moreover, Dufrenne posits the need to encounter the question of the other, through ongoing reflection on our relationship to self, one another, and the world—which he elevates to an ethical imperative. Dufrenne argues that this is particularly significant, given declarations of the *death of God* in Modernist philosophy—a declaration also accompanied with the asphyxiation of the self, which causes human beings to build defenses against our inevitable end.

Other existentialists: Karl Mannheim and Martin Buber

The Hungarian-born philosopher, Karl Mannheim (1952) is best recognized for his contribution to the *sociology of knowledge*. Mannheim incorporated Marxist ideas in his work, particularly in his efforts to demonstrate that "ideas were the product of their times and of the social statuses of their proponents" (Sagarin and Kelly 1970: 293). As such, Mannheim sought to explain why human beings "behave differently in the framework of different social groups and class situations" (294). "Truths," therefore, are linked to and influenced by the social context from which they emerge. In the *Problem of Generation*, for example, Mannheim (1952) asserts that when any major event (i.e., the Great Depression, the holocaust, the Second World War, Vietnam, and civil rights) collectively impacts a group of people, *particularly at adolescence*, they are likely to exhibit a *collective consciousness* about its meaning. Hence, generations can be grouped based on their collective sociohistorical experiences of a major event, which Mannheim believed had an impact on their thoughts and feelings

---

[19] Mikel Dufrenne (1953) can also be categorized in the tradition of phenomenology. His best-known book, *Phénoménologie de l'expérience esthétique* (*The Phenomenology of Aesthetic Experience*), expounds on the inextricable link between the larger dimension of human feeling and aesthetics. This is a book that Freire is bound to also have read, given his expressed interest in aesthetics with respect to the question of our humanity.

as a group and, in turn, influenced how they made sense of their existence and social identity. Despite the problem with Mannheim's effort to formulate "a value-neutral concept of ideology" (Stirk 1992: 66), his writings on "liberty, democratic planning, fundamental democratization of society, and the theory of democratic personality are critical issues in Freire's early writings" (Torres 1993: 120). Mannheim's sociology serves as a catalyst for those seeking to interpret society as a totality, beyond the specific interests of the ruling class. Furthermore, Mannheim's theory of the *awareness process* bears similarity to Freire's process of *critical consciousness* (Paiva 1979, 1980).

Martin Buber (1958), an Austrian, Jewish philosopher and educator, centered his work on religious consciousness, interpersonal relations, and community. Buber's major philosophical contribution was his notion of *dialogical existence*, where he points to the primacy and direct interactive quality of the *I-Thou* relationship, in contrast to an *I-It* relationship or monologue expressed through an indirect and mediated experience of the other. Moreover, in the I-It experience, the individual approaches all others (things or people) as instrumentalized objects—to be used, known, or experienced—dehumanizing the other and devaluing the meaning of existence. In contrast to positivist notions, Buber insisted that existence must be understood as an intimate dialogue between people *with* one another and the world: a relationship that could only transpire through openness and willingness to be responsive to others and in communion with all beings.

Phenomenology

Phenomenology, as a branch of existential study, seeks to be scientific in its objective study of social phenomenon, through employing a systematic method of reflection for determining the essential properties and structures of human experience. It is "above all, a meditation on knowledge ... [putting] consciousness face-to-face with the phenomenon and appears, thus as consciousness of the given" (Torres 2014: 31). At the center of this school of thought are five fundamental assumptions (Orbe 2009). Briefly and simply, the first rejects the belief in objective research, preferring to cluster assumptions through a process of phenomenological *epoché*—a process that seeks to block biases and assumptions, in order to make sense of a social phenomenon within its own system of meaning. Second, analyzing everyday behavior offers us a greater understanding of its inherent nature. Third, we can best understand human nature through studying the unique ways in which we reflect the world around us. Fourth, engaging conscious experience, rather than so-called objective data is preferred. And lastly, since the focus is on discovery, unrestrictive methods of inquiry are employed.

The first moment: Georg Wilhelm Hegel

Historically, phenomenology has been divided along three distinct moments. The first is associated with Georg Wilhelm Hegel's (1977) *Phenomenology of Spirit*. Hegel sought to break with the old order, arguing against the positivist epistemological tradition of modern philosophy that had prevailed from Descartes through Kant. In contrast to the idea that the individual mind controlled thought, Hegel argued that a collective human dimension is at work in the construction of knowledge and, as such, tension always exists between an individual's unique sense of things and the need for distinguishing universal concepts for societal integration. Herein are two movements—the first, *meaning* or "sense of certainty" and, the second, *perception*—that correspond to the first two of Hegel's three modes of consciousness. The third movement, *understanding*, arises through the negotiation of tensions, a process that becomes progressively more refined. This idea of knowledge as movement across oppositional and contradictory tensions signals the Hegelian *dialectic*, where it is understood as an interactive striving to arrive at stable and truthful categories of thought. Knowledge as *dialectical movement* is then a recurrent theme in Hegel's writings and sits at the heart of his innovative epistemology.

Hegel elaborates on *self-consciousness* as an awareness of another's awareness of oneself. Inherent to self-consciousness is found a struggle for *recognition*, caused by opposing tensions generated by different meanings. On one hand, there is the moment when self and other come together, which makes self-consciousness possible; and, on the other hand, the moment of difference arising when one is conscious of the *otherness*. For Hegel, this tension between selves and others, between mutual identification and estrangement, manifest in the field of social relationships. This struggle for recognition is magnified between two individuals (or groups) who are bound to one another in an unequal relationship of dependence. About this dialectical bond or relationship between the consciousness of master and the consciousness of the oppressed, Hegel argues: "The one is independent, and its essential nature is to be for itself; the other is dependent, and its essence is life or existence for another. The former is the Master, or Lord, the latter the Bondsman." This points to the struggle of *lordship and bondage* (111) or master and slave, and its various expressions, which are reflected in Karl Marx's analysis of social class and later in Freire's exposition of the oppressor/ oppressed contradiction in *Pedagogy of the Oppressed*.

Equally important to this discussion is Hegel's claim that social standards or laws do not reside in objects or in the mind but in the *organized social whole* (541). Within the context of this social dimension, each individual identity is also part of a collective, where values and moral conventions of the organized social whole are internalized as emanating from oneself. When political life fails to be the true expression of common ethical life, forms of social oppression result that seek to annihilate opposing forces. For Hegel, the ethical encompasses common or communal values, customs, and codes of conduct that determine how people act, their beliefs, and how they relate to the world—all which become deeply embedded in the collective culture. Nevertheless, Hegel argued that culture is a dynamic force always subject to change, an idea that is in sync with his view of history as a dynamic and unfolding collective force.

The second moment: Edmond Husserl

The second and most fundamental phenomenological moment is that of Edmund Husserl (1954, 2012), considered the father of phenomenology, in that his ideas had a widespread influence on philosophers who engaged questions of existence and beingness. According to Husserl, phenomenology encompassed "the reflective study of the essence of consciousness, as experienced from the first-person point of view" (Woodruff 2007). This approach to knowledge construction begins with the intuitive experience of phenomena, or what emerges through human reflection; and, by way of this expression, seeks to comprehend the essence of existence. Husserl rejected the abstraction and detached knowing of positivism, by focusing attention on questions of human perception, experience, and knowledge through the structure of consciousness. Husserl's underlying premise is that "All consciousness is consciousness of something."[20]

Husserl asserts that the only certainty we have is our own conscious awareness. Hence, this is the place from whence we must begin to know the world. However, our awareness and consciousness must always be understood as an awareness and consciousness of *something*—where *something* refers to any object, real or unreal, physical or psychical, which we reflect on—although experience, in and of itself does not discern *states of consciousness* from *objects of consciousness*. Thus, we cannot know whether objects of consciousness have an independent existence separate from us, although they do unquestionably exist as objects of our consciousness. It is precisely this relationship between experience, the world, and consciousness then that permits human beings to explore and understand our existence.

For Husserl (1954), consciousness does not exist outside of the *lifeworld* nor does the lifeworld exist separate of consciousness—radically confirming the dialectical relationship between consciousness and the world. "In whatever way we may be conscious of the world as universal horizon, as coherent universe of existing objects, we, each 'I-the-man [woman]' and all of us together, belong to the world as living with one another in the world; and the world is our world, valid for our consciousness as existing precisely through this 'living together'" (108). As such, the lifeworld, as the ground for all shared experience, is understood as fundamental to *ontological* (of being or existence) and *epistemological* (of the nature of knowledge or meaning) reflections and interrogations.

The last moment: Martin Heidegger

The last moment in phenomenology is attributed to Martin Heidegger (1962)[21] who is said to later have rejected phenomenology. Heidegger's (1962) central

---

[20] In an essay originally published in 1939 entitled "Une idée fondamentale de la phénoménologie de Husserl: l'intentionnalité," Jean-Paul Sartre makes reference to Husserl's famous phrase "All consciousness is consciousness of something." Intentionality: A Fundamental Idea of Husserl's Phenomenology first appeared in *Situations I* (Paris: Gallimard, 1947).

[21] Originally published in 1927.

focus is the ontological question: "What is 'being'?" In response, he sought to distinguish between human existence as beings (*Sein*) and the existence of things in general (*Seindes*). With this in mind, he centers his analysis on *Dasein* (Gorner 2007: 4), "the being" for whom a description of experience is essential to our engagement *with* and our ability *to-be-in-the-world* (Torres 2014). Heidegger also argues that human existence and time are inextricably linked, since human beings are always looking toward the future.[22] Hence, he reasons that being is really just a process of becoming, rejecting the Aristotelian claim that human beings possess a fixed essence.

Heidegger (1962) however, makes a distinction between *authentic* human beings, who have a distinct grasp of their humanity (i.e., farmers and rural workers); and *inauthentic* human beings (i.e., city dwellers) who are out of touch with their own individuality. In turn, this inauthentic state of being causes anxiety. This anxiety, according to Heidegger, is the result of subjugation to arbitrary cultural rules. Moreover, human beings respond in two ways: either to flee or face up to the anxiety. Heidegger proposes that facing the realities of our human existence, although limiting, is also liberating.

---

[22] At this juncture, it is useful to signal anew the Eurocentric philosophical foundations of the majority of thinkers discussed in this chapter. This is particularly apparent here in Heidegger's theorizing of time and being—conceived through a lens that corresponds to Eurocentric system of values.

> Eurocentrism, as it prevailed during European Enlightenment, was advocated in England by John Locke and David Hume, in France by A. R. J. Turgot and Voltaire, and in Germany by Gotthold Ephraim Lessing and Immanuel Kant, to give some examples. This means that during this period it was in play all over Europe. For the origin and dissemination of Eurocentrism, the idea of progress is very important. This idea means that world history as a whole, with all of its relevant developments, comes to its absolute peak in Europe in the second half of the eighteenth century. In this way it is possible to frame a concept of history that covers the whole world. However, this possibility comes at a high price. Although certain periods of history are judged in a differentiated way ... Europe is the standard within which all the different phenomena in space and time get their place as historic stadia. Europe of this period of time understands itself as superior with regard to all other times and cultures, and ... Europe defines what philosophy or science is. (Kimmerle 2014: 100)

This also points back to the earlier discussion on Latin American thought, which sought to challenge, destabilize, and transform the Eurocentric worldview in Latin America, fundamentally linked to the coloniality of power. Moreover, the racism (and sexism, for that matter) that underpins the worldview of the 1800s and 1900s when these theorists were writing is both inescapable and indefensible; yet, as critical education theorists like Phillip Kain (2005) and Peter McLaren argue, disrupting epistemological possibilities simultaneously exist within theories, particularly with respect to Hegelian dialectics and historical materialism.

Although Heidegger initially considered his concepts related to time and being as universal, he later posits that the actual time or period (or *epoch*)[23] in which we live impacts our way of being, providing the concept of Dasein *historicality* (Heidegger 1962: 41). This phenomenon also signals a historical condition or truth that may remain concealed, until a moment when the limits of inauthentic existence or a *fore-sight* (a guiding idea that redefines our sense of being) provoke ontological inquiry and "comports itself towards something possible" (306). Heidegger defines truth as *both revealing and concealing* ways of being-in-the-world ... "situations are not spatial; rather ... situations are determined by taking action, asking questions, re-creating the situation into which [one] has been thrown" (Petruzzi 1998). Human agency or freedom can only be expressed through the process of inquiry, in which one critically reflects upon ways of being-in-the-world.

The evolution of consciousness, for Heidegger, is then understood as key to our human existence, emerging from our *being-in-the-world* and, thus, historically motivated. However, different worldviews also create different interpretations of what it means to be. Linked to this, Heidegger also engaged questions of language and meaning, where language is not seen as an arbitrary construct nor does it solely correspond to or describe the outside world. Instead, he argues that our words actively name things into being and can have a powerful and transformative impact on the world. As a student of both phenomenology and the psychology of language, Heidegger's views would have been significant reference points for the evolution of Freire's own views on literacy.

Revolutionary Influences

The ideas Freire expresses in *Pedagogy of the Oppressed* clearly reflect the dramatic impact of his exile from Brazil, as well as a radical shift in his thinking,

---

[23] Freire makes note of the idea of *epoch* in *Pedagogy of the Oppressed*, referring to the critical work of German Sociologist, Hans Freyer (1958), who posited that history enters critical epochs in which the objective cultural forms are unable to contain the flux of life. As a consequence of the tension, the historical moment gives rise to the necessity of transformative change.

inspired by his relationships and associations with revolutionary intellectuals in Latin America and around the world. This arbitrary dividing line should not be taken as a hard demarcation, but rather as simply a logical one, given the historical conditions and pressing issues of his time. Freire's intellectual history resumes in this section, bringing together a discussion of Marxism, the Frankfurt School, and anticolonial thinkers who influenced his thinking.

Marxism

German philosopher, Karl Marx is considered one of the most enduring revolutionary intellectuals of all time—whether embraced or maligned, his ideas have been overwhelmingly engaged across all disciplines and social movements for liberation around the world. Marxist philosophy, as with many of the philosophies discussed earlier, must be understood against the backdrop of the Enlightenment,[24] which gave rise to the overwhelming belief that phenomena could be known *objectively* by way of the observing mind, which become the medium for liberating the human spirit.[25] Marx, as did other philosophers discussed earlier, challenged positivist claims. For example, although initially influenced by the phenomenology of Hegel, Marx (1933) came to challenge what he considered to be the *idealist* tendencies in Hegelian dialectics.

> The question of the relation of thinking to being, the relation of spirit to nature is the paramount question of the whole of philosophy .... The answers which the philosophers gave to this question split them into two great camps.

---

[24] The Enlightenment refers to an intellectual and scientific movement of eighteenth-century Europe that, in defiance of the autocratic rule of monarchy and the Roman Catholic Church, infused a rational and scientific approach to religious, social, political, and economic views. The ideas of this historical period led to the American Revolution and French Revolution and strongly influenced the Industrial Revolution. Thinkers that loom large in this period are Rene Descartes, John Locke, David Hume, Adam Smith, Spinoza, and Immanuel Kant.

[25] Key ideas of the Enlightenment age include: (1) The Individual is starting point for all knowledge and action and individual reason cannot be subjected to a higher authority; (2) Rationalism, where reason and rational thought, independent of experience, is innate within the human mind and the only basis for organizing knowledge; (3) Empiricism: the only valid way to gain knowledge about the world is through observation or sensory experience; (4) Scientific method is considered to allow the observation of facts and the discovery of laws that govern these facts; (5) Progress: knowledge gained by scientific methods can be used to explain or predict events; and (6) Universalism: scientific methods for acquiring objective knowledge are universal so they can be applied to all spheres of endeavor. These ideas are foundational to positivism, which was defined in note 17.

Those who asserted the primacy of spirit to nature … comprised the camp of idealism. The others, who regarded nature as primary, belong to the various schools of materialism. (329)

True to his material sensibilities, Marx developed a *dialectical materialism* that encompasses four key ideas (Stalin 2013).[26] First, we cannot understand the nature of phenomenon divorced from its totality, from "a connected and integral whole, in which things, phenomena are organically connected with, dependent on, and determined by, each other" (9). The aim here is to understand society as a whole. Second, nature is always in "a state of continuous motion and change" (9), simultaneously rising and disintegrating. So in addition to its interconnections, we cannot understand history, for example, apart from its constant movement. Therefore, history, as well as human ideas, knowledge, and culture, remain always unfinished and in a state of becoming something new (Roberts 2003). Moreover, knowledge, consciousness, and societies change to the degree that their movement is acknowledged and embraced. Third, change and movement in nature is not circular or redundant, but rather goes from "the simple to complex, from the lower of the higher" (11). And, fourth, contradictions are inherent to all phenomena. Things do not evolve as harmonious unfolding, but rather, "as the 'struggle' of opposite tendencies which operate on the basis of these contradictions" (13). In concert with this approach, Marx proposed a political and economic analysis firmly grounded on the indivisible link between theory and practice.

Marx offers a revolutionary reading of history that combines ontology and epistemology through the premise of class struggle (Roberts 2003). Marx and Engels (1972)[27] note, "As individuals express their life, so they are. What they are, therefore, coincides with their production, both with what they produce and with how they produce. The nature of individuals thus depends on the material conditions determining their production" (42). In light of this, Marx theorizes that the only viable means for transforming the oppressive and alienating conditions produced by a dehumanizing wage system of labor is a revolutionary process, which can collectively mobilize society toward a just

---

[26] First published in 1938.
[27] First published in 1854.

and equal redistribution of social and material wealth. Hence, "the economical emancipation of the working classes is therefore the great end to which every political movement ought to be subordinate as a means."[28] Nevertheless, "the emancipation of the workers must be the task of the workers themselves."[29] Essential to this revolutionary process then must be conditions for workers to participate as the historical subjects of their own knowing and liberation.

The power of Marxist ideas is consolidated in the theory of *historical materialism*—a dialectical theory of knowledge and analysis that focuses on historical processes and the societal causes of capitalist oppression. Marx contends that all forms of social thought (i.e., art, philosophy, science) and institutions (including the family) originate from the political economic superstructure[30] of the state. Hence, everything in life is economically determined. The flow of money informs our relations with one another, with nature, and with the world. Marx employs the category of *value* to signify basic relations of production in capitalism, where all social and material exchanges are organized on the basis of value (Postone 1996). The alienating structures of private property, for example, overwhelmingly shape our thoughts and aspirations, as capital dictates the boundaries of human activity (Marx 1998). About this Marx (1844) writes,

> Through *estranged, alienated labor*, then, the worker produces the relationship to this labor of a man alien to labor and standing outside it. The relationship of the worker to labor creates the relation to it of the capitalist (or whatever one chooses to call the master of labor). *Private property* is thus the product, the result, the necessary consequence, of *alienated labor*, of the external relation of the worker to nature and to himself.

---

[28] *Resolution of the London Conference on Working Class Political Action.* International Workingmen's Association written by Marx in 1871. See: https://www.marxists.org/archive/marx/works/1871/09/politics-resolution.htm.

[29] *The First Congress of the International* in Geneva, 1866, written by Marx. See: https://www.marxists.org/reference/archive/bakunin/works/1872/karl-marx.htm.

[30] Marx's theory divides society in two layers, which he terms the "base" and "superstructure." The base refers to the sphere of all the material, tangible aspects of life, along with the economic relations that capital generates. The superstructure refers to the sphere of political and ideological institutions; the cultural belief system, and the hopes, dream, and spirit generated by the capital. The superstructure is understood in terms of three aspects: (1) the legal and political expressions of society linked to relations of production; (2) the forms of consciousness that express particular class views of the world; and (3) the processes by which human beings become conscious of a fundamental economic conflict and wage struggle.

Accordingly, all societal institutions are established and reproduced *within* economic relations—economic relations that Marx claims can only be transformed through a revolutionary process of class struggle where the tyranny of capital is overcome. However, Marx also notes that it is precisely from *within* the limitations of class tensions and antagonisms—produced by the structural inequalities of the ruling class—that new possibilities for liberation arise.

Marx further argues that the dialectical necessity of human history points to the eventual dismantling of the oppressive state and the establishment of a just society. Essential to Marxist thought are questions of history and of workers-as-subjects (or makers) of history. "Historical materialism, by virtue of its emphasis on human productive practices and historical specificity, holds out the prospect of perceiving the present as history. Human beings can know the world, despite its complexity, because they have made it" (Roberts 2003: 174). Marx confirms that women and men make history, as much as we are made by history, although often not within conditions of our own making. Hence, to understand history, ourselves, and the world requires that knowledge be constructed within the material conditions of our historical continuity This challenges abstract, neutral, or prescribed views of history, knowledge, or consciousness, by reasserting our humanity as full and active participants in the revolutionary process—a process that must begin concretely where lived history, consciousness, and material existence intersect. Marx (1998) begins here in that knowledge, like history, does not exist divorced from our lives, but rather "the production of ideas, of conceptions, of consciousness is at first directly interwoven with the material activity and the material intercourse of men [and women], in the language of real life" (42).

However, Marx also notes that society's phenomenological sphere (or sphere of appearance) is often quite different from its essence. Thereby, pointing the way for the development of a theory of ideology that can engage the contradiction between the appearance and essence of society—a contradiction that benefits the ruling class. *Ideology*, in the Marxist sense, signifies the production, reproduction, and consumption of ideas and behavior that distort or illuminate the nature of reality (Giroux 1983), obscuring relations of power, entrapping our sensibilities, and obscuring existence. Moreover, since ideology is contradictorily situated and recreated within the sphere of appearance, it expresses not only social and material formations of domination but also resistance and affirmation. Marx uses the concept of *commodity fetishism*[31] to unveil the contradiction within a capitalist society, where the value of workers is gauged through a system of monetary exchange (accepted by the worker), while concealing the hidden extract surplus value (profit of the producer) and the workers' estrangement or alienation[32] from their labor.[33] For this reason, Marxists maintain that seldom is domination absolute within the capitalist

---

[31] In Marxism, the concept of commodity fetishism is used to explain how the social organization of labor is mediated through market exchange, the buying and the selling of commodities (goods and services). In *Capital*, Marx and Engels (1996) explain the concepts underlying commodity fetishism in the following manner:

> As against this, the commodity-form, and the value-relation of the products of labour within which it appears, have absolutely no connection with the physical nature of the commodity and the material relations arising out of this. It is nothing but the definite social relation between men [and women] themselves which assumes here, for them, the fantastic form of a relation between things. In order, therefore, to find an analogy we must take flight into the misty realm of religion. There the products of the human brain appear as autonomous figures endowed with a life of their own, which enter into relations both with each other and with the human race. So it is in the world of commodities with the products of men's hands. I call this the fetishism which attaches itself to the products of labour as soon as they are produced as commodities, and is therefore inseparable from the production of commodities. (83)

[32] "Alienation" refers to the process whereby workers are made to feel separate from the products of their own labor. In capitalism, workers are exploited insofar as they do not work to create a product that they, themselves, can sell to a real person; instead, workers, in order to live and survive, must sell their labor for a wage (as if their labor were itself a property or thing that can be bought and sold). Workers are alienated from their product (what they make) precisely because they do own the product they make, which belongs to the owners who have purchased the labor-power of workers in exchange for exclusive ownership over the workers' products and all the profit that comes by the sale of those products. However, the worker's production does not have to lead to alienation and can actually be very satisfying. This happens under conditions where workers can pour their subjectivity into what they make and even gain enjoyment from the fact that another person gains enjoyment or satisfaction from what they have made. The idea here is that the further workers are from the products of our labor, the more that we can become alienated and objectified, distanced from our creativity and opportunities to transform our world. Such estrangement serves to meet the objectives of capitalism, at the expense of the humanity of workers.

[33] It is in his discussion of estranged labor that Marx (1844) differentiates human beings from animals, which Freire takes up in *Pedagogy of the Oppressed*. Of this, Marx contends,

> The animal is immediately one with its life activity. It does not distinguish itself from it. It is *its life activity*. Man makes his life activity itself the object of his will and of his consciousness. He has conscious life activity. It is not a determination with which he directly merges. Conscious life activity distinguishes man immediately from animal life activity. It is just because of this that he is a species-being. Or it is only because he is a species-being that he is a conscious being, i.e., that his own life is an object for him. Only because of that is his activity free activity. Estranged labor reverses the relationship, so that it is just because man is a conscious being that he makes his life activity, his *essential being*, a mere means to his *existence*.

mode of production.[34] Rather, given the effectiveness of ideology in obscuring structures of oppression, the working class often became complicit in their own dehumanization.

Consistent with the discussion above and worth repeating, Marxism posits the existence of social classes, whereby human beings are separated into distinct segments of the population, according to their social and material wealth. The dynamics of a society can only be understood in terms of a system where the dominant ideas are formulated by the ruling class to secure control over the working class. The deep structures of human inequality perpetuate and reinforce class divisions, along with the inherent social class conflicts and contradictions of capitalist societies. However, the dynamics of class struggle can move us beyond the negative reading of ideology above, to an arena of critique where the oppressive ideas, structures, and practices of the ruling class are openly critiqued and *class-consciousness* evolves. Marx argues that it is through this evolution of class-consciousness and organized revolutionary action that the working class give birth to new theories, along with new social and political organizations.

For Marx, the historical class struggle of workers must be understood dialectically—where the interconnections, changes, and movements between and across individuals and societies, humans and nature, knowledge and practice all retain the revolutionary tension necessary for critical inquiry and the possibility of transformation. It is this feature of dialectical materialism that ruptures the bourgeois (or liberal) farce of individual freedom, in the absence of revolutionary aims. To this point, Marx argues, "In bourgeois society capital is independent and has individuality, while the living person is dependent and has no individuality." In contrast, Marxism expresses the importance of communal solidarity, by calling for "an association, in which the free development of each is the condition for the free development of all" (Marx and Engels 1848).

---

[34] "Mode of production" refers to "everything that goes into the production of the necessities of life, including the 'productive forces' (labor, instruments, and raw material) and the 'relations of production' (the social structures that regulate the relationship between humans in the production of goods)" (Felluga 2015: 180 - 81). According to Marx and Engels, (as stated earlier) for individuals, the mode of production is "a definite form of expressing their life, a definite *mode of life* on their part. As individuals express their life, so they are. What they are, therefore, coincides with their production, both with *what* they produce and *how* they produce" (Marx and Engels 1972: 42).

Given the fundamentally antidemocratic foundation of capitalist relations, Marxism considers democratic principles indispensable to overcoming our alienation (McLaren and Leonard 1993), as well as our efforts to engage critically across larger arenas of organized class struggle that extend beyond our daily tensions as individual workers. Marx contends, "social domination in capitalism does not, on its most fundamental level, consist in the domination of people by other people, but in the domination of people by abstract social structures that people themselves constitute" (Postone 1996: 30). Lastly, Marx responds to this universalism of worker oppression through a call for *Internationalism*, where the common interests and struggles of working people worldwide focus on the abolition of national interests and the formation of international communities where socialist values of human rights and economic justice prevail.

Marxist intellectuals

The works of Marxist theorists influenced Freire's ideas and are cited throughout *Pedagogy of the Oppressed*. These include Vladimir Lenin, Rosa Luxembourg,[35] György Lukács, Antonio Gramsci, and Louis Althusser, as well as Lucien Goldmann, André Nicolaï, and Gavrito "Gajo" Ptrovio. These socialist philosophers engaged Marx and expanded his ideas in a variety of ways, particularly with respect to questions of humanist praxis, ideology, consciousness, cultural hegemony, and language. In several instances, their writings challenge the Marxist orthodoxy of their time, in an effort to free Marxism from the vice of an exaggerated scientificity and economic determinism that betrayed its liberatory intent.

Vladimir Lenin

Bolshevik revolutionary leader, Vladimir Lenin is credited for the success of the *Great October Socialist Revolution*[36] of 1917. This Bolshevik offensive is considered to mark the birth of the Soviet Union. Lenin's *What Is to*

---

[35] Along with Simone de Beauvoir, Rosa Luxembourg is one of only two female intellectuals included in this intellectual pantheon.
[36] Also commonly referred to as *Red October*, the *October Uprising* or the *Bolshevik Revolution*.

Be Done?—a book fashioned as a blueprint, based on Lenin's tactics for revolutionary praxis—is considered his most formidable contribution to our understanding of strategic actions for societal reinvention. Lenin's central theme is built around three primary questions: (1) the character and main content of political agitation; (2) organizational tasks; and (3) the plan for simultaneously remaking society. Lenin points to the significant role of theory, arguing, "without revolutionary theory there can be no revolutionary movement" (12).

For Lenin, theoretical (or ideological) struggle is as significant to revolution as political and economic struggles. On this issue, Lenin is more pragmatic than Marx, in that he contends that beyond the spontaneity of class struggle, the revolution requires the active participation of committed organic intellectuals (which he calls *professional intellectuals*), who are in relationship *with* the working class. It is through this shared relationship of praxis, between intellectuals and workers that Lenin maintains political consciousness evolves and society is remade. Lenin, further, insists that *practical* participation in political life is key, for it is through our lived praxis (where theory and practice unite) that we come to truly understand the "relationships between *all* the various classes of modern society" (43). Such participation works to "clarify for *all* and everyone the world-historic significance of the struggle for the emancipation of the proletariat" (49).

Fundamental to revolutionary praxis, Lenin argues, is the need to eradicate "*all distinctions as between workers and intellectuals*, not to speak of distinctions of trade and profession" (71). This calls to mind Lenin's concern with the tendency of the Russian Social Democratic Party to instrumentalize the economic demands of workers for revolutionary struggle and "why any subservience to the spontaneity of the mass movement ... prepare[s] the ground for converting the working class movement into an instrument of bourgeois democracy" (59). For Lenin, the only real antidote to this dehumanizing objectification is revolutionary praxis, where workers are integrated in the process of intellectual formation and the practice of social democracy.

However, Lenin contended that to accomplish such a difficult endeavor requires leadership. In concert with this directive, Lenin asserts: (1) no revolutionary movement can endure without a stable organization of leaders maintaining continuity; (2) the broader the popular mass drawn spontaneously into the struggle, which forms the basis of the movement and participates in it, the more urgent the need for such an organization, and the more solid this organization must be; (3) such an organization must consist chiefly of people professionally engaged in revolutionary activity; (4) in an autocratic state, the more we confine the membership of such an organization to people who are professionally engaged in revolutionary activity and who have been professionally trained in the art of combating the political police, the more difficult will it be to unearth the organization; and (5) the greater will be the number of people from the working class and from the other social classes who will be able to join the movement and perform active work in it (79). Although there are aspects of Lenin's tactics that have been severely criticized as antidemocratic and refuted, no one can deny that his leadership and revolutionary vision ignited the liberatory aspirations of many worldwide.

Rosa Luxembourg

Socialist philosopher, Rosa Luxembourg, is best remembered for her passionate discourses that sought to move notions of freedom and truth beyond dogma or sectarian fixations, in an effort to recover Marx's dialectical insistence on an embodied revolutionary process. Hence, Luxembourg's (1906, 2006) deeply humanistic and revolutionary sensibilities fueled her critique of so-called reforms that betrayed the essence of working-class struggle. Similarly, Luxembourg (2007) challenges the antidemocratic tendencies of many Marxists of her time, who were mired in a lifeless, mechanistic, and "policemanlike materialism" (116). This she argues undermines Marx's own humanism, which calls for "a society in which the full and free development of every individual is the ruling principle" (Marx 1990: 739). In the face of an increasingly dogmatic Stalinism, Luxembourg confronted what she perceived as deceptiveness and dangerous "infallible authorities" of the party, who undermined and betrayed the communal participatory demands of Marxist praxis. In response, Luxembourg (1905) asserts in *The Political Leader of the German Working Classes*, true to historical materialist ideals,

> Social democracy is simply the embodiment of the modern proletariat's class struggle, a struggle which is driven by a consciousness of its own historic

consequences. The masses are in reality their own leaders, dialectically creating their own development process. The more that social democracy develops, grows, and becomes stronger, the more the enlightened masses of workers will take their own destinies, the leadership of their movement, and the determination of its direction into their own hands. (280)

György Lukács

The major contributions of the Marxist philosopher György Lukács include the development of a Marxist system of aesthetics that opposed political control of artists and, like Luxembourg, defended humanism. Through his writings, Lukács sought to elaborate on Marxist notions of ideology, alienation, and consciousness within the context of an ever-expanding industrialized society. In 1923, Lukács wrote *History and Class Consciousness* (1972), where he forged a unique Marxist philosophy of history, which laid the basis for a critical literary and artistic perspective, which inserted artistic expression *within* the theory and practice of revolution. Defying mechanistic tendencies to view Marxism as merely a scientific analysis of social and economic change, Lukács delineates Marxism as philosophy. Lukács notes an intrinsic dialectics within the consciousness of workers, given their class positionality as objects of the social process that shapes their lives. Lacking is a sense of self-consciousness, which generates an intrinsic tension. This constitutes three aspects: first is the worker's own reified existence as a product of social mediation; second, the social totality; and third, the workers as the subject-object of that totality. Lukács (1972) writes, "The act of consciousness overthrows the objective form of its object" (178) and, thus, the worker too can overcome objectification through practical engagement with the totality of life.

A significant Marxist idea that Lukács (1972) expands here is that of *reification*, an alienating process of *rational objectification* that detaches people from their labor and knowledge, converting everything and everyone—including living ideas, qualities, interests, relationships, and human practices—into consumable objects, in the interest of capitalist accumulation. Lukács reinforces the link of reification to the commodity-structure of capitalism, where social relationships between people are objectified and fetishized, as if "they possessed an autonomous power and objectivity" (Rooke 1998). "Its basis is that a relation between people takes on the character of a thing and thus acquires a 'phantom objectivity', an autonomy that seems so strictly rational and all-embracing as to conceal every trace of its fundamental nature: the relation between people."[37] Lukács points to the manner in which this process of commodification, across social, political, and economic spheres, perpetuates human alienation and our subsequent subordination, within capitalist society.

Antonio Gramsci

The Italian revolutionary thinker, Antonio Gramsci, who was incarcerated for much of his life by Mussolini, is another key intellectual who wrote in the Marxist tradition. The compilation of his writing, published in *Prison Notebooks*, provided a useful rethinking of several fundamental ideas associated with Marxist thought and the assertion that a genuine democracy, as a total and integral part of society, had to be the fundamental objective of revolutionary struggle. Through his *philosophy of praxis*, Gramsci moved to overcome what he considered to be the democratic limitations of economic determinism and, in so doing, expand Marxism's explanatory possibility. About this, Gramsci (1971) writes, "The philosophy of praxis ... does not tend toward the peaceful resolution of the contradictions existing within history. It is itself the theory of those contradictions" (196–197). Of particular concern, for Gramsci was the failure of the working class to enter into the revolutionary process, as Marx had theorized, and instead falling captive to the authoritarian rule of fascist regime (Giltin 1994). This conflict prompted him toward a theory of *hegemony*. Starting from the assumption that the historical process *has deposited an infinity of traces* (Gramsci 1971:326) within us, Gramsci's radical conceptualization of culture opens new theoretical ground from which to examine the structures of everyday life.

More specifically, "hegemony refers to the ideological control of dominant beliefs, values, and social practices that are reproduced and distributed throughout a whole range of institutions, including schools, the family, mass media, and trade unions" (Giroux 1981: 94). Here, the supremacy of the ruling

---

[37] See: https://www.marxists.org/archive/lukacs/works/history/hcc05.htm.

class manifests itself in two distinct ways: as material domination and as intellectual moral leadership. Through inquiry into the nature of hegemony, Gramsci unveils the contradictions and unravels the entanglements between structures of political power, ideology, and pedagogy that result in relations of domination. Important to a theory of hegemony is the complexity that governs the perpetuation of unacknowledged ideologies that both protect and conserve the inequalities inherent to capitalist societies. Gramsci affirms the need to engage dialectically with a variety of ideological ideas and meanings in the context of everyday social life—ideas that are both imposed from outside and *voluntarily* reproduced from within, through widespread *common sense* notions—unexamined ideas, beliefs, or assumptions that betray the interests of the working class, by reinforcing social and material relations of domination. Here, the question of social agency is paramount to Gramsci's analysis, which diverts from an essentialized Marxist economic determinism and, instead, gives centrality to the response of human beings to their world.

Gramsci's theory of hegemony also served as an important response to changing forms of capitalist domination in the West that were evolving in advanced industrial societies. With the rise of modern science and technology, social control was exercised less through the use of physical deterrents and increasingly through the distribution of an elaborate system of norms and imperatives. Gramsci (1971) noted that, unlike fascist regimes that control populations primarily through physically coercive forces and arbitrary rules and regulations, capitalist societies utilize forms of hegemonic control that function systematically to ensure the masses adapt to the authority of the dominant society. Gramsci characterized the capitalist state as being made up of two overlapping spheres, a "political society" (which rules through force) and a "civil society" (which rules through consent). Accordingly, Gramsci (1971) addresses the phenomenon of *spontaneous' consent*—"given by the great masses of the population to the general direction imposed upon social life" (306). "Gramsci saw mass culture as the primary tool for submission. The more mass culture infects the thinking and attitudes of the population the less the state has to use harsher forms of coercion for domination. Gramsci described mass culture, or civil society, as the trenches and permanent fortifications that defend the core interests of the elites" (Hedges 2017: 1).

The notion of *manufactured consent* is situated in Gramsci's view of "the apparatus of state coercive power which 'legally' enforces discipline on those groups who do not 'consent' either actively of passively" (307). At the heart of hegemonic control are dynamics of political power—power derived by control of social structures and material relations of production that embody routines and practices, resulting directly from the context, content, and manner in which knowledge is produced. Gramsci also draws attention to "the degree to which the class system is upheld not simply by unequal economic and political power but also by bourgeois 'hegemony', the spiritual and cultural supremacy of the ruling class, brought about through the spread of bourgeois values and beliefs via civil society[38]—the media, churches, [education], youth movements, trade unions and so on" (Heywood 1994: 100). This represents a power preserved by selective silences and manifested in the fragmentation of social definitions, management of information, and the subsequent shaping of popular attention, consent, belief, and trust (Forester 1987). However, what cannot be missed here, according to Gramsci (1971), is that

> hegemony presupposes that account be taken of the interests and the tendencies of the groups over which hegemony is to be exercised, and that a certain compromise equilibrium should be formed—in other words, that the leading group should make sacrifices ... But there is also no doubt that such sacrifices and such a compromise *cannot touch the essential*; for though hegemony is ethical-political, it must also be economic. (373, emphasis added)

With this Gramsci suggests how progressive or revolutionary ideas of subaltern groups are appropriated to gain mass consensus, but only in so far as the hegemonic culture, with its economic structure of dominance, is preserved.

"Education is central to the workings of hegemony in which every relationship is a pedagogical relationship" (Mayo 2010: 2). As such, Gramsci's insights into

[38] Gramsci's theory of hegemony has also been employed in debates about civil society. For those concerned with the ways in which liberal or bourgeois thought both narrowly defines and reduces civil society to an "associational" or lesser domain in contrast to the state and market, Gramsci's definition affirms that civil society, within a genuinely democratic context, can serve as a public sphere of political struggle and contestation over ideas and norms. As such, it also offers a public context for communities to collectively build their critical capacities to challenge oppressive assumptions, practices, and policies, as well as articulate new ideas and visions (Heywood 1994). For another interesting discussion into this question, see Marco Fonseca's (2016) book *Gramsci's Critique of Civil Society*.

how power is constituted within the realm of ideas and knowledge production are particularly salient to this discussion. There are four important educational themes that resound in Gramsci's thesis of cultural hegemony. (1) The role of educators (in *intellectuals and education*) is associated here with "intellectual and moral leadership" (249), as well as the need for "active participation in the practical life" (320) of the community. (2) The formation of counter-hegemonic intellectuals (in *intellectuals and education*) or "organic intellectuals ... that emerge from out of the group itself ... [so] more and more people share the tasks of mental activity, of organizing, deliberating and leading" (425). (3) The relationship culture, language, and knowing (in *language and common sense*), "every language contains the elements of a conception of the world and of a culture" (326). And, finally, (4) the historical significance of passion (in *knowledge and feeling*) where "one cannot make politics-history without this passion, without this connection of feeling between intellectuals and [the] people ..." (350).

Louis Althusser

Among Marxist scholars, there are two distinct views at play with respect to the concept of ideology. The first is apparent in the writings of orthodox Marxists who contend it is possible to get *beyond ideology*, in an effort to reach some essential truths about society and freedom. In this perspective, ideology is essentialized as creating *false consciousness*—a way of thinking that prevents individuals from perceiving the true nature of their social or economic situation, consequently obscuring relations of power. Louis Althusser (2001) breaks with this essentialism,[39] by arguing that ideology is profoundly unconscious and a deeply embedded aspect of our culture, which actively determines how we think about *reality*. By reality, Althusser refers to that world that we create around us, once we have become a part of the *symbolic order*.[40] Submerged in this order, our perceptions of reality become

---

[39] "Essentialism" refers to (1) a belief that things have a set of characteristics that make them what they are and science and philosophy is their discovery and expression; and (2) a view that categories of people, such as women and men, or heterosexuals and homosexuals, or members of ethnic groups, have intrinsically different and characteristic natures or dispositions.

[40] "Symbolic order" refers to the social world of linguistic communication, intersubjective relations, knowledge of ideological conventions, and the acceptance of the law. Althusser draws this concept from Jacques Lacan. See: Jacques Lacan's (1977) *Écrits: A Selection.*

so indistinguishably bound to how we think that as soon as we even try to articulate new truths, we easily can fall back into our old, conditioned view of the world. Hence, for Althusser, it is impossible to access the *real conditions of existence* due to our reliance on language, which is both generated by and generates the prism of our ideological lens.

Althusser's (2001) view on ideology is then constituted according to four key assumptions.[41] (1) Rather than the real world, ideology represents the imaginary relationship of individuals to their real conditions of existence. (2) Ideology has material existence and manifests through actions that become ritualized through human relationships and to social institutions. (3) All ideology hails or interpellates concrete individuals as concrete subjects. And (4) individuals are always ready-subjects, in that even before birth we are primed as ready-subjects to accept the hegemonic precepts of the society in which we are born. Hence, similar to Gramsci, Althusser sees hegemony as less reliant on the power of the state apparatus than on the power of ideology, where individuals consider themselves to participate solely through their own volition. In keeping with these assumptions, Althusser introduces the notion of ideological state apparatus—which denotes institutions such as education, churches, family, media, trade unions, and law, which formally exist outside state control but which served to transmit or interpellate the values of the state.

Within the context of education, Althusser (2001) maintains that the ruling class has made education its "dominant ideological State apparatus ... which has in fact replaced in its functions the previously dominant ideological State apparatus, the Church" (104). He argues that as each cohort of students exit educational institutions, they enter into the workforce "practically provided with the ideology which suits the role it has to fulfill in class society" (105). Moreover, Althusser argues, "no other ideological State apparatus has the obligatory (and not least, free) audience of the totality of the children in the capitalist social formation, eight hours a day for five or six days out of seven" (105). Despite this central ideological function, schools are portrayed as neutral settings "purged of ideology ... where teachers respectful of the 'conscience'

---

[41] See: Althusser's (2001) *Lenin and Philosophy and Other Essays* (109–123) for a full discussion of these key assumptions. The discussion here is drawn from this section of the book.

and 'freedom' of the children ... entrusted to them (in complete confidence) by their 'parents' (who are free, too, i.e., the owners of their children) open up for them the path to the freedom, morality and responsibility of adults by their own example, by knowledge, literature and their 'liberating' virtues" (105–106).

In *Pedagogy of the Oppressed*, Freire makes reference to Althusser's (1967) discussion of *contradictions*[42] and *overdetermination*.[43] It is through his theory of *overdetermination*, that Althusser posits a double-edged epistemological challenge to all binary claims of absolute truth, whether these arise from idealism or materialism. For Althusser, truths are not objective, detached, absolute or homogenous; but rather are constructed across a multiplicity of affirming, contradictory, *and* opposing practices and theoretical perspectives, which result from an "active intervention in the construction of multiple truths" (Shin 2012: 4). In seeking to enliven the Marxist dialectic, Althusser offers us a "decentered structure" that is both multidimensional and multifaceted (Shin 2012), extending our revolutionary field of engagement, as well as providing greater conviviality in the context of class struggle. Further, in contrast to notions of political purity, Althusser argues for a way of comprehending culture as a superstructure, where traces of the past persist within the substructure, even in the process of revolutionary change. As such both conditions of domination *and* liberation are understood as existing within a complex whole of contradictions, informed by unevenness.

Nevertheless, Althusser asserts that through rigorous critical engagement of society, politics, economics, and history, we can begin to understand how ideological beliefs are *interpellated* into every aspect of our material lives and how they persist. This notion of *interpellation*, introduced by Althusser, signals

---

[42] For Althusser (1969), it is important to recognize that "the contradiction is inseparable from the total structure of the social body in which it is found, inseparable from its formal conditions of existence and even from the instances it governs; it is radically affected by them, determining in and the same moment, and determined by the various levels and instances of the social formation it animates, it might be called overdetermined in its principle" (101). Althusser draws this idea from Mao's Tse-Tung (1965).

[43] Althusser uses the idea of *overdetermination* as a way of thinking about the multiple, often oppositional, forces active at once in any political situation, without falling into an overly simplistic idea of these multifaceted and multidimensional forces being simply "contradictory." Moreover, "overdetermination of a contradiction is the reflection in it of its conditions of existence within the complex whole" (254).

a powerful social process in which we encounter cultural values and internalize them, as if they were solely ours. In the course of our socialization, ideas and assumptions of the world are presented to us, commonsensically, for our acceptance without questioning. For example, beginning from birth, gender roles are assigned to us by the culture in which we live; these are presented in such a way that we are encouraged to *accept* them as immutable. How we engage with (or disengage from) these commonly held societal beliefs and attitudes positions us in relation to power within our society (i.e., our location related to our class, gender, and sexuality). However, through our rigorous engagement with the world, Althusser posits that we can come to see the ways in which we are interpellated by ideology, as we move critically toward a more complex process of recognition and possible transformation. By so doing, women and men come to better understand the oppressive conditions we face, the decisions we choose, and commitments we must make to transform these conditions. Here, Althusser (1967) is consistent with Marx who contends that "it is in ideology that human beings 'become conscious' of their class conflict and 'fight it out'; in its religious, ethical, legal and political forms, etc., ideology is an objective social reality; the ideological struggle is an organic part of the class struggle" (11–12).

Other Marxist Philosophers

Freire also draws on Lucien Goldmann, André Nicolaï, and Gavrilo "Gajo" Petrović's humanist Marxist perspectives on consciousness and praxis. Goldmann begins from his opposition to the *scientificity* of what he considered to be Marxism in need of reinvention. The absolutizing of history and the specter of authoritarianism which had befallen it had to be tempered by restoring the dialectics of Marxist humanism. This constituted a major concern for Goldmann, given his opposition to the individualism of bourgeois rationalism and empiricism. In *The Human Sciences and Philosophy*, Goldmann draws on Lukacs's notion of ideology and consciousness, to distinguish between "real consciousness" and "potential consciousness." For Goldmann (1969), *real consciousness* is "the result of the multiple obstacles and deviations that the different factors of empirical reality put into opposition and submit for realization by potential consciousness" (118).

Through engaging the *obstacles and deviation*, human beings construct new knowledge and evolve in consciousness. Goldmann (1968) asserts "that on the level of individual consciousness, what corresponds to the dialectical conception of history is the immanent act of faith" (18). In *Comportment Économique et Structures Sociales*, André Nicolaï (1960) argues that economic facts are not independent of social, political, psychological, historical, and anthropological contexts and, thus, economics only make sense of our class struggle to overcome scarcity. Nicolai also develops a method of dialectical engagement—built on the idea that structures impact social behavior—which can uncover *unperceived practical solutions*. This idea is similar to Lucien's notion of real consciousness, discussed above.

Gavrilo "Gajo" Petrović was one of the main theorists involved in the Praxis School in Yugoslavia. The Praxis School primarily engaged Marx's early writings on his theory of alienation. Petrović also served as the editor of the journal *Praxis*, which published works congruent with the Marxist humanist stance of the school. The members of the Praxis School clashed with orthodox Marxist-Leninists of the Communist Party and were subjected to much criticism by zealous supporters of Stalin's regime. In response, Petrović and his comrades called for freedom of speech, pointing to Marx's insistence on the importance of *ruthless critique of all that exists*.[44] The underlying intent was a return to "the real" Marx, in contrast to Stalin's authoritarian right-wing philosophy, which had diverted from the human essence of praxis and thus fallen into dictatorship.

In his essay, "Why Praxis?," Petrović (1964) argues that "Socialism is the only human way out from the difficulties in which humanity has entangled itself, and Marx's thought—the adequate theoretical bases and inspiration for revolutionary activity." Moreover, he was concerned that an authentic, humanist socialism was simply impossible without revitalizing Marx's

---

[44] This expression, *ruthless criticism of all that exists*, is used by Marx in a Letter to Arnold Ruge of September 1843. The whole expression states:

> If constructing the future and settling everything for all times are not our affair, it is all the more clear what we have to accomplish at present: I am referring to ruthless criticism of all that exists, ruthless both in the sense of not being afraid of the results it arrives at and in the sense of being just as little afraid of conflict with the powers that be. (Petrovic 1964)

humanist philosophy and moving toward an understanding and practice of a Marxism that could step beyond a dogmatic authoritarian posture. He argued again the alienation and instrumentalization of human beings, under "the pressure of mass impersonalism and of the scientific method of 'cultivation' of the masses [which] is more and more opposed to the development of a free human personality." Petrović and his comrade also fought against the notion of a "correct" or "pure" form of Marxism; but rather, "to develop vivid revolutionary thought inspired by Marx." Ultimately, Petrović saw his work and that of the Praxis School as "a political project committed to 'the development of philosophical thought and realization of a humane community.'"

Critical theory

In *Pedagogy of the Oppressed*, Freire makes reference to several authors associated with the Institute for Social Research (*Das Institute fur Sozialforshung*), often referred to as the Frankfurt School. Under the direction of Max Horkheimer, theorists like Theodor Adorno, Walter Benjamin, Leo Lowenthal, Herbert Marcuse, and Erich Fromm, whose works have been loosely referred to as *critical theory* (or critical social theory), sought to radically challenge and transform positive forms of rationality that defined the construction of meaning and knowledge in the West. Toward this end, the Frankfurt School provided a substantive critique of *instrumental reason*,[45] through an incisive analysis of modernity's unwavering allegiance to Enlightenment rationality. Rather than

---

[45] Although Freire does not mention French philosopher Emmanuel Lévinas (1979) or German philosopher Jürgen Habermas (1987), both are considered important thinkers with respect to a critique of instrumental reason (Smith 2008). Lévinas points to the manner in which ontology, by its very nature, attempts to create a totality in which what is different and "other" is necessarily reduced to sameness and identity. This proclivity for totality is a basic manifestation of "instrumental" reason, where reason is used as an instrument for determining the best or most efficient means to achieve a given end. Through its embrace of instrumental reason, Western philosophy displays a destructive and objectifying "will to domination." Moreover, because instrumental reason does not determine the ends to which it is applied, it has been used in the pursuit of goals that are destructive or evil. In this regard, instrumental reason was responsible for much of the crises of Europe the twentieth century, particularly with respect to advancing totalitarianism (Wolin 2017). "According to Habermas' staging, all the participants in the discourse of modernity see the division between subjects, and the petrification of sociality due to instrumental reason, as the defining pathology of the times" (Smith 2008: 646). For Habermas (1987), "Since the close of the eighteenth century, the discourse of modernity has had a single theme under ever new titles: the weakening of the forces of social bonding" (139).

overcoming ignorance and suffering in the world, Adorno and Horkheimer (1972) argue, "the enlightened earth radiates disaster triumphant."

Writing during a critical moment of advancing capitalism and social unrest, a common philosophical thread across their writings is an underlying ontological and epistemological commitment to the idea that theory, as well as practice, must inform our philosophical and political efforts to transform the brutal structures and conditions of human oppression in the world. In its early years, the Frankfurt theorists, influenced by Marx, were primarily concerned with an analysis of the base structure of bourgeois society; but with time, their interest developed into a closer analysis of the cultural superstructure (Jay 1973). This shift was, undoubtedly, a result of the disruptions and fragmentations experienced in the process of their emigration and repeated relocation in the 1930s and 1940s—a process precipitated by the threat of Nazism, the member's avowedly Marxist orientation, and the fact that most of them were Jews. Hence, their contributions to critical social theory cannot be understood in the absence of the historical context that influenced the development of their ideas and shaped their theories.

The Frankfurt school

The work of the Frankfurt School came into being as a direct response to key political and historical transformations taking place in the early part of the twentieth century. The political shifts in Germany's governing structure had a significant impact upon its founders. During this tempestuous era Germany had managed to temporarily contain class conflict. But within two years following the First World War, the foundations of the German imperial system were undermined and a republic was declared in Berlin (Held 1980). What followed were thirteen years of chaotic political struggles between the German Communist Party (KPD) and the more conservative forces of the Social Democratic Party (SPD). As the KPD became increasingly ineffective in their efforts to organize a majority of the working class, the Social Democratic Leadership of the Weimar Republic supervised the destruction of the competing radical and revolutionary movements. In the process, the SDP did not only fail to implement the promised democratization and socialization of production in Germany, it also failed to stop the monopolistic trends of German industrialists and the reactionary elements which eventually paved the way for the emergence of Nazism. As the Nazis seized power in Germany under Hitler's rules, Italy and Spain came under the fascist leaderships of Mussolini and Franco. A similar fate befell the worker's struggle in these countries, where all independent socialist organizations were suppressed, which is what led, for example, to the imprisonment of Antonio Gramsci as noted earlier.

In light of the Marxist orientation shared by the members of the Frankfurt School, "the emergence of an antidemocratic political system in the country of the first socialist revolution" (Warren 1984: 145), consequently, had a profound impact upon the evolution of critical theory. The Russian revolution had been systematically weakened by foreign interventions, blockades and civil war; and Lenin's revolutionary vision was rapidly losing ground. After Lenin's death in 1924, Stalin advanced in Russia with the expansion of centralized control and censorship, a process created to maintain European Communist parties under Moscow's leadership, a phenomenon that prompted the critiques of Rosa Luxembourg, as previously discussed. In 1939, the Hitler-Stalin pact was enacted representing an ironic historical moment for those committed to the struggle of the working class and the socialist principles espoused by Marx.

A final event that influenced the development of critical theory was the nature and impact of the unbridled advance of capitalism in the West. The rapid development of science and technology and their overwhelming penetration into the political and social systems resulted in new transformations in the structure of capitalism, accelerating the development of an advanced industrial-technological society. Both the major historical and political developments of capitalist society, as well as the rise of bureaucratic communist orthodoxy affirmed for the members of Frankfurt School the necessity to address two major issues. First, the need to develop a new critical social theory within a Marxist framework, which could contend with the complex changes arising in an industrial-technological, post-liberal, capitalist society; and second, the need to recover the power of Marx's dialectical approach, which had undergone a major economic and materialistic reduction by a new authoritarian Marxist orthodoxy (Warren 1984).

The intent of the Frankfurt School was to become a material force in the struggle against domination of all forms, by addressing through their writings and political participation the following questions (Held 1980: 35).

- The European labor movements did not develop in a unified struggle of workers. What blocked these developments?
- Capitalism was a series of acute crisis. How could these better be understood? What was the relation between the political and the economic? Was the relation between the political and the economic? Was the relation changing?
- Authoritarianism and the development of the bureaucracy seemed increasingly the order of the day. How could the phenomena be comprehended? Nazism and fascism rose to dominate Central and Southern Europe. How was this possible? How did these movements attain large-scale support?
- Social relationships, for example, those created by the family, appeared to be undergoing radical social change. In what directions? How were these affecting individual development?
- The arena of culture appeared open to direct manipulation. Was a new type of ideology being formed? If so, how was this affecting everyday life?
- Given the fate of Marxism in Russia and Western Europe, is Marxism itself nothing other than a state orthodoxy? Was there a social agent capable of progressive change? What possibilities were there for effective socialist practices?

Efforts to respond to such questions centered on the manner in which ideology, in the context of capitalism, functioned to obstruct the capacities of human beings to act in their own interest. As such, the work of the Frankfurt School challenged traditional positivist definitions of culture that defined it as autonomous and unrelated to the political and economic structures of power that shaped everyday life.

Theodor Adorno

For Theodor Adorno, a major contributor to the Frankfurt School's investigation into the relationship of culture, power, and ideology, conventional views of culture failed to engage the decisive role of ideology in constructing both difference and social conflicts. In *Negative Dialectics*, Adorno (1973b) critiques the idea of *identity thinking* (us versus them) and its ties to the exclusionary universalism of the Enlightenment. He argues that identity thinking constructs "the other," by including dominant cultural values and ways of being as legitimately human, while excluding those cultural values and ways of the "other" that would counter this legitimacy. Hence, he posits that this cultural phenomenon of exclusion is, in fact, not a "natural" manifestation, but rather is constructed by the powerful in order to justify domination.

Adorno, therefore, criticizes philosophical notions that reify (objectify) the logic of culture as somehow independent of history, materiality, and social context, arguing, "culture ... cannot be fully understood, either in terms of itself ... or in terms of the so-called universal development of the mind" (Giroux 1983: 22). Here, Adorno (1991) problematizes authoritarian historical forms of Marxism that place "capitalism into a naïve narrative of progress and freedom [which] becomes, through its attempt to unify and integrate history, complicit with its object" (3). Informed by this critique, he developed a critical analysis of culture that makes it central to the development of historical experience, as much as in the social and material processes of everyday life. Adorno, similar to other theorists of the Frankfurt School, concluded that repressive forms of positivist rationality redefined the idea of culture in Western society, resulting in the objectification of the cultural realm.

This reification of culture permitted its appropriation as a new locus of social control, under which the domination of nature and society preceded technological progress and economic growth. To describe this phenomenon, Adorno (1991) used the term "culture industry" in response to the institutionalization of culture as an industrial force, which not only produces goods but also legitimates the logic of capital and its institutions. It is this hegemonic mechanism of rationalization, standardization, and commodification of culture, which consolidates, reinforces, and perpetuates dominant values and beliefs, that he termed "ideology." Moreover, Adorno asserts, "the effectiveness of the culture industry depends not on its parading an ideology [or] disguising the true nature of things" (10), but rather in fueling the belief that there exists no "alternative to the status quo" (11).

Max Horkheimer

Max Horkheimer (1972), often associated with a critique of ideology, also draws on the negative ideology of Marxism—the idea that ideology, as an individual or set of claims, perspectives, and philosophies masks or conceals the social contradictions in society, on behalf of the ruling class. More simply put, Horkheimer viewed ideology as "the veil over the contradictory character of society" (cited in Stirk 1992: 66). For Horkheimer and the other Frankfurt school thinkers, ideology spoke to forms of consciousness that become standardized and homogenized as representing everyone's general interests but, in fact, conserve the interests of those in power. This is accomplished in society by way of reinforcing the notion that "societal outcomes represent *natural* ones when they are the result of particular constellations of human relations; and/or … glorify the social situation as harmonious when it is, in fact, conflict-ridden" (Held 1980: 186). Hence, ideologies are not mere illusions, but rather the outcome of reified social relations that mystify and distort the truth about how and why there exist gross power differentials in society. Ideologies, moreover, embody "symbols, ideas, and theories through which people experience their relation to each other and the world" (Held 1980: 186). Hence, the need made for a critique of ideology to unveil the structures of our dehumanization and domestication is at the heart of critical theory.

For Horkheimer, ideology underpins capitalist social relations based on class interests that in practice (essence) negate individual autonomy, despite ideological adherence (appearance) to the doctrine of individualism. Hence, the individualism of capitalist ideology simultaneously emphasizes and denies the individual's subjectivity. On the one hand, the individual subject, freed from the bondages of feudalism, is now free to buy and sell on the open market. The individual's material success, therefore, becomes a guideline for judging right and wrong; and consequently, this success also becomes both the sign and reward of individual value. On the other hand, the individual subject is negated and alienated in a system of buying and selling. Hence, as mentioned earlier, the process of exchange becomes the mode by which individuality is organized and claimed. Pursuit of self-interest is equated with pursuit of individual material gain. Through this scheme, the liberal or bourgeoisie defense of individual freedom becomes ideology, in that it masks capitalist's interests and the underlying motivation that inform its origins (Held 1980).

Herbert Marcuse

Also critical to an understanding of how ideology works on and through individuals is the Frankfurt School's notion of depth psychology developed by Herbert Marcuse (1955). Influenced by the more progressive strands of Sigmund Freud's[46] theories of the unconscious and instinct, Marcuse conceived of ideology as existing at the depth of the individual's psychological structure of needs, common sense, and critical consciousness. Thus, instead of limiting his notion of ideology only to external social processes, Marcuse (1955), in *Eros and Civilization*, dialectically defines it as forms of historically rooted domination that exist both in the socioeconomic structure of society as well as in the sedimented history or psychological structures of the individual. In this manner, he seeks to explain "that the struggle against freedom reproduce[s] … in the psyche of man [and woman] as the self-repression of the repressed individual, and his self-repression in turn sustains his masters and their institutions" (16). Marcuse's view of ideology connects with Gramsci's notion of cultural hegemony, in that it points to the manner in which human domestication results from dominant forms of social control encased in a myriad of contradictions and unresolved conflicts that permeate everyday life. However, for Marcuse, this is also linked to eros—an erotic instinctual need for freedom significant to the struggle for liberation (Katsiaficas 2011).

In his writings, Marcuse also sought to imagine a society in which all aspects of our humanity—our work, play, love, and sexuality—could function in sustaining a free society, by first considering the ways in which these are disrupted in modern society. In *One Dimensional Man*, considered to be one of the most important books of its time, Marcuse (1964) asserts that, despite the one-dimensionality of human existence within capitalist society, there actually exist dimensions of our humanity that have been eroded and that we must recover. Part of this erosion includes destruction of the intimate spheres of life (i.e., sexuality), which have been appropriated and commodified in ways that facilitate domination, without critique or protest. The society, Marcuse writes, turns everything it touches into a potential source of progress *and* exploitation,

---

[46] See, for example, Sigmund Freud's (2002) *Civilization and Its Discontents* written in 1930 and Marcuse's (1955) *Eros and Civilization*.

of drudgery *and* satisfaction, of freedom *and* of oppression. The outcome of this contradictory rationality is "the conquest of the unhappy," where any sense that something is wrong and that change is needed or possible is suppressed. Proceeding on the basis of *negative* (or dialectical) thinking, Marcuse stresses the political necessity of overcoming "the oppressive and ideological power of given facts" (227), if human beings are to recover the multidimensionality of our existence.

Erich Fromm

Socialist psychoanalyst and philosopher, Erich Fromm sought to combine the explanatory powers of Marxism with Freud's more progressive psychoanalytical ideas, in ways that could breathe new life into the inextricable relationship that exists between human beings and society. Central to his life's quest was an unwavering commitment to illuminate the dynamics of psychological repression and social domination, by revealing the complex relationship that exists between the individual and society. Fromm (1955) argues that human beings, in the context of modern capitalist society, have been violently uprooted from our organic connection to nature; and, thus, have been left poorly equipped to adapt to in a rapidly changing world. He further notes that since human beings have simultaneously developed the ability to reason and recognize our increasing alienation—or separation from nature—the *human situation* of our objectification causes us an existential dilemma.

Fromm's writings are anchored in a *radical humanism* that throughout his life potentiated his steadfast emancipatory politics. Fromm (1966) contends,

> Radical humanism considers the goal of humankind to be that of complete independence, and this implies penetrating through fictions and illusions to a full awareness of reality. It implies, furthermore, a skeptical attitude toward the use of force, precisely because during recorded history it has been, and still is, force—creating fear—which has made humans ready to take fiction for reality, illusions for truth. It was force which made people incapable of independence and hence warped their reason and emotions. (13)

Hence, the human condition, our potential physical and intellectual capacities, and the evolution of consciousness are all themes interwoven across the landscape of Fromm's psychology of liberation. In a world Fromm perceives as steadily driven by technology toward a soulless and mechanistic existence, he seeks to both critically understand and recover the essence of our humanity, the spirit of our existence, and the possibility for an emancipatory purpose to human life.

In *The Art of Loving*, Fromm (1956) takes up a central theme of his life's work: *Love as the answer to the problem of human existence* (7), particularly within the dehumanizing context of capitalist society. For Fromm, "to analyze the nature of love is to discover its general absence today and to criticize the social conditions ... responsible for this absence" (133). Fromm, further, argues, "In a culture in which the marketing orientation prevails, and in which material success is the outstanding value, there is little reason to be surprised that human love relations follow the same pattern of exchange which governs the commodity and the labor market" (4). Underlying his critique of capitalism as *disintegrating society* is the assertion that the unbridled commodification of human beings, as market objects of exchange, has not only separated us from nature but from one another.

Fromm (1956) asserts, "the *principle* underlying capitalist society and the *principle* of love are incompatible" (131). The anxieties produced by this incompatibility have generated a culture of lovelessness and alienation; which effectively perpetuates, on one hand, repression of individual freedom and expression, while on the other, promotes increasing concentration of wealth and power among the dominant class. Accordingly, "in contemporary capitalistic society the meaning of equality now refers to the equality of automatons—human beings who in fact are devoid of their individuality" (Fromm 1964: 15). Central to Fromm's efforts to challenge this phenomenon is his historical materialist engagement with human relationships, which he perceives as essential to the future of our humanity. Love as an individual and collective political force is, therefore, viewed as capable of disrupting our alienation, recovering our humanity, and propelling human existence toward greater emancipatory consciousness.

From this sense, "love is not primarily a relationship to a specific person; it is an attitude, an orientation of character which determines the relatedness of a person to the world as a whole, not toward one 'object: of love'" (46); and, as such, Fromm (1956) maintains, that love is at the root of human solidarity.

Indispensable to this idea of love is a "communication with each other from the center of [our] existence."

> Love, experienced thus, is a constant challenge; it is not a resting place, but a moving, growing, working together; even whether there is harmony or conflict, joy or sadness, is secondary to the fundamental fact that two people experience themselves from the essence of their existence, that they are one with each other by being one with themselves, rather than by fleeing from themselves. There is only one proof for the presence of love: the depth of the relationship, and the *aliveness* and strength in each person concerned. (103, emphasis added)

In theorizing emancipatory relationships of love, Fromm identifies several qualities he deems *indispensable* to love—discipline, concentration, patience, concern, and responsibility. Essential to *knowing and being* in a relationship are the *indispensable qualities* of love, humility, faith, courage, and action. In his work, Fromm speaks to the reciprocal aliveness (or *biophilia*[47]) and horizontal nature of relationships—human interactions that affirm life—where faith and respect to for the other abide; where "The teacher is taught by his [or her] students" (25), relating "to each other genuinely and productively" (25).

Conversely, Fromm (1973) theorizes the deathlike (or *necrophilic*)[48] quality of loveless relationships where indispensable qualities of love are absent, particularly with respect to those groups perceived as problematic to advancing principles of profit and consumption. Here, Fromm makes reference to an alienating culture of exclusion, which results in the suppression of the objectified other—whether through ideological signification of inferiority or violent forms of repression. Fromm (1955) associates this necrophilic phenomenon to the manner in which "religious and racial minorities, as far as they are powerless, offer vast opportunities for sadistic satisfaction for even the poorest member of the majority" (290). Similarly, Fromm argues that possessive mechanisms of "extreme submission and domination" make people

---

[47] From defines biophilia as "the passionate love of life and all that is alive; it is the wish to further growth, whether in a person, plant an idea, or a social group" (Fromm 1973: 365).

[48] From defines *necrophilia* as "the passion to destroy life and the attraction to all that is dead, decaying, and purely mechanical" (Fromm 1973: 6).

"insane," to the point that all relationships become "dependent on those to whom he submits, or whom he dominates" (31). Such forms of narcissism, rooted in social and material relations of capitalist production, promote dehumanization and "lost contact with the world" (34). In the process, the other is perceived and treated as an object of domination, transformed "into a thing, something animate into something inanimate" stripped of that "essential quality of life—freedom" (32).

In *The Fear of Freedom*, Fromm (2001) undertakes a historical examination of the psychological dynamics associated with freedom and its impact on human beings. Central to his argument is that true freedom can only be predicated on an organic relationship of human beings to the world, within the spontaneity of love and productive work. In the absence of this relationship, the alienation and isolation brought on by human insecurities and anxieties diminishes the possibilities of freedom and unravels the integrity of the self. Fromm, therefore, asserts that true freedom or *freedom to* requires true connection with others—a connection that allows us both to enter into *spontaneous activity*, and, as such, experience a "spontaneous realization of the self " that with each interaction, unites us "anew with the world …" (224). Hence, freedom is not an individual stagnant construct or object to be obtained, but rather it is a living process generated *within* the relational structures in which we reside. Fromm contends that the contradictions of capitalism, in conjunction with Calvinist values, violates the necessary conditions for freedom by trampling human agency, in order to preserve its social and material domination. This, Fromm maintains, occurs through a mode of production that both objectifies and instrumentalizes human beings, alienating us from one another and our social environment. Fromm complicates this analysis by suggesting that even when human beings are freed from structures of domination, there is a *fear of freedom* (or *freedom from*) and a tendency to experience a new set of anxieties that can result in feelings of hopelessness—a hopelessness that can only be overcome when we can work together spontaneously to use our *freedom to* in the process of remaking our world. Unfortunately, Fromm also notes, that a common response to anxieties associated with the fear of freedom is to move toward authoritarianism, destructiveness, and conformity, which ironically become associated with a greater sense of security and safety.

Dismissed from the Frankfurt School by Horkheimer in 1939 and accused by some of the Frankfurt School members of having "emptied psychoanalysis of its revolutionary content by abandoning Freud's[49] essential premise that libidinal drives[50] are deeply embedded biological entities that energize human personality" and bypassing the "modernist agenda," (Friedman and Schreiber 2014: xxiii), Fromm, nevertheless, remains widely read and is one of the most cited critical theorists in *Pedagogy of the Oppressed*. And, of all the philosophers discussed, Fromm is one of the closest to resemble what we today call a public intellectual; for apart from his scholarly writings, he was consistently involved as an activist in a variety of social movements throughout his life.[51] Fromm also had a strong connection to Latin America. In 1950, Fromm moved to Mexico to accept a post at the UNAM (the Mexican National Autonomous University) in Mexico City, where he taught for fifteen years. As an active psychoanalyst, he also assisted with the establishment of the Mexican Institute of Psychoanalysis and served as director until 1976 (Burston 1985).[52] Therefore, it is not surprising that Fromm and Freire's paths crossed over the years.

---

[49] Although Fromm (1941) acknowledges that "Freud went further than anybody before him in directing attention to the observation and analysis of the irrational and unconscious forces which determine human behavior," in the *Art of Loving* (1956), he points to "Freud's error" or "his physiological materialism" rooted in an undialectical reading of the relationship between psychology and biology. This, according to Fromm, results in deterministic conclusions of, for example, psychosexual stages of development. About this, he accused Freud of ignoring the psychobiological aspects in his conclusion of male/female sexuality, which he chalks up to "Freud's extreme patriarchalism, which led him to the assumption that sexuality per se is masculine, and thus made him ignore the specifics of female sexuality" (36).

[50] "Libido" refers to the sexual or erotic drive. For Freud, this is analogous to the drive for hunger. Freud views it as a fundamental human instinct that is evident already at birth. All the libidinal impulses, for Freud, are inherently attached to vital bodily functions (e.g., nourishment, voiding of waste). What distinguishes the libidinal dimension from the functional aspect, as pure bodily necessity, is the pleasure with which the activity is associated. Thus the libidinal drive is tied to the pleasure principle. In his theory, Freud essentializes these drives as biologically determined, which is reflected in his libidinal phases psycho-sexual behavior, which are categorized as oral, anal, phallic, latent, and genital. See Freud's (1949) *The Ego and the Id* and *Sigmund Freud: Examining the Essence of His Contributions* by Stevens (2008).

[51] Apart from being a civil rights activist, Fromm also led vigorous movements against nuclear weapons, participated in anti-Vietnam war protests, and worked with movements for the protection of the environment.

[52] Although, there is a tendency to only speak about Fromm's influence on Mexican Psychology and humanist revolutionary ideas in the region (Burston 1985), I would argue, that Fromm's evolving sensibilities were also deeply influenced by his association and friendships with thinkers rooted in an early Latin Americanism or Southern epistemological tradition, including Paulo Freire.

Karel Kosik

The Hungarian Marxist humanist, Karel Kosik, is often overlooked with respect to his critical influence on Freire's ideas. In Prague, Kosik became a leading voice for democratic socialism in the period referred to as the Prague Spring of 1968; his on-the-ground political involvement, however, resulted in his dismissal from his university post in 1970. Kosik's (1974) major work, *Dialectics of the Concrete*, came to be regarded globally as a major contribution to critical theory, particularly in Latin America. In the Spanish translation, *Dialéctica de lo Concreto*, published in 1968, Adolfo Sánchez Vásquez asserts in the prologue, "Kosik is not only one of the most important philosophers of the second half of the twentieth century, but also one of those who best understood the spirit of resistance of critical thinking."

Kosik undertakes a masterful reexamination and critique of Heidegger, while providing a reworking of Marxian categories of humanist phenomenology. At the heart of his analysis is a criticism of reductive Marxism, in which he argues that we can only grasp the reality of anything through our practical activity. He contends this *praxis* is, in fact, the opening by which we gain a sense of being. Kosik introduces the notion of the *dialectical disunity* of everyday life to offer a rational critique of everyday intentionality, within the contentiousness of modernity. "The dialectical disunity is lived as a social conflict—the conflict of master and slave, ruler and ruled, of exploiter and exploited, manipulator and manipulated—and as the spirit of man and nature—subject and object, freedom and necessity, intent as causality" (Bakan 1983: 83). Given that human beings have become divided by the deeply hierarchical nature of capitalist relations of labor, Kosik asserts, uncompromisingly, that it is only by way of "historical dialectical struggle that the essence of being human can be developed, transformed and realized" (83).

Anticolonial theory

When one reads *Pedagogy of the Oppressed*, from a Latin Americanist perspective, there is absolutely no doubt that Freire's central thesis is intimately tied to an anticolonial perspective—a vital discursive dimension of many Latin American philosophers of his time. Both the works of Frantz

Fanon (1952) and Albert Memmi (1957),[53] whom Freire cites in *Pedagogy of the Oppressed*, are writ large in his theoretical formulation of the oppressed/oppressor dialectic and contradiction. Both these agile thinkers, often categorized as "postcolonial,"[54] root their analysis amid respective experiences of colonial relations in the Caribbean, France, Tunisia, ad Algiers—Fanon as Martinique-born colonialized subject and Memmi, as the son of a Jewish-Italian father and Berber mother, who grew up in Tunisia, within a Muslim context.

However, according to Cassirer and Twomey (1973), "Starting from similar experiences Memmi and Fanon developed widely divergent perspectives on the conflict between colonizer and colonized, between oppressor and oppressed.[55] While Fanon sought to involve himself in the conflict by denying and transcending the identity imposed upon him by historical circumstances, Memmi tried to combine involvement of the diverse elements that constitute his historical identity" (9). Despite these differences, their writings emerged during a most contentious historical moment of national liberation movements around the world. Particular to their writings are the Algerian War of Independence (Fanon) and the Tunisian National Movement (Memmi)—struggles inspired and fueled by organized working class people, who had long been oppressed by the French colonial system of capitalist rule. However,

---

[53] Memmi and Fanon knew each other when both men were working in Tunis. See the essay by Memmi (1973) titled "The Impossible Life of Frantz Fanon," where Memmi draws on mutual points of contact in a testimony to Fanon's contributions, viewing Fanon's life "as one possible model for the dominated individual's revolt against the conditions of his oppression" (Cassirer and Twomey 1973: 10). However, it is important to note critiques that have been issued regarding Memmi's analysis and characterizations of Fanon's process. For an excellent discussion, see Charles F. Peterson's (2007) *Dubois, Fanon, Cabral: The Margins of Elite Anticolonial Leadership*, where he argues that "Memmi's questions of Fanon's racial, cultural and geographical identifications reveal a mind unable to move beyond oppressive frameworks. Fanon's heresy of not sticking with his own kind disrupts Memmi's vision of nation, race, and culture" (100).

[54] Briefly speaking, "postcolonialism" refers to an area of study that analyzes, explains, and responds to the cultural legacy of colonialism and imperialism. As an area of study, postcolonialism engages the human consequences of external control and economic exploitation of native people and their lands. "The 'post' of Colonialism is both the after-time of a historical period and the critique of the episteme or mind set that led one small part of the world to dominate the Other" (Willette 2013). In addition to Fanon and Memmi, other key authors often associated with this academic tradition are Michel Foucault, Edward Said, Gayatri Charkravorty Spivak, and Homi Bhabha.

[55] It is precisely of this phenomenon of the oppressed to develop different responses patterns to the subaltern experience of the oppressor/oppressed or colonizer/colonized contradiction that is at the heart of the radical bicultural theory of cultural democracy developed in *Culture and Power in the Classroom* (Darder 2012)—first published in 1991.

as with most writers discussed earlier, their radical discourses conserve the patriarchal gaze, despite their significant contributions to our understanding of human oppression.[56]

Frantz Fanon

Frantz Fanon, an Afro-Caribbean psychiatrist, philosopher, and revolutionary, is considered one of the leading anticolonial thinkers of the twentieth century. Although revolutionary movements embraced his passionate anticolonial writings, his forthright challenge to the immorality of colonial rule was viewed as a threat to the white establishment.[57] By expounding on the racializing dynamics at the heart of what later would be referred to the coloniality of power, Fanon expanded the revolutionary ideas of Marxists and critical theorists to forge a significant philosophical assault against the brutality of the colonizer's gaze and its impact on the colonized. In the *Wretched of the Earth*, Fanon (1963) takes the European colonizing societies to task for their violence and wholesale disregard for the racism and suffering they perpetrate on the colonized, even when confronted. About this, Fanon writes, "In the war in Algeria, for example, the most liberal-minded French reporters make constant use of ambiguous epithets to portray our struggle. When we reproach them for it, they reply in all sincerity they are being objective. For the colonized subject, objectivity is always directed against him [or her]" (37).

On the question of *decolonization*, Fanon (1963) views it as a historical process, "an encounter between two congenitally antagonistic forces that in fact owe their singularity to the kind of reification secreted and nurtured by the colonial situation ... the colonized and colonizer are old acquaintances ... [however] it is the colonist who *fabricated* and *continues to fabricate* the colonized subject (2) ... [and who] is the bringer of violence into the home

---

[56] For feminists discussions on Fanon and Memmi, see: *Frantz Fanon: Conflict and Feminisms* by T. Denean Sharpley-Whiting (1998) and Maria del Guadalupe Davidson's (2012) essay, "Albert Memmi and Audre Lorde: Gender, Race, and the Rhetorical Uses of Anger" in *Journal of French and Francophone Philosophy*.

[57] In 1959, the seriousness of this threat becomes abruptly evident when a car "accident" in Morocco and a car bomb in Rome were both speculated to be attempts on Fanon's life (Cherki 2006). Nevertheless, Fanon persisted in his articulation of his anticolonial thesis until his death in December 1961 from leukemia.

and into the mind of the [colonized]" (37). Inherent in Fanon's politics of decolonization is an urgency to confront the divided and exploitative world, perpetuated by the colonial regime, where capitalism colludes with the forces of violence and education serves as a primary vehicle by which to perpetuate the status quo. For Fanon, "challenging the colonial world is not a rational confrontation. It is not a discourse on the universal, but the impassioned claim by the colonized that their world is fundamentally different" (6).

In *Black Skin White Masks*, Fanon (1967)—still agonized and conflicted by his own internal anxieties rooted in his identity struggles as a colonized subject[58]—examines the dehumanizing psychological impact of racism under colonization, while retaining a Marxist analysis that situates colonialism at the center of a racializing political economic project of social and material domination. The mechanism of *cultural assimilation* is of particular concern for Fanon, in that it speaks to a colonizing process in which the culture of the colonized is invaded by the exploitative culture of colonial power. Here, Fanon employs Marxist dialectics to show that this disabling impact is both a collective and an individual phenomenon. His analysis systematically uncovers the manner in which the colonizer/colonized dichotomy is profoundly predicated on an ideological fantasy of white superiority and Black inferiority, which is consciously and unconsciously at work in the theories and practices of white psychiatry and psychoanalysis.

Fanon contends that one of the most destructive dimensions of the oppressive colonizer/colonized contradiction or *dependency complex* is the manner in which the negation of Black identity becomes deeply internalized by the colonized, resulting in their social and material alienation. Fanon further argues that this internalization of self-hate and inferiority—propagated at the hands of the colonizer—leaves colonized subjects fragmented and estranged from the very essence of our humanity. At the heart of colonization, Fanon argues is a ruthless racializing mechanism that denigrates and maligns the worthiness of the culture, language, and knowledge of the colonized. *To*

---

[58] See the essay "The Impossible Life of Frantz Fanon," written by Memmi (1973) that provides some discussion of the dilemma's Fanon grappled with around this question. However, also see Jadallah's (2012) incisive critique of Memmi's perceptions of Fanon in her essay, "The Shibboleths within Albert Memmi's Universalism" in *Jadaliyya*.

be human is to be white; a commonsensical "truth" rooted in a Eurocentric taxonomy, which signifies *white faces* as pure, good, and worthy of power; while *black faces* are deemed bestial, violent, and irredeemable.[59] Fanon argues that the debilitating impact of the agonizing twoness[60] that ensues, often functions to destroy the self-determination of the colonized, who are thrust into a futile dilemma at the mercy of the colonizer—socialized to reject our own essence and to aspire to a whiteness that is unattainable, regardless of the level of education attained or loyalty expressed to the colonizer.

In speaking to this latter point, Fanon takes up Aime Cesaire's (1955) notion of *negritude*, which deems assimilation into the culture and language of the colonizer—rooted in a dependency that subordinates black humanity— as inherently harmful. Of particular concern here is the manner in which the aggression and violence of the colonizer becomes internalized by the colonized against one's own people. However it is important to note that Fanon is not a determinist, in that history does not determine the fate of a people; nor does he essentialize the colonized/colonizer contradiction as a prison from which there is no escape. Instead, Fanon (1967) proclaims, that for the colonized, we must be our own foundation and, thus, "the real leap consists in introducing invention into existence" (229). For Fanon, it is "by going beyond the historical and instrumental that [we] initiate our cycle of

---

[59] Although some would dismiss the validity of Fanon's analysis in today's context, we need only examine the overrepresentation of violence perpetrated on the Black population at the hands of police officers in the United States. In 2015, police killed 102 unarmed Black people, nearly twice each week. Thirty-seven percent of unarmed people killed by police in 2015 were black, despite the fact that only 13 percent of the population in the United States is African American. Unarmed black people were killed at five times the rate of unarmed whites. A police officer was only changed in less than 10 percent of these cases; and in only two instances were officers convicted. Moreover, as investigations into some of the most violent police departments in America have shown, police violence reflects a lack of accountability in the culture, policies, and practices of the institutions of policing, rather than crime rate levels. See *Mapping Police Violence* at: https://mappingpolicevi olence.org/unarmed/.

[60] In *Culture and Power in the Classroom* (Darder 2012), where I engage the notion of twoness through a radical redefinition of "biculturalism," I have noted "the early 1900s, writers, educators, and social theorists of color have made references in their work to the presence of some form of dual or separate socialization process among their own people. These references have included a variety of terms used to describe the personality development, identity, or traits of non-whites socialized in a racist society: double consciousness (DuBois 1903), double vision (Wright 1953), bicultural (de Anda 1984; Ramirez and Castañeda 1974; Rashid 1981; Red Horse et al. 1981; Solis 1980; Valentine 1971), diunital (Dixon and Foster 1971), multidimensional (Cross 1978), and other references that closely resemble notions of duality and "twoness" (Fanon 1967; Hsu 1971; Kitano 1969; Memmi 1957; Sue and Sue 1978)" (46).

freedom" (231) and forge *a struggle for a new humanism* (9). Underlying this new humanism is an emancipatory subjectivity that can unravel the colonizer/colonized contradiction.

In *Dying Colonialism*, we find a profound expression of Fanon's political radicalization as an anticolonialist, Pan-Africanist and internationalist, where he is "deeply wedded to a view of the development of the nation state and the creation of a new national consciousness as the legitimate goal of the anticolonial struggle to transform people and their culture" (Peterson 2007: 94). In this book, Fanon (1965) draws upon the colonial tensions and revolutionary dynamics of the Algerian War of Independence to conclude that "the essence of revolution is not the struggle for bread: it is the *struggle for dignity*" (12, emphasis added). And despite the historical impact of colonial rule in Algeria, Fanon engages across various intricacies of Algerian life to demonstrate how colonial subjugation of the population was negated, through a variety of revolutionary responses carried out by the colonized. Fanon bears witness to how the Algerian Revolution, like other mass struggles of the time, was intertwined with the everyday realities of the people. Every day and every action was framed within the revolutionary imperative of gaining the independence and liberation of Algeria. A significant feature of Fanon's work is the manner in which he depicts the revolution as a historical moment of dynamic change, where the social agency generated by revolutionary praxis not only transformed the people and society but also reinvented their attitudes toward those things *appropriated* from the colonial context, reinscribing these with liberatory meanings rooted in their social and material conditions. What Fanon powerfully affirms here is a socialist understanding of revolution, one that is unwaveringly grounded in a humanizing process that ensues through the actions of the people themselves; by which their self-determination, like *oxygen, creates and shapes a new humanity* (13).

Albert Memmi

The *Colonizer and the Colonized* is considered Albert Memmi's (1957) most influential work, where he provides an extensive analysis of the condition of both the colonizer and the colonized. Memmi's thesis engages with the manner in which both colonized and colonizer is entrapped in their respective role or in what Freire refers to as the oppressor-oppressed contradiction. As such, "a relentless reciprocity binds the colonizer to the colonized—his product and his fate" (24). Reminiscent of Fanon, Memmi too situates the impetus of his work in lived history: "I was Tunisian,[61] therefore colonized. I discovered that few aspects of my life and my personality were untouched by this fact. Not only my own thoughts, my passions and my conduct, but also the conduct of others toward me was affected" (4). However, unlike Fanon, Memmi's relationship to Marxism is present but more tenuous, stating "colonial privilege is not solely economic ... the life of the colonizer and colonized is to discover rapidly that the daily humiliation of the colonized, his [her] subjugation, are not merely economic" (8). However, this should not be surprising, given Memmi's deeply existential and literary roots.[62] Yet, despite his Modernist propensities, Memmi offers some key insights into the dynamics of colonial bondage and its impact on both the colonizer and colonized.

Memmi (1957) asserts that colonialism, as an economic and ideological phenomenon, is akin to fascism; and racialized violence its instrument of human oppression. Racism, in the colonial context, is understood as "ingrained in actions, institutions, and in the nature of the colonialist methods of production and exchange" (20). Hence, for Memmi, colonialism is predicated on the centrality of racism as a structural mechanism of colonial oppression, which results in the dehumanization of the colonized. Memmi also takes up the question of assimilation in the colonial situation, which he contends is an unattainable goal, given the deeply invasive and vertical relationship of the

[61] Tunisia became a colony of the French in 1881, gaining its independence in 1956. During the French colonial period, the country was home to French colonizers, Italians, Tunisian Muslims, and a minority Jews. The Italians, although not as well off as the French, were also privileged. The Muslim majority was the most oppressed. Although the Jews were also oppressed, Memmi describes the Jews as more willing to try to assimilate to the French. According to Memmi, colonialism was not as difficult for the Jews as it was for the Muslims because of their willingness to take on some aspects of the colonial cultural. Jews joined the French in the streets of Algiers during independence uprisings. Although Memmi joined the colonized rather than the colonizer, he contends that he understood why the Jews chose the side of the French. He writes, "Because of this ambivalence, I knew only too well the contradictory emotions which swayed their lives" (xiv). Moreover, it is important to note here that there has existed what some consider a long-standing historical relationship of conflict between Muslims and Jews in France (Mandel 2014), which surely was also felt in the Tunisian colonial context.

[62] It is interesting to note that in certain respect, Jean-Paul Sartre confirms this point when he writes in the foreword of *The Colonizer and the Colonized*, Memmi "attempts to live his particularity by transcending it in the direction of the universal. The transcendence is not toward Man, who does not yet exist, but toward a rigorous reason enforcing its claims on everyone" (18).

colonizer to the colonized. Within this profoundly ambivalent relationship of domination—requiring the labor and allegiance of the colonized, on one hand, and the social and political economic repression of the colonized on the other—results in an oppressive dynamic of ambivalence, leaving the colonized to survive within a wretched state of "painful and constant ambiguity" (59). Meanwhile, Memmi claims, even the lowliest from the dominant culture enjoys a "profound satisfaction of being negatively better than the colonized: they are never completely engulfed in the abasement in which colonialism drives them" (61).

However, in his *portrait of the colonizer*, Memmi also makes note of *the colonizer who refuses*; who despite expressed condemnation of injustice often lives "under the sign of a contradiction which looms at every step, depriving [them] of all coherence and all tranquility" (64). Forms of incoherence and contradiction are intertwined within an unacknowledged duplicity associated with their lack of genuine identification with the colonized—who, consciously or unconsciously, the colonizer regards as deficit. Of this, Memmi asserts the *benevolent colonizer* can be "both a revolutionary and an exploiter" (67), going "so far as to give [their] approval and even [their] assistance, [but their] solidarity stops here" (67); because they do not see the colonized as one of them nor do they have the desire to be one with the colonizer. Moreover, denial of the colonizing gaze leads them to rationalize their judgments of the colonized and their detachment from their struggle for liberation.

> How can one deny that they are under-developed, that their customs are oddly changeable and their culture outdates? Oh, he [she] hastens to reply, those defects are not attributable to the colonized but to decades of colonization which galvanized their history ... before colonization, weren't the colonized already backward? [And even when] he [she] has complete faith in the genius of the people, all people ... the fact remains, however, that he [she] admits to a fundamental difference between the colonized and himself [herself]. (68–69)

At the other end of the colonizer continuum, Memmi identifies the *colonialist*, referring to the colonizer who readily accepts and defends the colonial project, even if it means rewriting or *erasing history* or rewriting laws, in order to legitimate the usurpation and impunity of the mother country. This is carried out through an ideology predicated on the racialized supremacy of the colonizer, amid an ever-growing hostility toward the oppressed. Memmi argues that this oppressive relationship, mired in a growing contradiction, results in the *Usurper Role* or the *Nero Complex*, where this "intolerable contradiction fills [the colonizer] with a rage, a loathing, always ready to be loosed on the colonized" (110). The tensions and anxieties of the colonizer, according to Memmi, are deeply rooted in both the illegitimacy and injustice of the colonial project, on one hand, and the manner in which the colonizer cannot imagine human existence beyond the safety and security of the colonial condition.

In his *portrait of the colonized*, Memmi engages the impact of historical erasure upon the colonized, which begins early in the educational process. This dynamic of exclusion is repeated at all levels of power and decision making, which functions effectively to detach and alienate the colonized from their lived conditions. Moreover, this exclusion is accompanied with a deficit mentality toward the colonized, which when internalized reinforces a belief in their inadequacy to govern themselves and thus, promotes dependency on the colonial relationship, despite its fundamental violation of their freedom. Memmi also examines the question of schooling, language, and literacy within the colonial context and its impact on the colonized. He points to the manner in which the conflict between home and school culture creates a permanent *duality* in the colonized adolescent. With respect to language, literacy in the colonizer's language similarly results in a *linguistic dualism*, given that the mother tongue is not permitted to influence the larger spheres of power—making the colonized *foreigners* on our own land.

Memmi engages different aspects of the colonized, which although useful to understanding the cultural politics of colonialism, can at times fall into an essentialized portrayal, where greater dialectical engagement with issues of human agency and more open interpretations of human oppression might be useful. This may exemplify, where Memmi's classical lens can inadvertently betray his moral intentions, in ways that reify both the colonized and colonizer into inescapable bondage. This too may be why he offers only "two answers to the colonized" (163), by which escape from this colonial bondage is possible. The first is to *become like the colonizer*, which he argues is bankrupt; and the second is *revolt*, which he sees as the only logical step in the undoing of the colonial situation. While "the two historically possible solutions are tried in succession or simultaneously" (144), Memmi argues that it is only with abandonment of assimilation that *recovery of self and of autonomous dignity* can be achieved.

Comparisons of Fanon and Memmi

There has been a tendency to make comparisons between Frantz Fanon and Albert Memmi; however, some significant philosophical distinctions exist, which according to some scholars result in an uneasy correlation (Allensandrini 2014; Jadallah 2012). Beyond the fact that both anticolonial authors take up the subject of colonialism and posit theories about the relationship between the colonizers and colonized, it is at the place of respective methodological approaches that their roads divert. Perhaps one of the most significant distinctions is that Fanon uncompromisingly remains loyal to a Marxist humanist dialectic, grounding his arguments in his own subjective/objective praxis[63] as a psychiatrist and as a Black revolutionary, by way of examining oppressive social and material relations within the colonial context. As Fanon's work develops, his Western clinical training gives way to his revolutionary commitments, which intensify within both his political activities and philosophical interpretations. Memmi, on the other hand, retains his traditional orientation as philosopher[64] and novelist, whose sensibilities are more akin to the existentialist influences of Jean-Paul Sartre and Albert Camus. Moreover, it can be said that Fanon, as Freire, assumes a posture more akin to *epistemologies of the South* (Santos 2014).

Educational Philosophical Influences

Since Freire is primarily viewed as an educational philosopher, the following section provides a brief account of the three educational philosophers he

---

[63] About this point, Sharpley-Whiting (1998) notes in her book, *Frantz Fanon: Conflicts and Feminisms*, that "*Black Skin, White Masks* is at once a clinical study and an experimental narrative" (11).

[64] Memmi, on the other hand, seems to have remained more staunchly rooted in his classical perspective, to the extent that some scholars argue that Memmi has done an "about-face" in his last book, *Decolonization and the Decolonized* (Lieberman 2007). Nevertheless, many critical scholars continue to view Memmi's early writings as significant and salient to the continuing anticolonial debate.

references in *Pedagogy of the Oppressed*. Henri Bergson, John Dewey, and Pierre Furter compose a noteworthy trio,[65] in that each offers Freire an important degree of substantiation for his own insistence on acknowledging, both pedagogically *and* politically, the power of education as both a humanizing and democratizing force.

Henri Bergson

Henri Bergson was considered one of the most influential French philosophers of the early twentieth century. Although hugely popular in his time, his work was eclipsed after the Second World War by phenomenologists who built on his writings, yet received greater acclaim for his ideas. Bergson's epistemological claims—tied to the belief that "through intuition ... we probe reality—deform it—though for practical purposes" (Gunter 1995: 379)—have made important contributions to our contemporary philosophy of education. Bergson engages the reality of duration (process), where "things flow, are internal to one another, and exhibit unpredictable creativity" (379), along with its interaction (dialectic) of intuition and intelligence (Gunter 1995). In Bergson's writings on education, he protests the transmission of "dead ideas" and argues that education should never sacrifice the vitality and reflectiveness of intuition to the transmission of reified knowledge that is divorced of reflection and connection to the world.

Important to Bergson's philosophy are his distinctive treatment of the movement of time and his methodology of intuitionism that led him to posit a *method of multiplicity*, in which he recognized the epistemological disassociation, disharmony, differentiation, and divergences at work in the construction of knowledge (Mullarkey 1995), in an effort to bring together elements of heterogeneity and continuity, which he argued were inherently at work in all phenomena. Many have considered Bergson's notion of multiplicity

---

[65] Freire does not mention the writings of Croatian-Austrian author, Ivan Illich, in *Pedagogy of the Oppressed*. However, as both a radical Catholic priest living many years in Mexico and an acerbic critic of traditional schooling (Illich 1971), Freire and Illich's paths crossed over the years and their ideas have been engaged simultaneously in critiques and discussions of education. For examples see: Kahn (2010); Kahn and Kellner (2007); Rosiska and Domonice (1974).

as a revolutionary concept in that it inherently supports efforts in education to reconceptualize a pluralistic and diverse community.

Moreover,

> in order to define consciousness and therefore freedom, Bergson proposes to differentiate between time and space, 'to un-mix' them … On the other hand, through this differentiation, he defines the immediate data of consciousness as being temporal, in other words, as the duration (*la durée*). In the duration, there is no juxtaposition of events; therefore there is no mechanistic causality. It is in the duration that we can speak of the experience of freedom. (Lawlor and Leonard 2016)

Bergson (1911), in *Creative Evolution*, equates life with creation, in that he argues that creativity is what assists us to account for both the continuity of life and the discontinuity of its evolution. Hence, the integration of both intuition and creativity within the context of education must be considered essential features of an education in the interest of human emancipation.

John Dewey

American philosopher and educator, John Dewey, often referred to as the *father of the progressive education movement*, has influenced educators concerned with advancing democratic ideals. During the early 1900s, Dewey sought to articulate his pragmatic philosophy and expand on the idea of community to explain the purpose of education in a democratic society. His beliefs centered on a variety of basic principles, including the notion that education must engage with an enlarged experience; that thinking and reflection are central to the act of teaching; and that students must freely interact with their environments in the practice of constructing knowledge. Although there are those who have sharply criticized Dewey's faith in creative intelligence as eminently naïve and accused him of underestimating the sociopolitical and economic forces that shape inequality and injustice, Dewey's work is considered significant to the evolution of discourses on education, the individual, and democracy.

Dewey's writings are generally associated with *pragmatism*; a school of thought grounded in a view of knowledge that counters the dualistic epistemology and metaphysical abstraction of modern philosophy, while embracing a naturalistic approach wherein knowledge is seen as evolving from the process of *active* adaptation of an organism to its environment. In line with this perspective, Dewey's theory of knowledge focused on the interaction of the individual with his or her social environment. In *Education and Society*, Dewey (1916) argued, "Society exists through a process of transmission quite as much as biological life. The transmission occurs by means of ideals, hopes, expectations, standards, and opinions from those members of society who are passing out of the group to those who are coming into it. Without this, social life could not survive" (3).

Inquiry, for Dewey, is not rooted in passive observation of the world, from which truths are inferred. On the contrary, he saw inquiry as a dynamic process, which begins with an obstacle that prevents effective action; from there, it moves toward an active engagement with the environment, in order to discover new ways in which the individual can readapt to the environment, so that free action can be resumed. Dewey contended that traditional theories of epistemology had become estranged from this important connection to the world. In response, he endeavored to develop and refine a naturalist scientific approach that could restore a fundamental relationship between theory and practice. Dewey's naturalist approach was then most concerned with the product of interactions between organisms and the environment, in that he insisted knowledge had to be linked to a practical instrumentality or *instrumentalism*, which he identifies as the underlying motivation that guides social interactions. Hence, for Dewey, our experience of the world is constituted by our interrelationship with it, a relationship that must be anchored to practical significance.

Dewey's examination of societal, ethics, and aesthetics sought to expand on the significance of community and the purpose of education in a democratic society. His views of education are tied to three fundamental tenets for teaching practice, including: (1) the idea that education had to engage with the larger social environment; (2) that reflection must be at the heart of all teaching; and (3) that students need consistent opportunities to interact freely with their environment, in the process of knowledge construction. As such, Dewey attempted "to link the notion of individual and social (cooperative) intelligence with the discourse of democracy and freedom" (McLaren 1989: 199).

Dewey also brought to educational discussions of his time a new *language of possibility*, which challenged historical determinism, binary separations between knower and the world, reinforced the social agency of the teacher and student, and linked education to the possibilities of social change (Darder, Torres, and Baltodano 2017).

As such, Dewey (1916) saw moral and social questions in education as guiding human actions toward socially defined ends—democratic ends that in practical and concrete ways would result in productive and satisfying outcomes for both individuals and society. Hence, in contrast to an undesirable society, "which internally and externally sets up barriers for free intercourse and communication of experience," for Dewey, an ideal democratic society

> makes provision for participation in its good of all members on equal terms and which secures flexible readjustment of its institutions through interaction of the different forms of associated life is in so far democratic. Such a society must have a type of education which gives individuals a personal interest in social relationships and control, and the habits of mind which secure social changes. (99)

Pierre Furter

The Swiss educational philosopher, Pierre Furter, became known in Latin American through his long-term work in both Brazil and Venezuela. Similar to Freire, Furter served as a consultant for UNESCO. His work focused on worldwide education, regional disparities and their impact on impoverished communities. In *Educação e Vida*, Furter (1966) offers an alternative humanistic educational approach to economic educational models. He has made a much-needed contribution through a praxis of *androgeny*, a humanist concept of education specially focused on the learning needs of adults. Furter, however, viewed andragogy as a broader concept of education that applied to all human beings. Key to this approach is an understanding of everyday experience as the richest resource or fountain of adult learning. For Furter, learners are most motivated to learn when they experience the process of knowledge construction in ways that link it to their own needs and interests— interests that will lead to improving their well-being.

Furter's andragogical approach encompasses five key principles: (1) the learner has a need to know why they need to learn something and how much they will gain in the process; (2) learning requires a relationship that respects the self-concept of learners, so that they are seen as responsible for their decisions and their life and, thus, seen and treated as capable of being self-directed; (3) For the learner, experiences are the basis of learning and, as such, pedagogical approaches that take advantage of the many individual differences among learners will be most effective; (4) there needs to be a readiness to learn; that is, the learner must be willing to learn when the occasion demands some kind of learning related to the concrete conditions of day to day life; and (5) learners do best when there is guidance and concepts presented contextualized for actual use in their lives.

Furter considers these humanizing pedagogical principles as a means for creating an educational context where unknown possibilities can freely emerge and flourish in ways that are meaningful to adult learners. For Furter (1966), creating conditions for the "emergence of the awareness of our full humanity" (165) is an essential condition of any democratic educational effort. Moreover, he posits that education with adults had to address the common tendency of adult learners to hold on to that which they perceive as a "guaranteed space" through creating a pedagogical approach where: "The universe is revealed to [learners] not as space, imposing a massive presence to which [they] can but adapt, but [rather] as ... a domain which takes shape as [they] act upon it" (27).

Moving forward

This extensive, yet concise, intellectual history of the philosophers who influenced the ideas expressed in *Pedagogy of the Oppressed* is meant to assist the reader to better understand many of the underlying themes of the book. By referring back to this chapter, the reader will be able to make connections, which may not initially be apparent. In this way, the chapter will assist the reader to grasp more accurately the intent and possibility that inform Freire's liberating pedagogy.

In Dialogue with the Text

Major Themes, Chapter-by-Chapter

From these pages I hope at least the following will endure: my trust in the people, and my faith in men and women, and in the creation of a world in which it will be easier to love.

—Paulo Freire

In this chapter, each of the four chapters of Freire's *Pedagogy of the Oppressed* are summarized by way of a dialogical discussion[1] with the major themes that inform the composition of each chapter. The organization of each chapter summary also reflects my pedagogical sensibilities, influenced by four decades of interacting with the text. The rationale for this dialogical approach is that, although Freire engages with notions of oppression and, thus, the need for a pedagogy of the oppressed repeatedly throughout the entire volume, each chapter is sharply defined by a focused set of themes, which Freire articulates in juxtaposition to the overall purpose of his larger political project—namely the creation of a world grounded in an ethics of social and material liberation.

In summary, the focus of Chapter 1 is squarely placed on assisting the reader to understand the necessity for a pedagogy of the oppressed, given the conditions of social and material oppression that prevail in the society

---

[1] Given the dialogical approach that I have used for the chapter-by-chapter discussions of the major themes, all italicized words and phrases in this chapter are from *Pedagogy of the Oppressed* as they appear in the chapter under examination. Although this approach deviates from the standard APA format used in the earlier chapters, of this book, this stylistic devise permits Freire's voice to remain active and present throughout my direct engagement with his work. In essence, this approach is in sync with Freire's pedagogy of the oppressed.

and its impact upon subaltern populations. In Chapter 2, the focus is on the concept of *banking education* as an instrument of oppression, which Freire counters by way of a *problem-posing pedagogy*. In Chapter 3, the major focus is on Freire's conceptualization of dialogue and his dialogical methodology, which is tied to *generative themes*; linking dialogical praxis to the development of critical consciousness. And finally, in the last chapter, Freire focuses on an important comparison between *antidialogical* practices and *dialogical* practices, which he links to *cultural action* and a revolutionary vision of social transformation. Moreover, I engage the chapter discussions as interlocking parts of a larger revolutionary project, which seeks to set out underlying principles for liberatory pedagogy, methodology, and leadership.

Chapter 1

Without freedom [we] cannot exist authentically.

—Paulo Freire

In the first chapter of the book, Freire contextualizes the need for a *pedagogy of the oppressed* by engaging the historical and social conditions under which the oppressed exist, and juxtaposing these condition with the ruling class. Freire begins to carefully lay out the specifics of what he terms the *oppressor-oppressed contradiction* and how he theorizes the possibilities for engaging and transforming this contradiction—a contradiction anchored within particular attitudes, relationships, practices, and dynamics of oppression, perpetuated within the unjust structures of capitalist society. As his discussion unfolds, Freire makes it clear that liberation is neither a gift that can be bestowed upon others nor is it solely an individual pursuit. Rather, he argues, liberation is the outcome of collective social struggle, which must be carried out through a coherent commitment to a political project, in the interest of our humanity and the authentic democratization of society.

Humanization: *An inescapable concern*

> *The struggle for humanity is only possible because dehumanization, although a concrete historical fact, is not a given destiny but the result of an unjust order that engenders violence in the oppressors, which in turn dehumanizes the oppressed.*

Freire begins his seminal work with the *problem of humanization*, which he regards as *an inescapable concern* of those committed to a just world. However, key to his conceptualization of humanization, as both a pedagogical and political imperative, is also the manner in which this concern can lead us, conversely, toward recognition of dehumanization. Here, Freire does not essentialize either pole of the dialectical relationship between humanization and dehumanization, in that he argues that both are possibilities in the context of history and our human *unfinishedness*. What is particularly striking here is that Freire, in no uncertain terms, sets down one of his most important assumptions—an assumption clearly linked to his existential, phenomenological, and Marxist humanist formation—*humanization as the people's vocation*.

Although Freire is well aware of the manner in which this vocation is constantly negated and maligned, in concert with Marcuse, he affirms the *negation of the negation*. That is to say, that although it is true that this vocation is often negated by the injustices and violence of the oppressive order, it is also reasserted by our *yearning for freedom* and the struggles waged by the oppressed to recover our dignity and negate our alienation and disaffiliation as subjects of history and citizens of the world. Freire, however, does not only see this struggle as an existential concern but also one that is directly linked to social and material conditions that require the emancipation of labor, the overcoming of our alienation, and the affirmation of our humanity. Nevertheless, for Freire, this *historical task of the oppressed* is not solely about our liberation but also the liberation of *the oppressors as well*. This is a point that often creates some confusion for new readers, in that it is read through the linear and dichotomous lens of Western positivist thinking. However, Freire signals here the dialectical relationship between oppressors and oppressed. So, if one side of this relationship shifts, then so will the other. Freire's Marxist view of totality is clearly at work, in that when he speaks of liberation he is speaking of the totality of the human condition that encompasses oppressors and oppressed. As such, there is no way the oppressed can truly be liberated, without also the oppressors being liberated in the process.

For Freire, dehumanization is the direct result of the injustice and violence perpetrated by the dominant class—a phenomenon that distorts the humanity of both, oppressed and oppressors. The culture of hegemony normalizes and reifies the unjust hierarchy of the ruling class, as asserted by Gramsci and other critical theorists, while social and material forms of manipulation and repression uphold its one-dimensionality. Accordingly, asymmetrical relations of power are rendered common sense and serve to reinforce adherence to and reproduction of social and material domination. The educational system, according to Freire, becomes an *instrument of dehumanization* in that the self-determination and empowerment of students from oppressed communities is systematically thwarted.

Freire thereby speaks to the difficulties faced in the struggle for liberation, given that those in power are seldom motivated to radically alter conditions of inequality that benefit them; while those who suffer the concrete consequence of oppression are far more inclined to do so. Hence, Freire maintains that the oppressor, *who is himself dehumanized because he dehumanizes others, is unable to lead this struggle.* The immorality of unjust power is insufficiently suited for the task. In contrast, Freire notes, it is through the power generated by the oppressed, who recognize and assert the need for change, that an authentic struggle for liberation can be forged; and, in so doing, the oppressor is compelled to enter into a new relationship.

It is for this reason that Freire links critical thought directly to the *pursuit of our humanity*, in that our capacity to think critically is a vital precursor to the kind of social action necessary for overcoming, as Althusser argues, false ideologies of oppression that have become interpellated across society. Through the awakening of critical awareness, Freire contends, the oppressed can come to perceive the causes for injustice and, in so doing, generate social action that will create a liberating situation from which our humanity can freely unfold. It is precisely through our persistent critical engagement with the dehumanizing conditions we face, that our fixation with the culture of hegemony is shattered and new possibilities for humanizing power relations can emerge. This idea is essential for readers to grasp, in that Freire, in concert with staunch critics of authoritarianism, issues a firm warning: exchanging places with the oppressor does not overcome the oppressor-oppressed contradiction, which colonize the hearts, minds, bodies, and spirits of the people.

Alienation: The colonized mentality of oppression

At a certain point in their existential experience the oppressed feel an irresistible attraction towards the oppressors and their way of life. Sharing this way of life becomes an overpowering aspiration. In their alienation, the oppressed want at any cost to resemble the oppressors, to imitate them, to follow them.

In his varied discussions on the phenomenon of alienation—expressed as dehumanization, colonization, domestication, mechanization, oppression, cultural invasion—throughout the book, Freire brings together Marxism and the anticolonial writings of Memmi and Fanon, in his analysis of the colonized mentality. Within the structure of racialized capitalist relations, the oppressed have been interpellated, as Althusser would argue, with the ideologies of the ruling class. The consequence is an abstraction of our humanity, constrained by the wishes and desires of the powerful. Often this process of estrangement is accompanied by the internalization of deficit views toward self and community, inherently shaped by the scorn, hostility, and resentment of the dominant elite toward subaltern populations. This, Freire argues, is demarcated by an underlying distrust and denunciation of one's cultural sensibilities and knowledge, an aspiration to emulate the oppressor, and a growing dependency on the wealthy and powerful.

Dependency: The more that the oppressed internalize the attitudes and ways of the oppressor, the more estranged we become from self, from one another, and the world. Hence the lived histories, wisdom, and knowledges of the oppressed become submerged in the consciousness of the oppressor, where the *inauthentic worldview* that drives our objectification and subjugation produces a state of ambiguity and disempowerment. Simultaneously, there often exists a belief in the *invulnerability of the oppressor*—a belief that immobilizes and thwarts our self-determination and social agency. Freire suggests, the deeper our submersion into the oppressor worldview, the more likely the oppressed will experience confusion, doubt, fear, or guilt, if action is initiated that counters the status quo. This *emotional dependence* and adherence to the oppressor worldview generates what Fromm terms *necrophilic behavior*—action that extinguishes life. Moreover, this colonizing dependency can manifest as the *fear of freedom*, which Freire argues must be acknowledged and engaged in the liberatory formation of oppressed communities, in ways that do not *create still greater dependence.*

Fear of Freedom: In moving back and forth in his discussion of oppression, Freire asserts, *freedom is not an ideal located outside of us* but the manifestation of concrete social relations; therefore, freedom is essential to dismantling the duality of estrangement. Freire, who draws from Fromm's *Fear of Freedom*, reminds us there are two opposing tensions: the oppressed can be hesitant to embrace freedom, while the oppressors fear losing their freedom to oppress. Hence, the *fear of authentic existence* prevails in both oppressed and oppressor. Still, Freire insists that the *freedom to be*—key to the process of humanization—is vital to self-determination and liberation, suggesting that, as the oppressed engage critically with the power to act in the world, the contradictions that underlie the fear of freedom are potentially resolved by liberatory action.

However, a concern for Freire is the manner in which the oppressed may work to overcome their fear of freedom by seeking to reverse roles with the oppressor. This strategy unfortunately reinforces a prescription to domination—where the dominant group prescribes the boundaries of existence, while the colonized must conform. Unfortunately, the oppressed submerged and resigned to an oppressive consciousness are inhibited from acting on their own interest, feeling incapable of waging the risks necessary in the struggle for freedom. Yet, Freire argues, *If the humanization of the oppressed signifies subversion, so also does their freedom*; hence the necessity for the powerful to exert social and material control. As this culture of hegemony is intensified, Freire expresses concern over a *fatalism* that can befall the oppressed, reinforcing docility and domestication.

Fatalism: Freire laments the manner in which fatalism has become *a trait of national character*, within oppressive societies. He points to the manner in which human suffering is falsely rendered inevitable destiny or fate—whether consequence of *God's will* or a belief in the unworthiness of the subaltern. Here again, Freire points to the duality of alienation that permits the sham of fatalistic assumptions to remain veiled in the colonized mentality. Freire argues, "*As long as the oppressed remain unaware of the causes of their condition, they fatalistically 'accept' their exploitation. Further, they are apt to react in a passive and alienated manner when confronted with the necessity to struggle for their freedom and self-affirmation.*" The colonizing impact of fatalism, rooted in the violence of oppression, can often manifest itself, according to Fanon, in contradictory ways, including aggression by the powerless toward our own people.

Violence: Freire's perspective on violence is another of those key ideas that has been widely cited. He draws here from Fanon's *The Wretched of the Earth* to assert, *Never in history has violence been initiated by the oppressed.* Freire stresses, violence is founded upon a dehumanizing ideology that transfigures the living into "things," which can then be controlled, manipulated, eclipsed, or extinguished. In this way, concrete conditions of violence against the oppressed—perpetrated through subtractive schooling, labor inequalities, labor discriminations, policing abuses, or mass incarceration—are created, which support despotism, alienation and the negation of humanity. Hence, Freire argues, *It is not those whose humanity is denied them who negate humankind, but those who denied that humanity.*

In concert with Althusser, Freire maintains that the exclusionary and violent worldview of the oppressor *engenders an entire way of life ... for those caught up in it—both oppressed and oppressor. Both are submerged ... and both bear the marks of oppression.* However, this should not be in anyway interpreted to mean that both share equal responsibility for the violence. Nothing could be further from the truth, in that it is the cultural hegemony instituted by the oppressor that spawns and provokes violence—including the *horizontal violence* that the oppressed may manifest upon one another. Moreover, in line with Fanon, Freire clearly distinguishes between a possessive violence perpetrated *upon* the oppressed that negates life and those conscious or unconscious acts of rebellion by the oppressed meant to affirm life, by opposing the inhumanity or false generosity of the oppressor.

False Generosity: *False generosity* is another key Freirean idea often cited in the literature. Freire introduces the concept early in the chapter, when he admonishes those who would *attempt to "soften" the power of the oppressor in deference to the weakness of the oppressed*. Freire views the culture of hegemony in society as a permanent wellspring of false generosity, in that its charitable practices on behalf of the oppressed generally whitewash both the impact of poverty and the underlying deficit views, which blame the people for their own oppression. Employing Fromm's notion of necrophilia, Freire contends that false generosity actually fosters the perpetuation of death, despair, and poverty among the oppressed, given the necessity of an oppressed mass within capitalist society.

For Freire, false generosity constitutes then a form of violence, in that *it interferes with the individual's ontological and historical vocation to be more fully human*—and, so, deepens the dependency of the oppressed on the "benevolence" of the oppressor. False generosity shrouds the lovelessness of the oppressor who, Freire contends, sustain welfare programs for the people, as long as these do not tamper with the unjust system of labor, which assures power and privilege remains in the hands of a few. To drive this point home, Freire contrasts false generosity with *true generosity*, which fundamentally emerges from the pursuit of freedom. Within the dynamics of a true generosity, the oppressed are never expected to humiliate and erode their dignity, in supplication for that which should rightly be ours. In contrast, a true generosity is founded upon a loving relationship of communion *with* the people that nourishes respect, freedom, and self-determination.

In direct contrast, the beneficiaries of an unjust system of domination and exploitation generally refuse to acknowledge that to keep women and men socially, politically, and materially impoverished, despite their so-called charity, is to interfere with the capacity of the oppressed to be fully human. Hence, *the oppressors do not perceive their monopoly on having more as a privilege, which dehumanizes others and themselves*. Instead, they see their wealth as an inalienable right, which they've earned through their wherewithal and intelligence. Meanwhile the *have-nots* are seen through a victim-blaming lens, where they are deemed *incompetent and lazy, and worst of all is their unjustifiable ingratitude towards the "generous gestures" of the dominant class.* It is precisely the violence of this alienating dynamic and its impact on the oppressed that solidifies and intensifies *the tragic dilemma* of the oppressed.

The tragic dilemma: Oppressor-oppressed contradiction

The conflict lies in the choice between being wholly themselves or being divided; between ejecting the oppressor within or not ejecting them; between human solidarity or alienation; between following prescriptions or having choices; between being spectators or actors; between acting or having the illusion of acting through the action of the oppressors; between speaking out or being silent, castrated in their power to create and re-create, in their power to transform the world. This is the tragic dilemma of the oppressed which their education must take into account.

Freire articulates the oppressor-oppressed contraction as a condition of oppression that results in deep-seated duality, dichotomy, and ambiguity—all responses to tragic conditions of dehumanization that prevent the authenticity of human existence. To understand this key concept in Freire's work requires an epistemological understanding of the Marxist dialectic discussed in the previous chapter. It is, in fact, dialectical[2] thought that aids in shattering the duality and dichotomy of human relations, in an effort to restore totality and resolve tension

---

[2] Often students struggle to understand the difference between *dialectic* and *dialogic*. In a *dialectic* process, describing the interaction and resolution between multiple paradigms or ideologies, generally, one presumed solution establishes primacy over the others. The goal of a dialectic process is to merge point and counterpoint (thesis and antithesis) into a compromise or other state of agreement via conflict and tension (synthesis). It encompasses then a synthesis that evolves from the opposition between thesis and antithesis. In a *dialogic* process, various approaches coexist and are comparatively existential and relativistic in their interaction. Here, each ideology can hold more salience in particular circumstances. Changes can be made within these ideologies if a strategy does not have the desired effect. Whereas dialogic processes, especially those involved with regular spoken conversation, involve a type of listening that attends to the implicit intentions behind the speaker's actual words. Unlike a dialectic process, dialogics often do not lead to closure and remain unresolved. Compared to dialectics, a dialogic exchange can be less competitive, and more suitable for facilitating cooperation. Hence, this helps to explain Freire's preference for a dialogical approach in a problem-posing pedagogy. See: Chapter 17 of *Critical Thinking* (Paul 1993).

in the interrelationship between that which is often considered disparate or oppositional. Central to overcoming the oppressor-oppressed contradiction is an engagement with the dialectics of objectivity and subjectivity, which can expand an understanding of the oppressor-oppressed contradiction.

Dialectics of Objectivity/Subjectivity: Positivist thought constructs a false binary or separation between subject and object, between human action and the world, between the oppressor and oppressed. This points to an epistemology where objective reality or the material object is privileged in the construction of knowing. As such, the body, feelings, and intuition are either maligned or marginalized. It is this dichotomous worldview that bolsters false conditions of separation, by dismissing the role of human subjectivity. In direct contrast, Freire argues: *One cannot conceive of objectivity without subjectivity. Neither can exist without the other, nor can they be dichotomized.* What this means is that in order to transform the world, we should not fall into subjectivism, where objective reality is denied and only the individual subjective experience prevails. Nor should we fall into objectivism, which strips objects of their context and connection to humanity. In both instances, our transformative capacity to collectively struggle against oppression is hugely undermined by either inaction or actions that, wittingly or unwittingly, perpetuate the myths and false perceptions that preserve the oppressor-oppressed duality.

Oppressed/Oppressor Duality: Freire engages the suffering that results from the oppressor-oppressed duality from the standpoint of both poles. For the oppressed, this suffering is the outcome of internalizing an inauthentic sense of being that denies our humanity, in that it is rooted in the consciousness of the oppressor. Hence, Freire argues: *They are at one and the same time themselves and the oppressor whose consciousness they have internalized.* Until the oppressed are able to unveil this *existential duality*, a false sense of being can prevail, which may be expressed through fatalistic resignation and adherence to the situation of alienation. Of particular concern for Freire is when the oppressed prefer to maintain the *security of conformity*, rather than to risk overcoming this contraction, informed by the social forces of oppression.

On the other side of the pole is the oppressor, who holds dehumanizing views that objectify the oppressed as violent, ferocious, subversive, envious, or stupid. At this end, being human is considered the domain of the privileged, who accumulate wealth and power, in the name of productivity and progress. However, Freire insists, those who oppress others also exist in a state of dehumanization, hence, they too are inauthentic beings. To step out of their duality would also require them to discover the conditions of their situation—which can provoke guilt and suffering. More often than not, unfortunately, this dynamic does not move the oppressor to overcome the contradiction, but rather to better rationalize the inequalities and injustices that preserve their domination. Here, Freire turns to both Fromm and Lukács' arguments, in that what tends to prevail is a reification of the oppressor-oppressed contradiction, in that without possession of *power over the oppressed*, their sense of "normalcy" is shattered.

Resolution of the Contradiction: According to Freire, the central problem to be resolved is the fundamental expulsion of the internalized culture of social and material domination, which requires the authentic participation of the oppressed in cocreation of the world. This, inherently, reflects a Marxist critique, which admonishes the capitalist mode of production that perpetuates the slave-master dynamic. Hence, the contradistinction of the oppressed and oppressor must be overcome, if our liberation is to unfold as day-to-day existence. Nevertheless, Freire argues that the greatest obstacle to liberation is the internalized culture of domination that systematically functions to submerge the consciousness of human beings in the imagination of the ruling class. Accordingly, many of the oppressed, rather than to fight for their liberation from an unjust system aspire, instead, to wealth and power, reinforcing the hegemonic culture of domination. For this reason Freire contends, the struggle for liberation must be engaged as both a material and ideological fight for our *autonomy and responsibility* over our destiny—a destiny beyond the tyranny of racialized class inequalities.

Notwithstanding, this revolutionary process entails a deeply serious and committed political project, in that both the oppressed committed to liberation and the oppressor committed to *conversion* will face a multitude of struggles in order to supersede the essential contradiction. Freire, reflecting radical Catholic roots, notes that this conversion *requires a profound rebirth* and confirms the converted oppressor has a historical role, in abandoning their culture of exploitation and indifference to the oppressed. However, whether for the oppressed or the convert who fights at their side, Freire maintains, as did Althusser, the sedimented traces of domination will require our self-vigilance as we move through different stages of struggle—from oppressed objects to subjects of history—and endeavor to reinvent a *liberatory praxis* for humanity.

Pedagogy as revolutionary praxis

> *No pedagogy which is truly liberating can remain distant from the oppressed by treating them as unfortunates and by presenting for their emulation models from among the oppressors. The oppressed must be their own example in the struggle for their redemption.*

Freire's pedagogy of the oppressed must be first and foremost understood as revolutionary praxis that counters capitalist relations of production and colonialism, in that it is committed to a larger political project of societal liberation. Thus, a political project emerges from an enduring relationship of dialogue *with* the people and constitutes a pedagogy that is forged *with* not *for* the oppressed. Oppression and the social forces that perpetuate its existence become the objects of reflection, from which transformative action can be made and remade. The root of this revolutionary praxis is a dialogical relationship that is fueled by critical reflection and the sustained intervention of the people in the fight for liberation. Moreover, Freire makes it resoundingly clear that the *pedagogy of the oppressed cannot be developed or practiced by the oppressors*, but rather requires the participation and leadership of the oppressed. Essential here is a deep sense of faith in the people, by those *who fight at their side*. This delicate issue, unfortunately, has often remained obscured or ignored historically within impoverished communities around the world—hence, the oppressor-oppressed contradiction endures.

Two Distinct Stages: Freire identifies two major stages in the pedagogy of the oppressed. In the initial stage, the major concern is unveiling the culture of domination, dealing with the concerns of the oppressed, and working toward transformation of the concrete conditions. At this stage, the pedagogy must be *of and by* the people, not *for* the people. The second stage begins when *the reality of oppression has been transformed*. It is at this point, and only then, when it can become a pedagogy of *all* people, *in the process of permanent liberation*. The latter assumes ongoing expulsion of oppressive myths tied to a legacy of oppression, which can still surface unexpectedly to negate the social and material conditions of the new historical moment. Furthermore, Freire notes that the common dimension of both stages of the pedagogy is *action in depth*, through which oppression is challenged and transformed. Similarly, Freire confirms that at all stages of liberation, *the oppressed must see themselves as men and women engaged in the ontological and historical vocation of becoming more fully human.*

Praxis: In this chapter Freire also introduces the notion of praxis, which he links to critical reflection and action *with* the people—concepts that he develops in Chapter 2. Here, Freire asserts, at the core of a revolutionary praxis is critical dialogue fueled, as Che Guevara contends, by love for humanity and the world. And such dialogue begins with the concrete concerns and conditions that emerge from and with the people. This presupposes a humanizing relationship guided by mutual respect, love, care, trust, and commitment. In contrast to the domesticating dynamics of oppression experienced by oppressed communities that demand our passivity and silence, dialogue is a co-intentional and co-creative act of human interaction focused on the transformation of the concrete situation. Revolutionary praxis, moreover, recognizes the dynamic nature of humanity where *thoughts will change and new knowledge will be created*—knowledge from which new forms of understanding and action will be engendered. Freire, as does Fromm, distinguishes revolutionary praxis as *biophilic*—a life-affirming expression of love and solidarity *with* the oppressed.

As such, liberating praxis becomes *raison d'etre*—the underlying purpose for existence or literally, reason for being—of the oppressed. Freire extends this *raison d'etre* to revolutionary leadership, who understand liberation implicitly as a pedagogical *and* political undertaking. He argues here that revolutionary praxis, *which inaugurates the historical moment of this raison d'etre*, is not feasible without the conscious participation and commitment of the oppressed. With this in mind, Freire reminds revolutionary leaders that *their own conviction of the necessity for struggle (an indispensable dimension of revolutionary wisdom) was not given to them by anyone else*—if it is authentic. In this manner, he reaffirms the underlying purpose of a pedagogy of the oppressed, where teachers and students or leaders and communities exist as historical subjects, in the fight for liberation.

The fight for liberation

The conviction of the oppressed that they must fight for their liberation is not a gift bestowed ...

On the question of liberation, Freire draws from Fromm to argue that when the oppressed forge the fight for their freedom and humanity, they also must, in turn, embrace their *total responsibility for the struggle*. This process entails a refusal to exist as objects to be manipulated by the oppressor and, instead, take on the struggle as fully present and committed subjects of history. It is through this process that the oppressed unveil conditions of oppression and, in this way, become both objects and subjects of transformative action. As our collective criticality and political sensibilities evolve, we can more consciously activate our participation in history, and in so doing, overcome the oppressor-oppressed contradiction that incarcerates our humanity.

Freire argues, in order to wage the struggle for liberation, the oppressed must recognize the reality in which we are immersed as never a *fait accompli*, but a limit-situation that can be transformed. Freire maintains, it is precisely from the vantage point of our *unfinishedness*—and recognition that the oppressor cannot exist without the oppressed—that radical hope and liberating action can ensue. Our concrete commitment to enter into the struggle for our liberation initiates our unshackling from the oppressor-oppressed contradiction. More important, through a revolutionary praxis of collective struggle, the oppressed (and those who fight in solidarity at their side) build the critical awareness necessary to, step by step, vie for a liberatory vision of our collective human existence. Freire reminds us that at all stages of our liberation, we must see ourselves as women and men engaged in an ontological and historical vocation of becoming more fully human. In this way, Freire pronounces one of the most important, yet often missed, dialectical principles of his pedagogy: *while no one liberates oneself by one's own efforts alone, neither is one liberated by others.*

Questions for reflection and dialogue

1. What does Freire consider to be our most important vocation? In what ways does this impact how we think of education and society?
2. Freire connects alienation to the colonial mentality. What are major expressions of alienation and how do these impact the oppressed within schools, community, and society?
3. How does Freire theorize the dialectics of objectivity/subjectivity? How is this related to the oppressor-oppressed contradiction and how does Freire propose its resolution?
4. What are the two distinct stages of pedagogy of the oppressed? How are these related to revolutionary praxis?

Chapter 2

For apart from inquiry, apart from the praxis, individuals cannot be truly human. Knowledge emerges only through invention and re-invention, through the restless, impatient, continuing, hopeful inquiry human beings pursue in the world, with the world, and with each other.

—Paulo Freire

In Chapter 2, Freire sets out to unveil the manner in which education functions as an *instrument of oppression*. Motivating philosophical ideas that enliven his critical analysis come from the works of existentialists, Marxists, and critical theorists who engage questions of ideology, cultural hegemony, consciousness and oppression in ways that distinguish presuppositions that underlie structures of domination *and* liberation. From the onset, Freire begins a discussion of the *narrative character* of an educational system rooted in perpetuation of a colonizing and capitalist worldview. This entails a *banking concept* of education where *knowledge is a gift bestowed by those who consider themselves knowledgeable upon those whom they consider to know nothing.* In response, Freire proposes a *problem-posing pedagogy*, where a clear commitment to revolutionary praxis and a coherent purpose for humanizing inquiry are unapologetically centered on reinventing *education for the practice of freedom.*

Banking education

> *The "humanism" of the banking approach masks the effort to turn women and men into automatons—the very negation of their ontological vocation to be more fully human.*

At the heart of a banking concept of education is a deficit view of subaltern populations as *pathology of the healthy society*. Central to its aims is the need to conquer the minds and hearts of "deficient" students, so they willingly adopt and adhere to the unjust mentality of the ruling order. Hence, students from oppressed communities are expected to "integrate" into definitions of self and the world, as well as aspirations, prescribed by the dominant class. Those who resist the hegemonic process of integration are seen as "marginals" who resist the *gift of education* and, thus, require greater social containment. One of the ramifications of this colonizing (or racializing) mind-set is the systematic exclusion and expulsion of "troubled" students, who are an obstacle to the fluidity of social control. In contrast, those who eagerly comply are deemed a "good fit" and, often enlisted, knowingly or unknowingly, as neocolonial subjects[3] of the ruling order. Freire notes here that, while some may express commitment to liberation, those who remain immersed in the oppressor-oppressed contradiction can normalize the climate of banking education,

---

[3] The term *neoliberal subjects* is used here to refer to individuals from the oppressed class who become educated or "accomplished" within the status quo and, hence, affiliate themselves with the oppressor class and participate in the social control and management of oppressed populations.

without perceiving its alienating intent. *Paradoxically, then, they utilize this same instrument of alienation in what they consider an effort to liberate.*

Instrument of Alienation: To understand education as an *instrument of alienation,* Freire notably relies on both Marx and the Gramscian idea of cultural hegemony, where common-sense notions of society and the myth of education as a "humanist" project effectively conceal the underlying reasons for the persistence of social and material inequalities. Here, the dominant view of history and the world, as it currently exists, are blurred to support views of poverty, social inequalities, and academic failure as permanent or biological phenomena—divorced of its contemporary societal apparatus and rooted in a legacy of colonial power and capitalist oppression. Freire returns, once again, to Fromm, by asserting, *the banking concept of education, which serves the interests of oppression, is also necrophilic,* in that it stifles the creative power of the oppressed and *produces contents, whether values or empirical dimensions of reality, [that] tend in the process of being narrated to become lifeless and petrified.* Ultimately, Freire maintains, this lifelessness produces suffering that, according to Fromm, is the direct outcome of *human equilibrium disturbed.*

Freire details how this fragmenting, objectifying, and mechanizing pedagogy inhibits student creativity and imagination, by reinforcing alienation, fatalism, and submersion in a worldview of domination, discouraging critical thought and transformative action. He denounces the manner in which banking education presents reality as a *motionless, static, compartmentalized, and predictable world,* to which human beings must adapt. The issues and topics of classroom study, for example, are often alien to the realities of students from oppressed communities and, thus, have little consequence or meaning to their lives. Education isolated from their daily existence and set apart from *the totality* of oppressive societal conditions promotes students' immobility and disempowerment, by domesticating their *intentionality of consciousness.* As their credulity is stimulated, their social agency is disabled by the educational dictates of the dominant class, *who care neither to have the world revealed nor to see it transformed.*

Drawing on Simone de Beauvoir's work, Freire asserts that banking education is focused on *changing the consciousness of the oppressed, not the situation which oppresses them.* Indeed, the paternalism of banking education expects that students be passive and willing recipients, accepting and altering themselves to whatever is presented as "truth." In the process, he argues, education is reduced to *words [that] are emptied of their concreteness and become a hollow, alienated, and alienating verbosity*—hence, lifeless and powerless to transform conditions of human suffering. Also important to understand is that *the means used are not important*, in that when human beings are fundamentally denied the right to decide about our own lives, we are objectified—a phenomenon tied to the epistemology (theory) and methodology (practice) of oppression *in combination* that informs banking education. This results in an overarching pedagogical expectation that students *memorize mechanically the narrated content*, becoming *receptacles' to be "filled" by the teacher.*

Teacher-Student Contradiction: In his discussion of the banking concept of education, Freire draws on Jean Paul Sartre's critique of *digestive* or *nutritive* education, where the teacher feeds knowledge to the student to *fill them out*. Here, students exist as objects to be manipulated and coaxed by the teacher, in order to facilitate the students' passive receptivity to whatever knowledge teachers (or the state) deem worthy. In this oppositional dynamic, a *teacher-student contradiction*[4] is solidified in that the teacher and student are considered to exist at opposite poles. The depositing teacher is the knowing subject: the student depository the ignorant object. Implicit to this dichotomy is a view of students as spectators—apart from the world and apart from others. Unbeknownst to most educators, the capacity to manage spectating students is often a mark of good teaching. A good student, meanwhile, embraces—*as meek receptacle*—the knowledge dispensed by the teacher, without objection. To disagree with the teacher's truth is perceived as antagonism, regardless the validity of the student's objection. To explain the power of this alienating dynamic, Freire returns to the Hegelian dialectic of slave-master, where the student must *accept their ignorance as justifying the teacher's existence but, unlike the slave, they never discover that they [too] educate the teacher.*

---

[4] The reader should recall here the earlier discussion of the oppressor-oppressed contradiction, in the immediately preceding discussion of Chapter 1.

The teacher's task in banking education is to fill the students with their narration, without concern for who the students are or what they bring to the classroom. In essence, students are regarded as clean slates, whose cultural and linguistic histories and everyday lived experiences mean little in a mechanized culture of teaching and learning, built on abstracted, fragmented, and instrumentalized views of knowledge. Here, students are allowed to act only in the interest of *receiving, filing, and storing the deposits.* Anything outside this assimilative epistemology is perceived erroneous, irrelevant, misguided, or an obstruction to the student's academic or material achievement. Accordingly, students' creativity and imagination are sidelined by an approach that seldom proposes that they think critically about the concrete conditions of their own lives. As a consequence, the oppressor-oppressed contradiction—enacted through verticalization of the teacher-student relationship and inherent *in the deposits themselves*—is preserved. The outcome is a system of educational attitudes and values that preserve and fortify the contradiction, *mirroring the oppressive society as a whole.*[5]

However, Freire contends that neither the domestication of consciousness nor the teacher-student contradiction comprise essentialized forms of existence from which there is no exit. In fact, he argues that the anguish and tensions generated by the teacher-student contradiction, for example, can invoke students who were formally passive to resist and reject against their dehumanization. Nevertheless, Freire reminds readers that, as historical beings, when the organic movement of students' ideas and participation is stymied in the classroom, this constitutes a violation of their humanity. Here, he confirms that the oppression of human beings cannot be understood apart from the

---

[5] Here, Freire connects the following attitudes and values with the mirroring of oppressive society:
    a. the teacher teaches and the students are taught;
    b. the teacher knows everything and the students know nothing;
    c. the teacher thinks and the students are thought about;
    d. the teacher talks and the students listen—meekly;
    e. the teacher disciplines and the students are disciplined;
    f. the teacher chooses and enforces his or her choice, and the students comply;
    g. the teacher acts and the students have the illusion of acting through the action of the teacher;
    h. the teacher chooses the program content, and the students (who were not consulted) adapt to it;
    i. the teacher confuses the authority of knowledge with his or her own professional authority, which she and he sets in opposition to the freedom of the students;
    j. the teacher is the subject of the learning process, while the pupils are mere objects.

dehumanizing conditions that engender alienation. Moreover, Freire suggests, in line with Fanon, that when students resist or push against this violation it is simply a logical response to the psychological violence of oppression. In fact, *the rebellion they express as they emerge in the historical process is motivated by that desire to act effectively.* Given the social and material consequences that inform banking education, Freire decisively declares that educators committed to liberation must *reject it in its entirety*—and, in its place, give rise to a pedagogy guided by a problem-posing approach, where the *practice of freedom* lies at the heart of its purpose.

Problem posing education

> *Problem-posing education ... breaks with the vertical patterns characteristic of banking education ... [fulfilling] its function as the practice of freedom ...*

Problem-posing pedagogy as revolutionary praxis is Freire's response to the oppressive educational culture of the banking concept of education. It is an educational approach grounded on a dialogical praxis, with the explicit intent of promoting liberatory educational projects aimed at not only the resolution of the oppressor-oppressed contradiction but the generation of a living pedagogy for establishment of a permanently free society. The ideas in the first chapter of *Pedagogy of the Oppressed* serve as an important foundation for understanding a problem-posing pedagogy. First and foremost, the pedagogy is informed by a humanizing praxis, where the relationship of human beings to the world is central to teaching and learning.

Problem-posing pedagogy entails a *horizontal* approach that welcomes student participation as free thinkers and actors within their world, with an eye toward the development of critical thought. As such, a problem-posing pedagogy is generated through dialectical engagement of teacher and students, where teaching and learning are understood inseparable to a (subjective-objective) revolutionary praxis within schools and communities that supports *conscientização*—a communal process of evolving social consciousness. Freire suggests that central to this approach are fundamental questions related to culture and power that generate new and open interactions between teachers and students, which support unveiling and transforming oppressive values, attitudes, and practices that thwart dialogue.

Dialogue

A problem-posing pedagogy acknowledges the meaningfulness of human communication and communal relations in our lives. For this reason, Freire considers pedagogical dialogue as *indispensable* to developing relationships of cooperation and collective action within schools and society. He argues that a problem-posing educational approach provides students with the foundation for cultivating liberatory sensibilities and establishing the solidarity necessary for social transformation. Hence, dialogue is essential to a revolutionary praxis, in that without it students are left at the mercy of a brutal domesticating worldview and a mode of production that interferes with their authentic human existence. Through dialogue, a problem-posing pedagogy creates the conditions for new pedagogical relations to emerge, where teachers are also students and students are also teachers. In this liberatory dynamic, the hierarchical banking method of the teacher, as the only one who teaches, is ruptured. Instead, the teacher is also taught in dialogue with students, *who in turn while being taught also teach*. In this way, a sense of joint responsibility *for a process in which all grow* is established and nurtured between teacher and students.

It goes without saying, that for Freire, dialogue as a communal activity seeks to establish a democratic process of engagement that can ultimately lead to transformative action and greater critical awareness of the concrete conditions that impact our lives. The dialogical relationship, therefore, precludes dichotomies between teacher-student and student-teacher. The cultural and historical knowledges that both teachers and students bring must be allowed to intermingle organically with texts and materials (*cognizable objects*). In this liberatory environment of knowledge production, teachers and students are always *both* cognitive and narrative subjects involved in study. An important concept that Freire raises here, influenced by Marxism, is our need to overcome a view of both knowledge and cognizable objects *as private property*. Instead, the knowledge, texts, and materials introduced become objects of reflection by teachers and students alike, brushed against the realities of our lived histories.

This organic dialogical process of knowledge construction provides the pedagogical space for educators to, time and again, rethink our reflections, *within* the reflections and contributions our students make to the dialogue. Hence, passivity of students as docile listeners is overcome, as they become *critical co-investigators in dialogue with the teacher.* This approach to critical dialogue encourages the regenerative and ongoing consideration of ideas and themes of study that emerge from *both* teacher and students in the teaching-learning context. *The role of the problem-posing educator,* Freire steadfastly affirms, *is to create, together with the students, the conditions under which knowledge at the level of the doxa*[6] *is superseded by true knowledge, at the level of the logos.*[7] Hence, Freire identifies *authentic thinking* as one of the fundamental outcomes of critical dialogue—a way of thinking that intimately grounds us in and with our world.

Teacher—student as revolutionary partner

Freire insists, revolutionary teachers *must be partners of the student.* This principle is linked to the resolution of the teacher–student contradiction—a phenomenon where the role of the teacher is not only hierarchically conceived but is also situated at the opposite pole in an absolute and permanent dichotomy. In contrast, the teacher-student as revolutionary partner encompasses the dialectics of teacher *and* student simultaneously, *exchanging the role of depositor, prescriber, domesticator, for the role of student among students.* Here, the teacher-student as revolutionary partner engages *with* the student—teachers in a humanizing relationship that supports their *mutual quest* for liberation. This partnership also points to dismantling of an *authoritarian and alienating intellectualism*; which, by so doing, enables teachers and students to unveil and challenge the unjust structures and deficit myths that obstruct their consciousness as free *beings for themselves.* Freire rightly argues that revolutionary partnerships between teachers and students can only generate liberating praxis when there exist *a profound trust in people and their creative power.*

---

[6]   In brief, Freire is referring here to *Doxa,* the place where common beliefs or opinions guide human thought.

[7]   Again, briefly speaking, Freire is referring here to *Logos,* the place where rational principles, grounded on thoughtful reflection, guide human thought.

Praxis revisited

With a dialogical enactment of praxis, a problem-posing pedagogy creates the space, place, and time for teachers and students to discover and rethink together the social and material contradictions that impact their world. Freire contends that it is precisely through this critical dialogical approach that the oppressed come to identify together actions that will support efforts to resist, counter, and challenge oppressive conditions within schools, communities, and society that rob our humanity. Revolutionary praxis, as an existential human necessity, makes this possible; in that—through reflection, naming of the world, and action—human beings come to understand ourselves interdependently *within* history and *within* the world. And, with this discovery, we come to know our history, our world, and ourselves as, indeed, interrelated, living, organic beings, existing always as *unfinished* and in the process *of becoming*. As such—no matter to what extent the situations of our existence may conceal or limit the power of our creativity and capacity to speak and act against injustices, we nevertheless, exist in the ever presence of historical possibilities for transformation. It should be no surprise, then, why Freire insists, *problem-posing theory and practice take the peoples' historicity as the starting point* of their education.

Anchored in dialectical thought, revolutionary praxis *as a transforming principle transcends the theory–practice contradiction* and enhances the pedagogical interaction of action and reflection. In the process of reflection, Freire inspired by Husserl notes, teachers and students enhance the landscape of their perceptions and begin to appreciate the *background intuitions and background awareness*, which in the past may have been obscured by the oppressor-oppressed contradiction. Now, praxis gives rise to new awareness and an evolving consciousness of the self as subject of history. Similarly, such reflection, in conjunction with action, breaks through the dichotomy of the contradiction, in that it also brings a greater realization that practice never exists independent of theory, because one is the foundation and consequence of the other. Grounded, thereby, in this recognition of the ever-present *interplay of permanence and change*, the oppressed engage the world as the object of transformative action, through which liberation is forged. Hence, Freire affirms that revolutionary praxis is the foundation for a critical consciousness that seeks to transform oppression *as an action pursuing freedom*.

Conscientização

The evolution of critical consciousness or conscientização is one of the underlying aims of a problem-posing pedagogy. Freire's concept of conscientização signals an understanding of critical awareness and the formation of social consciousness as both a historical phenomenon and a human social process, linked to our emancipatory necessity as human beings to participate as *both* cognitive and narrative subjects of our destinies. It is vital that we keep in mind that conscientização does not occur automatically, naturally, nor should it be understood as an evolving linear phenomenon. Instead, Freire speaks to an emancipatory consciousness that arises through an organic process of human engagement, which requires critical pedagogical interactions that nurture the dialectical relationship of human beings with the world. This entails a grounded appreciation for the dialectical tension that must be retained between the empowerment of the individual and the collective empowerment of the people.

Whereby, banking education seeks to undermine the liberatory consciousness of the oppressed, Freire calls for the development of a living pedagogy that affirms life, through engendering a liberatory consciousness. In concert, Freire reaffirms, "*a deepened consciousness of [our] situation leads people to apprehend that situation as an historical reality susceptible of transformation.*" In this way, women and men committed to liberation create the conditions for empowerment and their mutual liberation. A problem-posing pedagogy, through the power of embodied revolutionary praxis, supports the *intentionality of consciousness*, in a way that displaces the estrangement of alienation by ushering in a new consciousness of self and the world. It is here that Freire makes reference to the *Jasperian split—or consciousness of consciousness*—which in actuality refers to the moment when the oppressed begin to experience the eclipse of their unconscious acceptance of the oppressor-oppressed contradiction and become aware (or conscious) that a new liberatory consciousness has emerged in their lives and their relationship to the world. Hence, it is the moment within revolutionary praxis when the oppressed become *conscious of* the revitalization of their humanity—a revitalization rooted in *the practice of freedom*, where fatalism gives way to empowering perceptions of reality and to communal relationships, rooted in solidarity and hope for the future.

Education as the practice of freedom

Education as the practice of freedom—as opposed to education as the practice of domination—denies that [humankind] is abstract, isolated, independent, and unattached to the world; it also denies that the world exists as a reality apart from people.

In positing a view of *education as the practice of freedom*, Freire again challenges educators to embrace a humanizing purpose—a relationship that extends outside the classroom. Moved by his radical Catholic values, Freire signals the *prophetic* and *revolutionary futurity* of a problem posing pedagogy, where authority must reside *on the side of freedom, not against it.* Freire affirms here the capacity of men and women, to transcend the immobility and fatalism of the alienating conditions that shape our lives. To do this effectively, we must be able to engage our current conditions not as unalterable fate *but merely as limiting*—and therefore a challenge we can overcome. This also entails an awareness of our incompletion, which lies at *the very roots of education as an exclusively human manifestation.* Freire notes, with a debt to Marx, that one of the starting points of a humanizing education is also found in the historical conditions that shape and are shaped by our lives. Hence, in alliance with our humanizing vocation, Freire asserts, *the oppressed must fight for their liberation.*

Freire again reminds us that it is only through overcoming the contradictions of the oppressor-oppressed dynamic that we step into the practice of freedom. Through the emergence of consciousness and our critical intervention in the world, we come to better understand how our consciousness of the world impacts both our actions and how we perceive our place in the world. With this in mind, Freire invites us to exchange a controlled, static and *well-behaved* present, as well as a predetermined or predestined future for a dynamic and life-affirming present, rooted in a revolutionary future, which necessitates our active participation in the reinvention of a genuinely free society. This struggle against oppression, however, must be guided by a liberatory praxis that supports our conscious emergence from the contradictions that once ruled our lives as colonized populations. Freire draws on Sartre to express that, within a revolutionary praxis of education, *consciousness neither precedes the world nor follows it.* Therefore, the point of departure for a liberating praxis, whether in schools or communities, lies in the people themselves and a consciousness that exists, steadfast, in the *here and now.* This practice of freedom as true communication must also engender solidarity, in that pursuit of our humanity cannot be a solo endeavor, but rather the praxis of the people. With all this in mind, Freire warns: *In the revolutionary process, the leaders cannot utilize the banking method as an interim measure, justified on grounds of expediency, with the intention of later behaving in a genuinely revolutionary fashion. They must be revolutionary—that is to say dialogical—from the onset.*

Questions for reflection and dialogue

1. How does Freire define the banking concept of education? How does the banking educational model function as an instrument of alienation?
2. Describe what Freire means by the teacher-student contradiction. How might you envision teachers and students as revolutionary partners in the educational process?
3. How does Freire define problem-posing education? How can teachers integrate a problem-posing approach in the classroom? What obstacles might they face?
4. How do you understand the development of critical consciousness (conscientização) and what is its pedagogical role in the practice of freedom?

Chapter 3

Through their continuing praxis, men and women simultaneously create history and become historical-social beings.

—Paulo Freire

In Chapter 3, Freire continues to deepen his articulation of a revolutionary praxis through engaging dialogue as an essential theme to the practice of freedom. Themes discussed in the early chapters, including humanization and dehumanization, alienation, fatalism, banking education, the student-teacher contradiction, false generosity, problem-posing education, and conscientização reappear scattered throughout. In addition to the dialogics of *the word* and *naming the world*, Freire focuses on a *methodology of the oppressed* that emerged from his literacy work. Here, again, Freire connects the significance of the major themes to the praxis of revolutionary leaders. Most important to Freire's dialogical formulation, however, is the manner in which dialogue *with* the people serves to disrupt the *culture of silence* perpetuated through structures of social alienation and material oppression. Freire's Catholic roots give rise to indispensable qualities of critical dialogue that pave the way for the *horizontal relationship* that can nurture and sustain the *indivisible solidarity* required, in order to participate collectively in transformative praxis. This chapter also takes the reader outside the classroom and into a *thematic universe* of critical inquiry, where the values of problem-posing pedagogy are integrated into a methodology of the oppressed that gives voice to concrete concerns and issues of alienation that obstruct the liberation of the oppressed and offers a participatory approach for investigation *with* and *of* the oppressed.

The word

Human existence cannot be silent, nor can it be nourished by false words, but only by true words, with which men and women transform the world.

Freire begins the discussion of dialogics with the concept of *the word*, which he considers to be the *essence of dialogue itself.* Engaging its constitutive elements, Freire argues, the word becomes truly the means by which dialogue is possible. Here, as he does in his discussion of praxis, he insists that if the radical interaction of *reflection and action* is sacrificed, an authentic or *true word* and, therefore, praxis is nullified. This is essential to understand, in that Freire conceives of *true word* as a transformative requirement. Inherent, is the idea that, on one hand, with absence of action there is no transformation; and, on the other, action without dialogue negates true praxis. Of course, the reason for this is that Freire equates the true word to be the underlying work of praxis. Moreover, Freire upholds both an egalitarian and communal view of the word;

insisting, *the word is not the privilege of [the] few, but the right of everyone. No one can say a true word alone nor can they say it for another.*

Freire identifies *an inauthentic word* as one that perpetuates alienation and the oppressive dichotomy of the subject-object contradiction. This occurs when the word is stripped of any possibility of transformative action, since the reflection required to produce the true word is distorted. He links the lifelessness of the inauthentic word with an alienating *verbalism*, where the empty word has no power to *denounce* the world and therefore unable to support the action required for transformation. Similarly, he speaks of an *activism*, where action occurs for action's sake, negating true praxis and making dialogue impossible. Hence, any dichotomy of reflection and action leads to expressions of inauthentic existence, reinforcing the *culture of silence* produced by the oppressor-oppressed contradiction.

Culture of silence

To glorify democracy and to silence the people is a farce;
to discourse on humanism and to negate people is a lie.

For Freire, *to silence the people* constitutes a form of dehumanization predicated by social and material structures of domination. Reinforced by the culture of silence is a sense of fatalism, hopelessness and despair, which can lead to the intensification of oppression. However, Freire refuses to essentialize these debilitating responses, by suggesting that finding hope, despite conditions of oppression, can also lead *to the incessant pursuit of the humanity denied by injustice.* However, he does make clear that dialogue is impossible within *a climate of hopelessness.* In fact, without hopeful conditions to speak the true word, our encounters become expressions of alienation—*empty and sterile, bureaucratic and tedious.*

The culture of silence must be understood as an extension of the phenomenon of alienation, discussed in the first chapter. Here, Freire ties alienation to conditions where dialogue is absent and, thus, the true word of praxis can find no expression. He argues that the concrete conditions of alienation impair the capacity of human beings to exercise their right to speak the true word, which reflects the realities of their oppression and exploitation.

As such, the culture of silence functions to preserve the dehumanization of the oppressed, in that Freire unwaveringly maintains that dialogue cannot exist between those who seek to *name the world* and those who would thwart their right to do so. In light of this tension, Freire argues, *Those who have been denied their primordial right to speak their word must first reclaim this right and prevent the continuation of this dehumanizing aggression.*

Naming the world

To exist, humanly, is to name the world, to change it.

Within Freirean thought, the means by which women and men name our world is through our participation in critical dialogue. In this way, naming the world opens up the transformative possibilities for unveiling the oppressive conditions of our existence and, by so doing, renaming our world. Freire rightly asserts that we have not been *built in silence*; but, rather, through dialogical action and reflection, we imbue our word and our labor with the essence of our existence. Here, Freire employs Pierre Furter's notion of authentic human existence: that which *permits the emergence of the awareness of our full humanity, as a condition and as an obligation, as a situation and as a project.*

It is, therefore, through the dialogical emergence of awareness that the true word is spoken and possibilities for humanizing praxis manifest. It is with this in mind that Freire reaffirms: *Dialogue is thus an existential necessity.* Critical dialogue, as the means for purposeful reflection and action with one another and the world, must be understood as a communal undertaking. It cannot *be reduced to one person "depositing" ideas in another, nor can it become a simple exchange of ideas to be "consumed."* Freire also distinguishes dialogue from polemic arguments or hostile debates, informed by an authoritarian culture of conquest—where epistemologically only certain truths are given legitimacy, while others are marginalized, ignored, or rendered invisible.

Instead, dialogue provides ample opportunity for naming the world, as mediated and expressed by the oppressed, to be addressed as legitimate and worthy acts of cognition. Dialogue as the practice of freedom commences only when the oppressed (or the students-teachers) can begin to ask: What shall we dialogue about? This preoccupation signals, as Freire notes, a step toward greater autonomy and responsibility for the content of dialogue. This reflects a profound step in the naming of the world, as the oppressed become subjects of the learning experience, rather than persisting as silenced objects of domination. Freire connects this expression of liberatory consciousness—born of struggle—with *the supersedence of slave labor by emancipated labor, which gives zest to life*. In essence, the verticalization of oppression is stymied through the communal establishment of horizontal relationships—a dynamic implicit to revolutionary praxis.

Horizontal relationships

> *Founding itself upon love, humility, and faith, dialogue becomes a horizontal relationship of which mutual trust between the dialoguers is the logical consequence.*

In order to establish genuine dialogue, Freire firmly contends that educators must transform vertical relationships rooted in authoritarianism. This entails dismantling the colonizing ethos of domination by establishing the conditions for horizontal relationships within schools and communities. In this discussion, as noted earlier, Freire's theological influences provide him a language of humanization from which to articulate what he considers to be the horizontal nature of genuine dialogue—namely *love, humility, faith, and trust*. These indispensable qualities, in combination, serve as an emotional, political, and spiritual foundation for the establishment of what he terms *indivisible solidarity*.

Love: Freire returns to the question of love, asserting it is impossible to name the world without the presence of profound love; in that the act of naming the world is part of a creative, life affirming and authentic praxis, for which love is indispensable. In fact, Freire notes, in concert with Che Guevara, the true revolutionary *must perceive the revolution, because of its creative and liberating nature, as an act of love*. For Freire, love constitutes the very foundation through which dialogue must unfold. In its absence, domination as alienation of our humanity reveals what Freire terms the *pathology of love*, where a destructive sadist-masochist contradiction emerges. In direct contrast, dialogue founded in love, generates the courage, responsibility, and discipline of women and men committed to the struggle for liberation. However, Freire warns, *as an act of bravery, love cannot be sentimental; as an act of freedom, it must not serve as a pretext for manipulation. It must generate other acts of freedom; otherwise, it is not love.* Hence, it is only through the resolution of the oppressor-oppressed contradiction, that we restore love and defy the lovelessness of asymmetrical relations of power that defy our humanity.

Humility: Freire makes the case for the manner in which the unjust verticalization of human relationships results in false humility, authoritarian fixations, and disabling alienation—for both the oppressor and the oppressed. Arrogance and paternalism, fueled by a sense of superiority and supremacy are features of oppressive relationships that interfere with open human expression and the people's right to recreate our world. In the process, banking educators, researchers, and leaders who lack humility enter into necrophilic encounters, obstructing the possibility of any partnership in the naming of the world. Hence, Freire asserts, men and women who lack humility and *cannot acknowledge [themselves] to be as mortal as everyone else, still [have] a long way to go before [they] can reach the point of encounter.*

Faith: Freire speaks to the indispensability of faith in humankind that must engender the horizontal relationship of dialogue. To enter into dialogue without faith in others, Freire notes, makes a mockery of dialogue, inevitably degenerating into *paternalistic manipulation.* This signals the need for a profound faith in the capacity of the oppressed to find our own way, to recreate our world, and to generate the human autonomy and responsibility required for personal and collective self-determination. Freire insists that this right to self-determination, inherent in our humanity, is *not the privilege of an elite, but the birthright of all.* However, he counsels, this is not a naïve faith, in that we cannot pretend arrogantly that submersion in the consciousness of domination has not caused us all impairment or has not left behind the traces of our histories of oppression—whether oppressor or oppressed. Nevertheless, rather than undoing our faith, Freire contends, horizontal relationships of dialogue encourage thoughtful commitment and embodied action in the name of human liberation.

Trust: Freire conceptualizes the climate of mutual trust as a direct dialogical outcome of a horizontal relationship grounded in love, humility, *and* faith. The interrelationship of these qualities within, for example, liberation theology is considered paramount to the struggle for community empowerment and societal transformation. Without the genuine presence of these indispensable qualities (in combination), Freire maintains, trust cannot flourish in schools or communities. So, although faith, as noted earlier, exists as an *a priori* condition for dialogue, trust is not the same, in that trust can only be generated and established *within* the horizontality of genuine dialogue—where people are heard, their intentionality respected, and the space and time exists *for being and becoming* free subjects of history.

Hope: Foremost for Freire is the recognition that the struggle for our humanity and our liberation is impossible without hope—for without hope, fatalism can overcome us, disintegrating our dreams and leaving us in the oppressive zone of antidialogical existence. What Freire is signaling here is the manner in which he conceives of hope as an existential necessity. This is so, for in an antidialogical climate of hopelessness, it is nearly impossible to envision our lives beyond the limit-situations that bind our humanity. Nor can hope manifest in a context of *crossing ones arms and waiting*. Instead, Freire affirms, *As long as I fight, I am moved by hope; and if I fight with hope, then I can wait.* Freire suggests, our tolerance for waiting is directly linked to our capacity to generate a sense of hope in our lives, despite the oppressive conditions that surround us. He also links this hope to communion: *Hope is rooted in [our] incompletion; from which [we] move out in constant search—a search which can be carried out only in communion with others.*

Indivisible Solidarity: To provide an understanding of dialogue beyond merely human communication, Freire culminates his indispensable qualities for dialogical horizontality, by calling again for an *indivisible solidarity*. This question of solidarity is often one of the most contentious, misunderstood, and undertheorized dimensions of revolutionary praxis. However, given Freire's Marxist humanist leanings, it is not surprising that he speaks to this question—a question that is fundamentally rooted in our human existential need for community and belonging, as well as the historical necessity for class struggle. Solidarity, then, is a key principle of praxis if we are to, indeed, transform the culture of domination and capitalist mode of production that fuels our estrangement from one another and the world. Freire notes that *self-sufficiency*—so much a part of the colonizing ideology of modernism—is deeply incompatible with dialogue. Accordingly, public spaces are destroyed or controlled by the political interest of the elite, in ways that prevent genuine public voice and true dialogue across the body politic,[8] as well as ample opportunities to mature in communal inseparability. Hence, a pedagogy with the oppressed is made possible through indivisible solidarity—a solidarity imbued by radical love, humility, faith, trust, and hope—where dichotomy between human beings and the world is overcome by dialogical praxis.

Dialogical praxis

Only human beings are beings of praxis ... only human beings are praxis.

Freire returns to the question of praxis as dialogical manifestation of critical knowledge and creativity, rooted in reflection and action for transformation. In Freire's view of praxis, it is not enough for people to come together in dialogue, in order to gain knowledge of the world. Intrinsic to dialogical praxis is collective human action grounded in reflection and the naming of the world, in order to transform it. Grounded in a Marxist view of human beings and Kosik's view of praxis, Freire initiates a discussion that distinguishes the praxis of human beings from animals.[9] He views human beings as *incomplete beings*, who treat our actions and ourselves as objects of reflection. This *capacity for human reflection* is what, Freire contends, distinguishes humans from animals who are *unable to separate themselves from their activity ... [nor] reflect upon it*. Freire fashions here a boundary in the *life space* of humans and animals, asserting *only human beings are beings of praxis*.

---

[8] *Body politic* refers to the people of a nation, state, or society considered collectively as an organized group of citizens.

[9] Freire's view of animals has been contested among animal rights activists and some scholars of indigenous knowledge. In his essay, "Toward an Animal Standpoint," Richard Kahn refutes the notion that "nonhuman animals are ... unthinking, unfeeling, and lesser objects, instead of rational, sentient, and equal beings" (4). Again see: *Critical Pedagogy, Ecoliteracy, and Planetary Crisis* (Kahn 2010) for an insightful discussion on this question.

Another difference Freire asserts is the historical nature and social agency of human beings, in that we instill the world with our *creative presence by means of transformation.* In contrast, he posits animal activity as being neither praxis nor creative transformation but, rather, an ahistorical activity of species who are *beings in themselves.* Hence, humans are capable of praxis precisely because we can be critically aware of our world and ourselves and, thus, exist in *a dialectical relationship between the determination of limits and [our] own freedom.* As such, it is through our capacity to be conscious of our autonomy and our responsibility for decisions and actions in the world that offers human beings the possibility of overcoming the limitations we face.

Freire maintains that true dialogue is impossible without critical thought, in which reality is understood *as process, as transformation, rather than as a static entity.* Here, critical thought is both inextricably tied to action and immersed in the progression of time—the past, present, and future of our existence— open to the risks of change this may involve. Hence, critical thought contrasts with *naïve* thought that, wittingly or unwittingly, invests in accommodation to the "normalized" and guaranteed space, seemingly ignorant of the injustices reproduced. Critical thinkers, on the other hand, are committed to the change required for our continued humanization. Freire draws on Furter's work to assert, *"the goal will no longer be to eliminate the risks of temporality by clutching to guaranteed space, but rather to temporalize space"* in ways that permit the world to be revealed.

Dialogical praxis generates the basic conditions for the development of critical thought, through opening the field for engaging the limitations that surround our lives. Without true dialogue neither communication nor education can generate critical thinkers. It is only through dynamic engagement of the world, by way of critical thought, that we unveil reality, unmask the myths that obscure oppression, and continue to generate and regenerate our critical faculties. In this way, Freire contends, *a critical analysis of a significant existential dimension makes possible a new, critical attitude towards the limit-situations. The perception and comprehension of reality are rectified and acquire new depth.* As critical thought expands, conscientização—as a communal social phenomenon—also evolves, in ways that deepen the collective possibilities for dialogical praxis and prepares women and men to struggle for our liberation. Herein also lies the investigative foundation for what Freire terms a *methodology of conscientização*, rooted in the dialogical praxis of problem-posing education.

Methodology of conscientização

> *When carried out with a methodology of conscientização the investigation ... introduces or begins to introduce women and men to a critical form of thinking about their world.*

A central feature of the second part of this chapter is Freire's discussion of his liberatory methodology. Here, the pragmatic dimension of Freire's ideas begin to crystallize in his efforts to articulate the aspects of a methodology embodied through *the concrete, existential, present situation of real people*. He provides an example of critical guidelines for the emergence of generative themes and the investigative stages that result in a liberatory pedagogical approach to community research with the oppressed, whether students in a classroom or people in community contexts. In contrast to banking approaches that reify the oppressed as objects of study, the lived histories of the oppressed are the starting point of his work in communities. Anything short of this, Freire notes, constitutes false generosity—a vertical structure of study that perpetuates the domestication and disempowerment of students and communities. About this Freire contends: *One cannot expect positive results from an educational or political action program which fails to respect the particular view of the world held by the people. Such a program constitutes cultural invasion, good intentions notwithstanding.*

Freire's methodology of conscientização affirms the various dimensions of people's culture as absolutely significant to informing both a humanizing educational praxis and a critical investigation into people's lives and their actual needs. As an empowering and liberating pedagogical force, Freire insists that the underlying focus of a methodology of conscientização is for the people to become *masters of their thinking*. Freire stresses repeatedly that such an approach can only be possible through the pedagogical inclusion of cultural knowledge and lived experiences formally suppressed; which through critically opening the epistemological field of engagement, now gives rise to the people's *generative themes*.

Generative themes

The concept of generative themes—which is *neither arbitrary invention nor hypothesis to be proved*—is at the heart of Freire's methodological approach. He utilizes the term *generative* to signify themes that hold the possibility of constantly unfolding and recreating into new and different themes, given that the historical conditions associated with themes are ever changing. This also means actions connected to particular generative themes will also change, as the new untested feasibly is identified. This organic and dialogical quality of generative themes merits some focus here. For if the methodology of study follows the hierarchical ethos of traditional research, there is no need to determine *the nature of the theme*, instead the emphasis will be placed on proving whether the theme is actually legitimate or not. In this supposedly neutral scientific pursuit of verifying the objective legitimacy of the theme— which is usually predicated on the prescribed criteria of the dominant class— *its richness, its significance, its plurality, its transformations, and its historical composition* are sacrificed.

In direct contrast, Freire proposes a methodology that is fundamentally dialogical, providing ample opportunity for the people to identify meaningful themes, through their participation *as subjects of their own study*. This dialogical approach cultivates and nurtures critical awareness about the meanings people attach to the themes generated. Freire also asserts that the very nature of the generative theme is best understood *through one's own existential experience* and critical reflection on the relationship between men and women *with* one another and our relationship with the world. Hence, the more actively engaged the people are in exploring their thematics, the more profoundly aware they become of their situation and their ability to *take possession of that reality*. In this way, their growing critical awareness or process of conscientização leads to new actions with the purposeful intent of transforming society.

Freire explains, however, that generative themes cannot emerge in a context of alienation, where human beings are *divorced from reality*. This is so, given that the formation of generative themes requires the space and place for freely naming the limit-situation and considering the collective impact of our perceptions and the realities of life. With this in mind, it is useful to clarify that the object of study is never the people themselves—*as if they were anatomical fragments.* Instead, the object of study must be the language and thoughts used to signify reality, how reality is perceived, and the worldview from which generative themes emerge. This indicates a participatory study of a people's praxis, guided by meaningful generative themes they use to name their world and the actions they take together to transform limiting conditions.

Freire also links meaningful generative themes to general and concrete facts, ideas, values, concepts, and hopes that characterize any particular *historical epoch.* As such, limit situations are anchored to conditions and challenges within broad to specific historical moments and broad to specific societal contexts. Here, Freire explains:

> Generative themes can be located in concentric circles, moving from the general to the particular. The broadest epochal unit, which includes a diversified range of units and sub-units—continental, regional, national, and so forth—contains themes of a universal character. Within the smaller circles, we find themes and limit-situations characteristic of societies (on the same continent or on different continents), which through these themes and limit-situations share historical similarities.

These historical themes exist always *interacting dialectically with their opposites.* Hence, it is precisely this *complex of interacting themes* in any epoch that comprises what Freire terms *its thematic universe.*

Freire also maintains, when people are confronted with a contradictory universe of themes, it is not unusual for reality to be mythicized and for an oppressive climate of irrationality to prevail; such is the case, for example, in epochs of colonial conquest or fascist dictatorship. He notes the existence of a *dominated consciousness,* which does not perceive the limit-situation in its totality, but rather as a secondary phenomenon without particular influence or cause. For Freire, this skewed perspective of casual factors as solely *epiphenomenon* is of deep concern in the investigation of generative themes, in that it tends to cause people to perceive reality as not only fragmented, but in ways that dichotomize and deaden the *interacting constituent elements of the whole.* Inherent in the contradictions of an epoch, for example, are a variety of limit-situations that become dichotomized, essentialized, and veiled, in the service of domination.

Limit-situations

Freire draws on Jaspers' idea of limit-situations as de-essentialized by Vieira Pinto, who provides a more optimistic reading of the concept. In this sense, a limit-situation is not an *impassible boundary* of which there is no escape, but rather *the frontier, which separates being from being more*. Hence, limit-situations point to those human situations that bind our humanity and, thus, become obstacles or challenges to dialogical praxis. Inherent to limit-situations are asymmetrical relations of power, where the dominant class benefits from perpetuating the limiting conditions. To overcome, for example, our dehumanization, which assumes the end of dehumanization, we have to overcome the limit-situation that converts human beings into things. To enter into a liberating praxis requires us to engage more critically with the dialectics of our existence as subjects and objects of our lives. In this way, we can come to reflect in new ways, with greater clarity about our individual and collective actions, as well as begin to accept greater responsibility for our decisions. In turn, we begin to overcome the limit-situations that demean and oppress our lives.

Freire posits dialectically that themes both *contain and are contained in limit-situations*. However, often limit-situations are not clearly seen nor understood; corresponding responses—*as historical action*—will then fail not only to transcend the situation but to see the untested feasibility that could overcome the contradiction. Nevertheless, Freire suggests that through critical engagement, a limit-situation's *true nature as concrete historical dimension of a given reality* can be unveiled. In so doing, the oppressive ideology that normalizes perpetuation of the limit-situation is disrupted by *limit-acts*—acts carried out by the oppressed to overcome the limitation. To transform and supersede the limit-situation in the concrete requires critical perception *embodied in action*. We must recall, however, that limit-situations occur within ever-changing historical conditions, which means that when limit-situations are superseded, new ones will surely appear, evoking the need for new limit-acts. Nevertheless, to carry out limit-acts requires that we are able to critically perceive the possibilities that exist beyond the limit-situation, in other words the *untested feasibility*.

Untested feasibility

Dialogical praxis serves as a pedagogical and political means by which the oppressed come to reflect critically on the conditions that limit our freedom, in order to discover the unjust conditions that engender limitations, as well as the untested feasibility. By untested feasibility, Freire is referring to those human possibilities that lie just beyond the limit-situations, which often remain obscured. Freire engages Goldmann's idea of *potential consciousness* and Nicolai's view of perceived/unperceived *practicable solutions* to bring complexity to his discussion of untested feasibility and its relationship to consciousness. He reminds us that limit-situations imply that there exist those who are served by the limitations and those who are *negated and curbed by them*. Fatalism and other responses to alienation interfere with our capacity to perceive the untested feasibility.

On the other hand, when limit-situations are perceived as *the frontier between being and being more human*, the oppressed begin to increasingly direct their actions toward *the untested feasibility implicit in their perception*. Freire does warn though that those served by the limit-situation will perceive the untested feasibility as a threat to the status quo and, therefore, block dialogical praxis. It is, however, through problem-posing investigation that the people engage conditions that limit their freedom and move more intently toward bringing an untested feasibility of liberation to the present.

Problem-posing investigation

Freire reasserts the problem-posing approach as the liberatory foundation for his *methodology of conscientização*—a methodology by which people's generative themes are critically engaged through a dialogical praxis of participation. Just as problem-posing education counters the lifelessness of banking education, a problem-posing approach to research with the people constitutes a life-affirming praxis founded in love, faith, and trust in the people's capacity to generate those themes that are truly meaningful with respect to their world. In this context, the teacher-student considers the program content neither a gift nor imposition, but content developed in relationship with the concrete needs and interests expressed by the people.

In discussing the authentic educational program of a problem posing investigation, Freire notes, *Authentic education is not carried on by "A" for "B" or by "A" about "B," but rather by "A" with "B," mediated by the world—a world which impresses and challenges both parties, giving rise to views or opinions about it.* Freire recognizes these views as generated through the entire human being, where anxieties, doubts, and hopes point to a variety of significant themes rooted in communal knowledge and through which a pedagogy (and methodology) of the oppressed can emerge dialogically—grounded in *the concrete, existential, present situation of real people.* In this way, the regenerating dimension of dialogical praxis supports the organic generation of themes and ongoing expansion and renewal of the content and its direction. Here, Freire also reminds us that the dialogical educator must engage the people's thematic universe not to lecture, but rather as issues to be decodified and studied collaboratively. To initiate this collaborative process, Freire turns to the *decodification* of the themes, which he contends *stimulates the appearance of a new perception and the development of new knowledge.*

Freire's thematic investigative approach is centered on *gathering information in order to build up a picture (codify) around real situations and real people.* The process of decodification begins at the point in the investigation when people begin to identify different elements of the lived situation, *exteriorize their view of the world*, and reflect critically on it in order to change it. Freire likens this process to a photographer working to bring a photograph into focus. He goes on to discuss different stages of decodification, with a clear intent on maintaining the *dialectical nature* of the process. He exemplifies the dialectical movement of thought in his analysis of a *concrete existential coded situation.* The important thing here is to understand decoding as a process that moves people from an individualized, estranged, abstracted, fragmented, and partial understanding of the situation to an understanding of the situation within *the whole* of our collective existence, in order to return to the situation with new insights, *together with other Subjects.* Freire contends that if the process of codification is done well, it will lead to new critical understanding of the coded situation—an understanding that emerges as alienation to the concrete limit-situation is overcome, a stronger sense of connection ensues, and an opening of perception to greater possibility for transformation is realized.

One of the underlying aims of a problem-posing investigative approach is the enactment of a revolutionary praxis that affirms the decodification of people's themes, as they critically move toward greater depth in their perception and comprehension of their individual and collective lives and new ways of thinking about the world. For Freire this signals a process by which human beings *emerge from [our] submersion and acquire the capacity to intervene in reality, as it is unveiled.* This growing awareness and capacity for intervention stems directly from the deepening of conscientização—which Freire considers *characteristic of all emergences.* Furthermore, it is precisely through the social agency ignited by critical consciousness that action is initiated and sustained. It is not surprising then that Freire would affirm problem-posing thematic investigation as a methodology of conscientização, where consciousness moves from "real consciousness"— where untested feasibility is imperceptible—to "potential consciousness" that strives to transform the untested feasibility into action. Freire's discussion of the various *stages of the thematic investigation* delineates an organic, life-affirming path forged by the investigative team *with* the people, as *co-investigators.*

Stages of the thematic investigation

Thematic investigation thus becomes a common striving towards awareness of reality and towards self-awareness, which makes this investigation a starting point for the educational process or for cultural action of a liberating character.

Prior to beginning his discussion of the four stages of the thematic investigation, Freire reminds us of the collaborative nature of this approach. He insists, fundamentally, that *we cannot think for others or without others.*

Even when people may be struggling with what may seem as superstitious or naïve perceptions of a situation, Freire maintains that deep faith in people's capacity to rethink the assumptions that inform their situation in community must be at the core of thematic investigation, in that how people express their situation at any given moment in time is inseparable from the larger social and material context in which they must survive. Freire contends, *Human beings are because they are in a situation. And they will be more the more they not only critically reflect upon their existence but critically act upon it.* The stages of investigation encompass a dialogical relationship between the investigative team and community people participating in the study. Freire warns that the process of investigation must never become mechanized, abstracted, or reductive, but rather retain its dialogical sensibilities, without losing sight of the totality from which the meaningful thematics of the people emerge. This also entails a liberatory relationship in which both investigators and the people work together in becoming *jointly educated* about the situations that impact the life of the community.

Stage one: Learning the people's perception of reality

The investigation begins with a process that requires the team to learn from the community and the different ways in which people perceive their situation. Freire notes that this stage can involve difficulties and risks for the team, as they work to initially gain an understanding of the conditions in community and to begin dialogue with the people about the objectives of the study. Freire confirms, moreover, the *investigation will be impossible without a relation of mutual understanding and trust.* Once representatives of the community agree to participate, their presence at every stage of the work is central to the integrity of the study.

As investigators engage with the people, it is important to be self-vigilant about not imposing values that transform the themes expressed by participants. This decoding stage begins as the investigative team seeks to decipher the *living code* of the community itself, engaging its totality, in order to understand how its different parts interact. As *sympathetic observers*, they note the varying circumstances of the community and prepare to enter into dialogue about impressions together, in order to consider and reconsider, in nonhierarchical ways, their shared perceptions of the limit-situations and contradictions at work, as well as to gain a better sense of the community's interpretation of the situations and contradictions they face. At this point, opportunities might arise to begin organizing educational projects.

Stage two: Preparation of codifications

In the second stage, preparation of codifications for thematic analysis is the focus of the study. As a team, the investigators now select the contradictions that will inform the codifications to be utilized for the thematic investigation. These may include, for example, sketches or photographs, which will support the team's critical engagement with the community. Freire, however, sets out several important requirements, meant to ensure the dialogical nature of the investigation. The first requirement is that the codifications must be familiar and reflect the lived experience of the community. An equally fundamental requirement is that codifications not be over enigmatic or oversimplified—which Freire argues suppresses dialogue—rather they should be "*simple in their complexity and offer various coding possibilities in order to avoid the brainwashing tendencies of propaganda.*" Freire also suggests that codification be organized as a *thematic fan*, which will help to assure a variety of possible perspectives to emerge in the decoding process. In the dialogical process of decoding, participants *externalize their thematics*; and, in so doing, discover opportunities to engage their contradictions in ways that may lead to new awareness of their reality. From here codifications are derived from the shared contradictions, which lead to what Freire terms *inclusive codifications*. In this way, the codifications begin to express dialectically the participants' sense of totality, which propels their thinking from *real consciousness* (which obscures totality) to *potential consciousness* (which engender the perception of totality).

Stage three: Returning to the people

Stage three of the thematic investigation returns the codification of the investigative team to the people for dialogical engagement, through what Freire calls *thematic investigation circles*, also known as *cultural circles*. At this point in the study, the codifications are discussed in ways that require the investigative team to *not only listen to the individuals but ... also challenge them, posing as problems both the codified existential situation*, as well as their own responses. These discussions are recorded to ensure that the investigative team can return to them for subsequent analysis. Freire also notes that it is at this stage in which the *cathartic force of the methodology* may surface, as participants express emotions, sentiments, and opinions related to their lives, which they would not otherwise share outside their home. As participants express their connection between self and their existential situation, Freire advocates for the *conscientização of the situation*, a process that prepares participants for actions that can counter obstacles to their humanity.

Last stage: Systematic interdisciplinary study

In the final stage of the investigation, the team engages in *a systematic interdisciplinary study* of the different aspects of the relationship with the community. This entails a process whereby the themes explored are now considered across different knowledge spheres, to allow for a more integral understanding of what has been learned. Freire, however, warns that the investigative team must remain wary of sacrificing the richness and power of the investigation to *strictures of specialties*. Instead, the team works to break down the themes in ways that can unveil the fundamental nuclei, which provide direction to materials for preparing teacher-students to carry out the ongoing community work in cultural circles. At this juncture, Freire presents the dialogical notion of *hinge themes*—themes developed by the investigative team to facilitate connections that may be needed in dialogue with the community. A key concern of the work in the cultural circles is that the themes should never be presented as an inflexible phenomenon or divorced of people's lives. Once, the thematic material of the people has been fully explored, it is returned to them again as problems now to be transformed through their actions. It is at this juncture in Freire's approach that humanizing educational programs can be developed and established in ways that reflect the essence of the community. For Freire, this thematic approach also serves to *link intellectuals, often well-intentioned but not infrequently alienated from the reality of the people, to that reality. It also gives the people an opportunity to hear and criticize the thought of intellectuals*—a situation that seldom exists within a banking approach to research.

Revolutionary leadership

> *Revolutionary leaders do not go to the people in order to bring them a message of "salvation," but in order to come to know through dialogue with them both their objective situation and their awareness of that situation.*

Freire's discussion of some of the issues and stumbling blocks of revolutionary leaders and political projects meant to engage the needs of the people prepares the reader for Chapter 4, where he unpacks the issue of cultural action and revolutionary leadership in a more explicit and expansive manner. Nevertheless, here, he speaks to those who would come to education and study with the people to support an expressed revolutionary project but yet fall prey to the hierarchical rationalizations of a banking education model. Instead, Freire insists that truly humanist educators and authentic revolutionaries must focus on the question of societal transformation in community with the people. He admonishes revolutionary leaders who come to the people with agendas and programs fashioned in complete absence of the people—the ones who will be most affected by their content. Freire argues, banking educators and revolutionaries who see themselves as *saviors of the oppressed* have forgotten that the *fundamental objective is to fight alongside the people for the recovery of [our] humanity, not to win the people over* to programs and campaigns that perpetuate alienation. Here it is useful to, once again, recall that *we cannot expect positive results from an educational or political action program, which fails to respect the particular view of the world held by the people.* Hence, Freire deems the dynamics and impact of such programs as perpetuating the colonializing and capitalist mentality of *cultural invasion.*

Lastly, Freire adamantly argues that to encourage the passivity of the oppressed through authoritarian revolutionary schemes—no matter the rhetoric—is indisputably *incompatible* with a humanizing culture of liberation. He argues, instead, that the task of humanist educators and revolutionaries is to engage in pedagogical and political cultural actions that are not only dialogically compatible but also intimately committed to the liberation of the oppressed. As such, our starting point for any educational program or community action must be *the present, existential, concrete situation, reflecting the aspirations of the people*—not as intellectual device but embodied revolutionary praxis.

Questions for reflection and dialogue

1. What does Freire mean by the true or authentic word? How does the culture of silence prevent the oppressed from naming the world?
2. For Freire, what constitutes humanizing dialogue? What are the essential components of dialogical praxis?

3. Freire maintains that through horizontal relationships, the oppressor-oppressed contradiction can be resolved. What does he mean by this and what are the indispensable qualities of horizontal relationships?
4. What is the underlying purpose of a methodology of *conscientização*? Describe, in particular, the idea of generative themes and limit-situations, as well as the four stages of Freire's thematic investigation.

Chapter 4

If true commitment to the people, involving the transformation of the reality by which they are oppressed, requires a theory of transforming action this theory cannot fail to assign the people a fundamental role in the transformation process.

Throughout the book, Freire suggests, in subtle and more direct ways, that pedagogy of the oppressed is, in fact, a pedagogy of revolutionary change and societal transformation that must be carried out by the people. In this chapter, he unapologetically asserts the revolutionary nature of *cultural action*, squarely examining the differences between *antidialogical* and *dialogical* approaches. Freire argues that antidialogical conditions, given their alienating purpose, serve as instruments of oppression; while a dialogical praxis, on the other hand, is enacted through a pedagogical and political commitment to the liberation of the oppressed. He expounds on the characteristics of antidialogical action, which enact a pedagogy and politics of conquest, divide and rule, manipulation, and cultural invasion. In direct contrast, he points to the characteristics of dialogical action, which enact radical cultural expressions of cooperation, unity, organization, and cultural synthesis. In a variety of ways, this last chapter serves as a synthesis of the book, in that it revisits and weaves together many of the central themes Freire has explored in the previous chapters, in ways that speak to authentic revolutionary leadership, whether it be within schools or communities. Freire, in particular, draws on Gramscian ideas of both moral leadership and the formation of organic intellectuals, to engage with the complexities of political authority and communal participation, both deeply essential to a revolutionary praxis of cultural action.

Freire reaffirms the central thesis of his work: human beings are *beings of praxis*; and, as such, authentic humanizing activity is the outcome of theory *and* practice—a praxis that is the outcome of the dialectical relationship between self, others, and the world. He posits the need for a dialogical relationship of leadership between those who are designated as leaders and the people who must participate as central figures in the process of transformation. Freire also undertakes a critique of hegemonic or antidialogical leadership founded on a banking concept, where leaders are the narrators and subjects of history, while the people are expected to merely serve as docile objects of a prescribed political agenda in which they are estranged from all decision-making. For Freire, this does not constitute true revolutionary leadership but rather the reformulation of the old oppressor-oppressed contradiction, with *the leaders as its "thinkers" and the oppressed as mere "doers."* Freire again maintains that revolutionary leaders, who invalidate the praxis of the people, inherently invalidate the legitimacy of their own praxis—a false, dichotomous, and oppressive praxis that imitates the dominant elites. In doing so, antidialogical revolutionary leadership is reduced to *a revolution without the people, [who are now] drawn into the process by the same methods and procedures used to oppress them.*

Freire further warns against a *mechanistic view of reality*, where there exists little awareness of the manner in which concrete situations impact consciousness and, therefore, how consciousness impacts our world. Freire notes the fallacy of *a mechanistic view of transformation*, where leaders ignore the need to *problematize false consciousness*, convinced that slogans and directives from an elite leadership is sufficient to changing historical conditions. Freire returns here to Marx and the historicity of humanity, asserting that there is no history without human beings and no human beings without history. Hence, to deny people the *right to participate in history* begets conditions of oppression, irrespective of rhetorical intentions.

In concert with Lenin, Freire adamantly insists that a *true commitment to the people* requires a revolutionary theory of cultural action, where the dialogical praxis of leaders *and* the people—in solidarity—engage critically *the structures to be transformed.* This necessitates authentic community relationships of struggle rooted in authentic dialogue, where revolutionary praxis emerges from a shared commitment and emancipatory vision, where leaders do not reify *the oppressed as their possession.* Freire calls for revolutionary leaders to *incarnate a genuine humanism,* grounded in principles of a *dialogical revolutionary process,* where leaders embody both a commitment and revolutionary solidarity with people as comrades in the struggle for our liberation.

The revolutionary process

> *The revolutionary process is dynamic, and it is in this continuing dynamics, in the praxis of the people with the revolutionary leaders, that the people and the leaders will learn both dialogue and the use of power.*

Consistent with earlier discussions of revolutionary praxis, Freire reaffirms dialogical principles that inform the revolutionary process. Freire repeatedly affirms that human activity grounded in action and reflection is the root of societal transformation. However, at this juncture, he notes the dialectical manner in which *theory is necessary* to the illumination of praxis; in that revolutionary theory is the living manifestation of a regenerating alliance that must persist in the making of a just society. In other words, we come to reflect on the world in order to act upon it in ways that inform democratic life; then we reflect on the actions taken and their emancipatory impact; and, from there, evaluate the outcomes from whence we then develop theory. In this way, theory remains rooted to the lived experience of communal praxis.

In terms of leadership, Freire acknowledges that leaders *bear the responsibility for coordination and, at times, direction.* However, he emphasizes the need for dialogical responsibility, which emerges from shared responsibility with the community and, therefore, cannot proceed without their voice and participation—particularly when the consequences of decisions directly impact people's lives. This is to affirm that *dialogue with the people is radically necessary to every authentic revolution.* In fact, Freire notes that it is this courageous dialogical praxis between leaders and the people that most distinguishes a true revolution from a coup d'état—an authoritarian form of seizing power. This speaks to a political and cultural leadership relationship accountable to the people, requiring open and honest dialogue about *its achievements, its mistakes, its miscalculations, and its difficulties.*

In this dialogical praxis, Freire asserts a central ethical tenet of his pedagogy and his politics: *Dialogue, as the encounter among men [and women] to "name" the world, is a fundamental precondition for [our] true humanization.* Hence, dialogue is not a concession or gift to be extended to the people, in order to yield consensus. Rather, it is the right of human beings, as subjects of history, to participate in self-determining our individual and collective destinies. If we understand the revolutionary process as a pedagogical force then it too must be rooted in the lived histories of the people and, thus, begin with their concrete existential situation. As such, the revolutionary process affirms what Freire considers *a radical need: women and men as beings who cannot be truly human apart from communication, for [we] are essentially communicative creatures.* Therefore, to silence our voices and active participation impedes communication and reduces the people to the status of "things."

Freire, again, reminds the reader that the oppressor-oppressed contra-diction is an essential requirement of domination, where the dominant pole and subordinate pole exist antithetically. In direct contrast, he speaks to the dialogical nature of revolutionary praxis, which shatters dichotomies, opening the way for reflection *and* action to emerge simultaneously—both fluidly and organically. In this way, actions, which may be feasible or infeasible *at the present time*, can be engaged critically in ways that openly support the evolution of conscientização. Communities work with the leaders to determine liberatory strategies and tactics that are in sync with both the concrete conditions of people's lives and the larger political project of liberation. A point often missed in discussion of the revolutionary process is that *critical reflection is also action.* This constitutes, in the Gramscian sense, respect for both the intellectual capacities and labor of the people, as well as the labor of organic intellectuals who are involved in articulating revolutionary theory—historically, politically, economically, and culturally—*with* the people as equal *Subjects of revolutionary action.* Herein lie the intercommunicative roots of the *Cultural Revolution* envisioned by Freire and other revolutionaries of his time.

Drawing from Althusser, Fromm, and others, Freire complicates his analysis by reminding us that, in the struggle for freedom, the moment when power is seized reflects only one moment of the larger revolutionary process; in that, revolution—as *a social entity*—comes into being within an oppressive society. Hence, a dialogical praxis of revolution must contend with *the potentialities [or traces] of the social entity in which it originated*, given the *interplay of contradictions*. Freire explains, *in a dynamic, rather than static view of revolution there is no absolute "before" or "after."* For this reason, he adamantly insists that dialogue must not be a promise for the future, but rather a constant and ongoing dimension of liberating action, at all stages of the revolutionary process.

This essential dialogical feature of liberatory struggle creates the space where the people and revolutionary leaders come to learn how to engage and exercise power democratically, in the interest of liberation. Conversely, it is through *denial of communion in the revolutionary process* and withholding opportunities to participate actively in the dialogical exercise of power and self-governance that disabling dependency of the oppressed on the dominant class is engendered. Consequently, antidialogical actions that reflect a *fear of freedom* and *lack of faith in the people* function as instruments of oppression, which have historically obstructed the expansion, development, and self-governance of oppressed communities—who exist under the shadow of dependency, the *absolutizing of ignorance*, and an interpellated view of genetic and cultural deficiency.

Antidialogical cultural action

> *The antidialogical ... aims at conquering ... increasingly and by every means, from the toughest to the most refined, from the most repressive to the most solicitous (paternalism).*

Of concern to Freire, within the context of revolutionary praxis, is the importance of a *theory of revolution* that arises from the lived histories of the oppressed, which can unveil the antidialogical nature of oppression. Freire contends, there do not exist oppressive conditions that are not, at their root, also antidialogical; *just as there is no antidialogue in which the oppressors do not untiringly dedicate themselves to the constant conquest of the oppressed.*

Freire goes on to discuss further what he means by antidialogical actions by presenting major pillars that bolster the structures of antidialogical action— namely, *conquest, divide and rule, manipulation, and cultural invasion.*

Conquest implies an inherently antidialogical relationship; where one group conquers and another is conquered. In this manifestation of the oppressor-oppressed contradiction, the vanquished colonized become the possession of the colonizer. Freire notes the symbiotic nature of antidialogical and oppressive sensibilities, which the oppressor simultaneous enacts in the world to preserve both their social and material domination. In fact, Freire maintains that once conditions of conquest are established, antidialogical action is the means by which these are preserved. Freire also notes how the fabrication of myths are employed to present the world as fixed and immutable, to which the colonized as passive spectators must simply adapt. This internalization of *deposited myths* across the society is *indispensable* to perpetuating the culture of domination. Freire notes several debilitating myths,[10]—including *the myth of the natural inferiority of the latter and the superiority of the former*—which may vary historically but are essential to a politics of subjugation and repression. Permeating, overtly and covertly, the landscape of society, Freire notes, the perniciousness of these myths reflect the *necrophilic passion to oppress.*

Divide and Rule signals intolerance for the unification of the oppressed, an act perceived as *a serious threat* to the dominant class. As a minority in number, the ruling class deems the struggle for liberation as a potential danger. In an effort to disrupt and silence the voices and participation of the people, the oppressor utilizes a variety of hegemonic strategies to isolate and alienate the oppressed or to garner their consensus. One strategy entails *a focalized view of problems*, which fails to go to the root cause, masking its totality. This focalized

---

[10] A few other myths Freire includes:

> that the dominant elites, "recognizing their duties," promote the advancement of the people, so that the people in a gesture of gratitude should accept the words of the elites and be conformed to them; the myth that rebellion is a sin against God; the myth of private property as fundamental to personal human development (so long as oppressors are the only true human beings); the myth of the industriousness of the oppressors and the laziness and dishonesty of the oppressed.

approach reinforces alienation, by making it more difficult to perceive the situation critically and, thus, keeping people with the same problems from coming together. Freire contends, *the more alienated people are the easier is to divide and keep them divided*. Hence, an underlying purpose of divide and rule is both to preserve social class inequities and obscure class conflict. Freire also illustrates how the oppressor-oppressed contradiction is steeped in a mode of production that perpetuates class divisions and racialized oppression.

Manipulation functions to bring the oppressed into hegemonic conformity with the interest of the ruling class. Freire signals the manner in which a deceptive myth that proclaims all people can ascent to the ruling class shrouds the structural nature of oppression. Often pacts that emerge between the dominant class and the dominated, particularly within historical moments of uprising, create a false impression of dialogue and change. In fact, such manipulative pacts often result in inauthentic organizations that compromise the dialogical necessity of revolutionary change. Hence, manipulation functions to deepen the submersion of the people into the oppressed-oppressor contradiction, leaving the structures of domination and exploitation untouched. Freire contends, moreover, that the paternalism of populist campaigns is rooted in anesthetic forms of manipulation that distract people *from the true causes of their problem*.

Cultural Invasion is the antidialogical phenomenon where the culture of the colonized is invaded and overrun by the colonizing culture. At the heart of cultural invasion is the dehumanizing and violent politics of conquest, which seeks to subjugate, socially and materially, the worldview of the oppressed, as a means to *inhibit the creativity of the invaded by curbing their expression*. In the process, the inferiority of the colonized is reinforced and the duality of oppressor-oppressed contradiction solidified, as the oppressed are forced into an inauthentic existence at the service of the dominant culture. Freire contends that cultural invasion serves as both an *instrument* of domination and the *result* of domination. As such all public and private institutions across the dominant society are implicated in its perpetuation, either through preparing future invaders or through schemes of false generosity that demand the assimilation of colonized populations. He points to the danger of assimilated or neocolonial professionals who, naively or astutely, perpetuate the interests of the dominant class by managing and containing the oppressed. However, Freire also reminds us that when the people have internalized the worldview of the oppressor, often heightened ambiguity and fear of freedom can stall revolutionary action.

Dialogical cultural action

Dialogical action is indispensable to the revolutionary ...

In response to antidialogical principles, Freire posits a set of dialogical principles, anchored in the ideas discussed in earlier chapters related to dialectical thinking and dialogical praxis. The four dialogical principles discussed are *cooperation, unity for liberation, organization, and cultural synthesis.* These principles represent the cornerstones of a revolutionary praxis, which support the making of cultural revolution as a living praxis.

Cooperation speaks to the relationship of revolutionary leaders and the people, as they work together for social change. Freire, more specifically, draws on Martin Buber's notion of "I and Thou" to describe cooperation as a dialogical relationship, where the coming together of I and Thou (Not-I) affirms our existence in the world. This dialectical sensibility of "I am because we are" also works to counter the trenchant individualism, competiveness, and objectification of the banking concept of pedagogical relationships. Cooperation creates the space where all can meet to name the world collectively, guided by a shared vision of societal transformation. This space also provides the people a place for problematizing conditions of oppression; and, by so doing, *fulfill [our] vocation as subjects* of our world. Within the dynamic of revolutionary cooperation, leaders do not own the people but rather exist as comrades and coauthors of struggle, working together in community to unveil and challenge structures of alienation. As such, cooperation is rooted in qualities of love, faith, trust, and communion, rooted in a life affirming revolutionary process.

Unity for Liberation is essential to dialogical cultural action, in that transformation without unity between leaders and the people, as *revolutionary partners*, is impossible. This process of establishing unity requires a break from the *divisive adhesion* to the dominant culture, as we confront the structures of dehumanization that plague our communities. Freire affirms here, dialectically, a key understanding: as we move toward greater unity and solidarity, we also, simultaneously, become true individuals, in that we shed our false identification with the oppressor. In other words, as we unveil the oppressor-oppressed contradiction and authentically move beyond it, our capacity for unity flourishes; in that we develop a deeper dialectical sense of autonomy and responsibility in our relationship with self *and* others. This sense of unity also entails an emergence of class-consciousness, where former contradictions and blindness to our alienation are overcome. With this in mind, Freire argues, *in order for the oppressed to unite, [we] must first cut the umbilical cord of magic and myth which binds [us] to the world of oppression*, in that the unity that now connects us must be fundamentally of a liberatory nature.

Organization, according to Freire, is a natural outcome of unity, where the struggle for liberation is our common task. Here, he speaks to the revolutionary necessity of *historical witness* in the process of organization. The task of being witness to our liberation constitutes, for Freire, one of the *principal expressions* of the cultural and pedagogical dimensions of revolution, in that it encompasses the spirit of consistency, boldness, radicalization, courage to love, and faith in the people—indispensable qualities to our labor as historical subjects. Witnessing, as a form of organizational expression, also requires the maturity to risk and to enact patience, in that the process of revolutionary change exists as an ongoing historical phenomenon. As such, Freire suggests that our organization with the people must be built on a long view of history; one that negates oppressive manipulation based on false calls to urgency and, instead, embraces the totality of our situation and revolutionary struggle. Within this revolutionary paradigm of organization, discipline does not equal rigidity or regimentation. Instead, the objective here is to create conditions of organization that support the development of our individual and collective consciousness—a consciousness rooted in our *naming the world* together. Here, Freire offers us another important axiom of his pedagogy of the oppressed: *There is no freedom without authority, but there is also no authority without freedom.* It is this powerful dialectic in the context of communal organization and leadership that distinguishes emancipatory authority from authoritarianism.

Cultural Synthesis is the result of dialogical cultural action. Freire reminds us, however, that cultural action can function both in the interest of domination or liberation. Freire draws on Bergson's ideas here to note that the crosscurrents of antidialogical and dialogical cultural actions create an ongoing human condition of both *permanence and change.* With respect to cultural synthesis, dialogical cultural action seeks to preserve this *antagonistic contradiction,* since the underlying purpose of dialogue is to courageously engage the human creative tensions at work in the process of forging a liberatory society. In the context of cultural synthesis, when revolutionary leaders engage with the people, they cannot do so as invaders, but rather as *revolutionary partners* who seek to learn together. Hence, this opens the way to confronting cultural actions that betray our humanity, so that we may move away from antidialogical actions of domination and toward liberating actions in the world. Freire's notion of cultural synthesis, moreover, challenges the passivity and invasiveness of imposed or prescribed models. Instead, he calls for cultural action and educational programs that are inextricably linked to the realities of the "here and now," which are inherently produced by subjects *within* the historical process. This initiates conditions for new knowledge and new actions that arise directly with the people as active participants—rather than as subjects of an alienating and hidden curriculum that stifles life. Moreover, cultural synthesis does not deny cultural differences among the people; rather, differences are integral to the process of transformation—affirming the *undeniable support* each brings to the other. As such, knowledge of *the totality* is indispensable to *cultural revolution* and the formation of collective consciousness across communities and societies.

Cultural revolution as living praxis

As the cultural revolution deepens conscientização in the creative praxis of the new society, people will begin to perceive why mythical remnants of the old society survive in the new. And they will then be able to free themselves more rapidly of these specters ...

Cultural revolution embodies a humanizing praxis of conscious transformation, carried out through *communion with the people*—a politically dynamic sphere for people to learn and grow together as subjects of history and cultural citizens of the world. And, it is, indeed, through the expression of *unshakeable solidarity* and labor with the people that, Freire maintains, revolutionary leaders are *authenticated in their praxis*. However, he does acknowledge that there are those who would judge such faith and commitment in the people *as naively and subjectively idealistic*. Yet, he refutes this notion, by affirming that there is nothing *more real or concrete* than human beings presently engaged in dialogue; and, inversely, nothing more deadening and antagonistic to dialogue than the verticalization of social and material power perpetuated and reinforced by the dichotomous contradiction of the oppressor class.

Freire argues *the road to revolution* can only be paved through the *plenitude of our praxis*. This speaks to a living revolutionary praxis that both makes and is made through the power of our collective consciousness and cultural actions, where our shared critical engagement assists us to interrogate oppressive myths, beliefs and practices, as we organize our thinking and knowledge in ways that bring us closer to the concrete reality of our lives. Within Freirean thought, the evolution of our living praxis is also linked to the process of our *radicalization*—where through the development of critical consciousness, the oppressed emerge from the oppressor-oppressed contradiction to refute prescriptions issued by the dominant class and, instead, embrace the struggle for our humanity.

In bringing this discussion to a close, it is worth recalling that revolutionary liberation and the cultural revolution Freire advocates necessitates a living praxis of revolutionary leadership—a humanizing approach that communally extricates the oppressed from the false generosity, manipulation, and paternalism of banking models of leadership. Essential to this revolutionary praxis is a powerful move away from thinking *about* the people to thinking *with* the people—whether within communities, schools, labor organizations, religious institutions, universities, or other entities of society. It is not surprising then that Freire ends his seminal tome by asserting: *Only in the encounter of the people with revolutionary leaders—in their communion, in their praxis—can this theory be built.*

Questions for reflection and dialogue

1. Describe the four pillars of antidialogical cultural action and what conditions do these engender with respect to the relationship of leaders to the people?
2. Describe what Freire means by a revolutionary praxis of leadership and how is this directly linked to dialogical cultural action?
3. Within the context of cultural revolution, how are leaders authenticated? In what ways is this essential to liberatory struggle?
4. What is the central purpose of a pedagogy of the oppressed and how does this purpose inform a living praxis of revolutionary leadership?

Impact, Influences, and Legacy

An Interview with Ana Maria Araújo Freire

The spirit that guides this book is very much connected with a desire to provide insights into Paulo Freire: the educational philosopher, international dignitary, revolutionary humanist, teacher, comrade, and friend. Underlying this commitment is also the realization that we make very specific choices in how we tell the story, for all books are, to one extent or another, the telling of a story—with the same characteristics of everyday stories, including what we

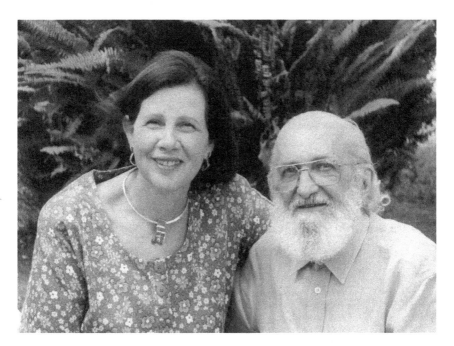

Figure 4.1 Ana Maria Araújo and Paulo Freire, circa 1990s.

focus on and what we do not; what voices are centered and what voices are not; stories filled with the humanity of our fuzzy memories and contradictions, as well as our insights and brilliance. With this in mind, this chapter presents an interview conducted in Brazil with Ana Maria Araújo Freire—or Nita, as she is known to friends—in May 2016.[1] From the following, I hope the reader will glean insights into Paulo's lasting influence and relevance, as well as a more intimate portrayal of the man from Recife, who would spark the imaginations and revolutionary dreams of educators around the globe for more than fifty years.

Paulo's background

A/D[2]: Can you tell us some things that you think were key in Paulo's background?

Nita: Paulo came to live in Jaboatão at an early age. In Recife, he lived in a big house, played in the backyard, and went to school, and had few friends. He lived primarily within the sphere of his family. But when he arrives to Jaboatão, he comes into conditions of a very poor child, an impoverished boy and he begins to share experiences with the children of the factory and farm workers, and to learn about this new reality from them. He also begins to realize how people, like his grandmother and friends of the family, would call the people "riffraff " (*essa gentinha*). It was said as if to condemn them, as if they were nothing but trash. In other words, as if the common people were not worth anything and could be exploited and subjugated. *Essa gentinha* was then used disparagingly to refer to the poor, as if they were the lowest level of people, in every sense. This did not strike Paulo right. So, he would ask, "But why? They are exactly like me. These boys are just like me. What is the difference?

[1] I extend my heartfelt gratitude to my comrade, colleague, and friend, Donaldo Macedo—considered to be the foremost translator of Paulo Freire's work—for his most generous assistance with this interview. This interview would not have been possible without his kindness, patience, and bountiful spirit of solidarity. Also many thanks to Alexandre Oliveira for his excellent translation of the recorded interview material.
[2] A/D refers to Antonia and Donaldo.

What is the difference between the factory worker's son and me in the world?" He was not able to understand why people said such things. Paulo would tell me, "I had a sensitive awareness of injustice as a child, but only at the level of my feeling and sensations; not on a rational level, not at a level of conscious reflection." Paulo could not understand the reason for such injustices in the world. So, by the age of twelve, he began to concern himself more seriously with knowing the reason for such things beings as they are and understanding social phenomena. This, of knowing the reason for being or why something is this way and not that, all of this was an important preoccupation for him.

A/D: When did Paulo begin to gain awareness of the circumstances of his life?

Nita: As I said, Paulo grew up in Jaboatão, which was an important hub of the railway in the Northeast of Brazil. At that time, Brazil had an excellent railroad system controlled by the English. Their operations center was located in Jaboatão historic center, near the house where Paulo lived as a teenager. At the time, this area was actually called "Little Moscow" because there were many communists and communist leaders living in the district. Through their organizing efforts, they begin to influence the working classes in the Northeast. Paulo lived among them as an adolescent and it was in association with them that Paulo began to reflect more deeply on his concern related to the differences in how people are treated.

Many of the workers who were considered more intellectually gifted were sent to the Soviet Union for political and intellectual formation. They would spend three to four years studying Russian; and after Russian, they would spend another three to four years studying Marxism. When they finally returned home, they were a little *like fish out of water*, completely disassociated from the Brazilian reality. They did not know how to address the people. When they held meetings with the workers, meetings would empty out, because they talked about things that had nothing to do with Brazilian everyday life. This is where Paulo's idea of starting from the given reality of the people begins for him. This is when he experienced this important realization.

Paulo also noticed, "The organizers had great theories that worked well in Russia, but the people here did not accept them." It made him wonder, "Are the people in Brazil less smart? Are our people less prepared? Aren't we all prepared to improve our own lives? What is the reason for the disinterest?" Then, Paulo began to think about conditions related to human submission. The organizers wanted to bring understanding to the people but under the guise of *saving* Brazilian workers. The organizers, in a sense, wanted to be the saviors of the people. But, that was impossible! The people were not accepting the ideas that were being transmitted. So this made Paulo begin to think more deeply about what people needed and wanted to improve their lives. With this what I want to say is that the deepest historic roots of Paulo's intellectual formation are connected to his constant questioning and realizations gained living within the northeastern reality in Brazil. It's here when he begins to think about the why and how of education and society Where he begins to ask, "In favor of what or whom? Is it against what or whom?" These became the fundamental questions of Paulo's epistemology—which cannot be separated from the historical context in which he grew-up and lived his life.

Impact of Paulo's work

A/D: What was the initial impact of Pedagogy of the Oppressed *in Brazil?*

Nita: *Pedagogy of the Oppressed* was published in the United States in 1970. The book was published in English even before it was published in Portuguese. And why was this? We, in Brazil, were in the heights of a dictatorship, back in the days of General Emilio Garrastazu Medici and it was impossible for the book to be published in Brazil. In fact, Paulo's name could not be spoken in public spaces, at the time. It was forbidden. If one wrote his name in any periodical, a newspaper, or magazine, you would have to justify this before the authorities that often employed torture on the people. So, Paulo's name was not mentioned. For that reason, it was first published in the US, even before Brazil.

Fernando Gasparian from *Paz e Terra* publishers did have copies of the original manuscript of *Pedagogy of the Oppressed*. How did the manuscript make its way to Brazil? Paulo had met a Swiss congressman at the University of Geneva. The congressman offered to take the manuscripts to Brazil, since he knew his luggage would not be opened. He was a foreign government official, who could enter and leave Brazil without being searched. He brought the copies and got them to Gasparian. But at that time, Gasparian said there was no possible way to publish the book in Brazil. At the universities, Paulo's work could not be discussed, as it was prohibited. It was forbidden in schools as well, and it was forbidden in the mainstream media.

Nevertheless, *Pedagogy of the Oppressed* did manage to find its way to a restricted audience of readers, and it became possible for the book to be published in 1974. Before then, however, some people had read copies of the English edition, and it had also come out in Spanish, Italian, and French. People did have copies of those editions, which had been smuggled into Brazil and read by them. After being published in 1974, the book became better circulated in Brazil. But it still had a restricted number of readers. The first edition in Portuguese was not the resounding hit it had been in the United States—where within a few weeks the entire first printing, which was expected to last a year, was sold out. So there was not that type of success in Brazil; especially because there was still fear and a very conservative society, as well as one of our cultural flaws—the tendency not to value what Brazilians accomplish, do, and say.

When Paulo first returned, there was an extremely positive reaction to his return, all came out to celebrate his return. At that time, Paulo began to reengage in a certain way, in a different manner than before he was exiled. He reengaged historically in a different manner with the popular movements. The grassroots education movement was eliminated by the military regime but the work was reemerging actively through the church, but no longer with literacy as the central goal. Nevertheless, there was within it, camouflaged, Paulo's idea of conscientization built into its pedagogical practices. Later, however, some intellectuals become aware of the shallow nature of their own theories. This is an issue that cannot be missed, even though Paulo seldom spoke of it; although Darcy Ribeiro[3] spoke a great deal about the issue—there was certain anger

---

[3] Darcy Ribeiro is the Brazilian author, anthropologist, and politician, whole ideas of Latin American identity influenced later scholars of Latin American studies. As Minister of Education of Brazil he carried out wide reforms, which brought him invitations to participate in university reforms in Chile, Peru, Venezuela, Mexico, and Uruguay, after his exile from Brazil after the 1964 coup d'état.

on the part of intellectuals related to Paulo's resounding reputation and the knowledge that he continued to develop during his years in exile. So, they began to accuse Paulo of never truly caring about Brazil; that he had enjoyed "the good life" abroad and now had come back to Brazil, wanting to impose his views and ideas. Paulo, however, never sought to impose his views. He would say that he might try to persuade others, but never to impose his ideas upon others.

In the 1980s, there was widespread dissemination of Paulo's ideas in Brazil, but where they had the most influence was not in the academic world. Paulo's ideas had the most impact among impoverished and oppressed communities, which were influenced by reading his books. Much of this happened through the creation of progressive Christian-based communities, which embraced Paulo's ideas. Another venue was through movements for popular education and a new understanding of popular education began to emerge during that period. Through Paulo's ideas, a more democratic understanding of popular education emerged, which was not focused on keeping the impoverished class in a position of inferiority. Rather, these movements worked for an education that supported workers to learn more than just how to carry out their craft; such, that they could gain the power of their own knowledge and also acquire scientific knowledge that could serve them as individuals and society. That was the new direction that popular education began to take; unlike the past, where the education of the workers was solely focused on teaching a trade or craft.

So, with Paulo's permanent return in 1980, he began to have a great deal of influence in Brazil. However, Paulo's return destabilized certain common beliefs among some notable intellectuals, considered advocates of Paulo's ideas in Brazil. When Paulo returned, he had no intention of humiliating them. He had no pretensions of being more than who he was, in that Paulo never thought one person is more or better than another; he believed that one person could simply be different from another. It is this attitude that, I believe, helped him to make greater contributions with his work. But I do think there was an atmosphere of envy, to such an extent that some intellectuals actually set out to put an end to Paulo's prominence in the field. They accused him of having spent the tough years of the military regime abroad, away from Brazil and, now, returning full of glory and privileges, to bask in the spotlight.

It did not matter that Paulo had not chosen to go into exile or that he had not wanted to leave Brazil. Paulo was forced to leave. He was forced to go into exile or be killed by the military regime. Paulo was one of the main targets of the military regime, in that the regime understood the power of his ideas. The mobilization Paulo was working to bring about among the impoverished classes was going to change relations of power in Brazil through literacy education; for in Brazil, in order to vote people had to be literate. They had to show they could read and write. The literacy campaign at the time of Paulo's exile was working to bring literacy programs to three million Brazilians—this was the goal for the National Literacy Program of 1964. It only existed briefly, but there had been much preliminary work done, prior to 1964; extensive development work with literacy workers had been in progress. The decree was issued in March, but by April the program had been eliminated. It was believed that among the three million people who would have been served by the literacy program, the great majority would have joined with leftist forces to change the rule of power. That, of course, was the regime's greatest fear; you see, and it is the same to this day. The powerful elite did not want to lose their hierarchy of power. The 2016 coup is the same. The 1964 coup was absolutely necessary from the standpoint of the right elite, "the heirs to the big house" where the slaves had not been entitled to literacy. So, a great fear persisted (and persists) that the impoverished masses could become literate and rebel against the status quo.

Paulo was very celebrated in the US. His concept of critical pedagogy, of an education that is not mere reproduction of something memorized, where one makes students repeat what has already been said. Rather, his pedagogy encourages the creativity and autonomy of individuals. Critical education is, above all, about that. It started in the US, but has spread through a large part of the world. Now, the concern with the term "critical pedagogy" is that it is very North American, and it is very much the same case in Spain as well. Here in Brazil, when one mentions *Freirean Pedagogy*, the idea that it is critical is understood. There isn't as much of an emphasis on "criticalness," as there seems to be in the US. It is a given here that you cannot have authentic education that is not critical. You are not educating for repetition and memorization; we are instead educating ourselves and other men and women for our critical participation in society.

Intellectual influences

A/D: Who were the intellectuals that influenced Paulo's ideas in Pedagogy of the Oppressed?

Nita: First, let me repeat, historically, Paulo's early experiences of poverty in the Northeast of Brazil were the greatest influence on the development of his ideas. It was not the most famous and competent authors who provoked Paulo to write *Pedagogy of the Oppressed.* It was the suffering he had lived and seen; his sensibility to injustice, which he felt with his entire body. It was the conditions he saw and experienced, in terms of the injustices of northeastern society that fueled his desire to change the world. That is the historical moment when he begins to think and say, "Only my ideas, my realization, my Christian spirit, my seeing in every oppressed person the semblance of Christ, that can lead me to understand and to find possibilities for changing the conditions of the oppressed." That is, then, when he begins to read other famous or not famous authors from all ideological currents in the world that he had access to.

From there, I would begin with the African authors. African authors like Amilcar Cabral, who was a leader referred to as a revolutionary pedagogue, who has a whole body of work about revolution. He starts by looking at the cultural revolution and writing a whole treatise on how to come to power through arms, which was the only means for fighting the Portuguese colonizer, at that point in history. So, I would include Amilcar Cabral, Frantz Fanon, and Albert Memmi. Paulo was greatly influenced by them because they dealt with the issue of the colonizer-colonized relationship, before Paulo did. They presented ideas that benefitted Paulo a great deal in his scientific comprehension of oppression.

He wrote *Pedagogy of the Oppressed* from the starting point of realizations he came to in Brazil and later confirmed and further developed in Chile. In 1969, President Eduardo Frei [Montalvo] accused Paulo of having written a work against the Chilean government, against the Chilean people, and against the Chilean president. With that indictment, Paulo decided the time had come for him to leave Chile. Paulo left Chile in 1969 with invitations to various posts. In fact, the World Council of Churches in Geneva created a department specifically to invite Paulo, so that he could be brought on board. It was the Education Department. Paulo went to Harvard and stayed there for nine months, and then, from there, he went to Geneva.

In addition to the African authors mentioned, I would say, the existentialists also influenced his perspective. He read Sartre. I have reading flashcards that Paulo would write out. There are many on Erich Fromm, whom he met in Mexico. He was with him in Mexico. Paulo was greatly influenced by Erich Fromm. The idea of biophilia and necrophilia is very present in *Pedagogy of the Oppressed*. He brought aspects to his work from Fromm. He was in the tradition of radical German thought. Then with the problem of the war, he had to leave Germany. For Paulo, Erich Fromm is one of the most important intellectuals of that time. With the advent of the war, Jews and progressive thinkers that did not endorse Nazism had to escape Germany. Many of them went to the United States, and some went to Mexico. Erich Fromm went to Mexico, and when he meets Paulo he says, "Paulo, *Pedagogy of the Oppressed* is a book I wanted to see, dealing with the issue of necrophilia and biophilia in educational terms, in educative terms." Fromm always acknowledged Paulo's work.

Phenomenology, I must say, is another strand of thought that influenced Paulo's thinking. There is the issue of humanism from Emmanuel Mounier. Above all from Mounier comes the issue of humanism, the necessity of treating the other as one wants to be treated. It is the issue that every human being, every human experience, every living thing must be respected. Paulo even loved rocks; he had a collection of rocks. Some, then, say he was an ecologist. No, Paulo was a humanist; and from there comes his attachment to all beings, above all living beings, and his deep value for life. For Paulo, it is this comprehension of humanism that supports an ethics of life; when today, ethics is the ethics of the marketplace—an ethics of that permeates all discourse and interpretations of society and the world. So, the humanist authors he read influenced Paulo's ethics; and always ethics for him was an ethics of life— where life must prevail over economic interests.

Paulo was both influenced and also had an influence on the development of liberation theology. Paulo is considered by some to be one of the founders of liberation theology. In fact, Friar Boff was once speaking about Paulo at a conference and someone from the audience asked, "Are you saying that Paulo Freire was a liberation theologist?" Boff responded, "Yes, I am saying that Paulo Freire is a liberation theologist." When liberation theology was first emerging out of the praxis of Gustavo Gutiérrez ... he was beginning to outline the precepts for a liberation theology, following the meeting in Medellin,[4] he sought Paulo out. He wanted Paulo to assist him in systematizing liberation theology, since Gutiérrez felt that liberation theory had much to do with the ideas Paulo had put forth in *Pedagogy of the Oppressed*. So, it can be said, Paulo was the one who helped to pedagogically systematize liberation theology.

Paulo, of course, acknowledged the influence of the church on his thinking, but he also critiqued the traditional church, which merely reproduces the fear of God and intimidates and mistreats, castigates and punishes the people. He also critiques the modernized church, where preachers can sing and gather their followers to sing and pray out loud and ritualizes, but does not deal with the essence of what it means to be in relationship with God. And then, for Paulo, there was the testimony of the church, where the death of the old makes way for the resurgence of a new comprehension of God as a magnanimous, compassionate God; and where people are worthy simply because they exist. I think this was Paulo's lucid and clear interpretation about the importance of the church and of religion in the daily lives of men and women. While that traditional church said, "You shall suffer, but you shall know the kingdom of the Lord. If you hunger for bread, you shall meet the Lord in the life after death." Paulo said, "No! I want to know God in this world ... the people need a God that is of this world, for them and with them ... a Church that fights at their side."

---

[4] Here, the meeting that Nita is referring to is the Conference of Latin American Bishops held in Medellin, Colombia, in 1968. At this conference, the bishops agreed that the church should take "a preferential option for the poor." The bishops decided to form Christian "base communities" to teach the poor how to read by using the Bible. The expressed intent was to liberate the people from the institutionalized violence of poverty, by informing the people that poverty and hunger were preventable. They pronounced that the poor were the blessed people and that the church has a duty to help them. The movement drew on the influence of Paulo, who was regarded as one of the great literacy teacher of the region. The movement eventually became known as *liberation theology* (discussed in Chapter 2).

Epistemological sensibility

A/D: Something apparent about Paulo was his epistemological sensibility. Can you speak to this aspect of his praxis?

Nita: I would say, perhaps immodest, because Paulo would never say this, but Paulo was a genius. Paulo had a sensibility that helped him to anticipate facts and things. He had a profound capacity for guessing what tomorrow might bring, in the sense of how people thought about issues. And, I believe, that was due to his radicalness of thought … his radical sensibility in both experiencing and making sense of the world. He used to say, "I plant my roots so firmly in the present that I can make use of the past to foresee the future." That's why I think of him always as a wise man. A wise man is in the present, but always remembers the past to also think about what might be. Paulo had a wisdom that was above the average person, not only the northeastern or Brazilian sensibility, but a sensibility of the world. When, he would set out to study, he used to say, "To me, just what I produce is not sufficient, my intuitions and realizations. I need to also find the scientific, theoretical substantiation from other authors." Paulo was very open-minded in that way.

Paulo's sensibilities may also be the question of culture. He was Latin American. The North American academic culture, in comparison, is not much given to certain sensibilities and to emotions; it does not value emotions in the act of knowing. Paulo's sensibility was one where he felt life and experiences within his body. He was also very compassionate and could put himself in the other's shoes. He was able to say, "What is this other man or woman feeling or experiencing?" It's about the capacity to put oneself in the other's place. That was part of Paulo's sensibility. A human sensibility that could value and take into account, as an important category of knowledge production, feelings, being emotional, experiencing indignation, facing up to it. For Paulo, those are necessary conditions for sharpening our sensibility and, therefore, our intellect. If a poor person on the street … for example, like a group of boys who killed an Indian man, and when asked about it said, "Oh, but he was just a beggar." Their actions showed no sensibility toward the man they killed, toward his condition. In their mind, he was a beggar … a thing.

Even here in Brazil, these days, many people do not want to consider the question of sensibility with respect to actions in the world that shock them, that frighten them, that causes them to be perplexed. To Paulo, it made him perplexed to see people making a living by working day and night, always barefoot, not even owning shoes. I remember downtown Recife, when people from the lower classes never wore shoes; they would have to walk around barefoot. They worked on their bare feet, even in the urban centers. So much so that, today, the popular classes are quite fanatical about buying shoes. A most profitable business in Recife is then shoe stores, which, I believe, comes from this legacy of not being able to own shoes. They have lots and lots of shoes, as if to make up for the time when their parents and grandparents went barefoot. Situations like this caused Paulo to wonder, "Why is it that I need shoes? I could not go out on the streets, tripping over on things, as my bare feet are not adept at walking on the ground and over rocks and poorly made sidewalks. How can they do this without shame or embarrassment?" It was because they were subjected to conditions of poverty; they had to adapt to it to survive; in a sense, they were educated since birth not to have shoes. This is an example of the way class difference deeply touched Paulo's sensibility. The issue of hunger, for example, was a major concern for him. Why is it that they have nothing to eat, and many don't complain. They are forced to live in conditions of starvation.

There is a poem by João Cabral de Melo Neto, a great northeastern poet, which says *they die each day*. And what do they die of? They die from being politically and economically ambushed before thirty, and they die of hunger. These conditions of poverty caused Paulo great pain and puzzlement. This again was part of his sensibility; the sensibility to recognize the things that are real in one's own reality … around a person, without fantasies, without camouflage, without justifications, "Oh, they are poor, but they revel in carnival; they are poor, but they have the religious festivals." In other words, Paulo did not romanticize poverty and misery. Instead, for Paulo, his sensibility caused him to notice that, in spite of hunger, in spite of their conditions of submission and homelessness and no sanitation, no clean water, they could make music of the best quality, and they could create and participate in carnival. Not because conditions of poverty did not have an impact on them or cause them suffering, but because they have an impetus for living that many in the middle class simply lack, even with their affluence. So, for Paulo, it was important to realize such things ... to be aware of the humanity of the poor. This was Paulo's sensibility to others and to the world. But Paulo's sensibility did not end there. He did not simply stop and cry over those who suffered. He set out to find epistemological resonances in philosophers and historians and sociologists and linguists, people from other sciences, to help him explain more profoundly, more scientifically, what his sensibility stirred him to see and experience in the world.

A/D: *Nita, this seems to be an aspect of Paulo's epistemological or cultural approach that is seldom grasped. Would you say this is an aspect of Paulo not well understood?*

Nita: Yes! I think it is a dimension that North American people do not understand. You hit it on the head; it is a question of culture. North Americans seem culturally quite superficial in this respect, that is, very mechanized, and to expect them to think at such a deep level of sensibility about what they experience seems very hard. They are taught to distance themselves from the world, in order to know it. This is the opposite of what Paulo lived. So, when students think, "Why should I worry about the poor? I'm not poor. My family is not poor." ... this reflects an extremely individualistic approach to society and to life. Such individualism justifies a lack of social sensibility for others. That's something Paulo had, as a result of shared experience ... through playing soccer, playing games, singing with others, listening to the radio news, participating in some way, critiquing the problem of war and violence. Through all those experiences, Paulo learned how to develop the sensibility of perception. Now, it is very funny because North Americans can be very courteous. When they greet you as you visit their homes, they are very welcoming, offering a glass of water or some wine. But really knowing them ... having a sense of how they experience or feel about the world and how this impacts the way they see the world is not so easy or apparent, especially in academic places. We, Brazilians do not tend to be so polite, shall we say [laughter], and don't usually take the same care to be courteous ... as in saying,

"Excuse me" or "I'm sorry," but we do place a high value on sensing, more deeply what is happening ... it's almost like a cultural reflex that effects our way of knowing the world ... our epistemology, which is different than North Americans and Northern Europeans.

I think that part of this difference is due to a sort of positivism, which has impregnated the North American intellectual context. But, there is also here in Brazil, intellectuals who say that Paulo's work has no value because he was too tied to the issue of sensibility. But Paulo did not stop at the level of sensibility. His ideas go beyond; in ways that his sensibility fuels his ideas ... his intellect. While in the United States, it seems that such level of sensibility has become dormant, in what is a positivist and reductive epistemological approach. So these human sensibilities are present but they tend to become latent due to the structure of the way they think. Paulo believed that it is up to teachers to awaken in their students this human sensibility that we all have; a sensibility that helps us develop a more profound concern for life ... for the "the other," for the society, for the country in which we live, for the world. How is it possible that a young adult, for example, not know about the many forms of North American exploitation that have been carried out around the world ... pillaging wealth and forbidding the self-determination of other countries ... imposing upon them self-serving rules and regulations. How could this not have an impact on how a young person is educated? For Paulo, he felt that teacher must work with students so that they can begin to ask, "How can all this take place around the world, and still we say we are a democratic country that teaches democracy?"

Another thing about this question of epistemology, Paulo would often say, "We must never be too sure of our certainty. Our certainties must always be put in check; we must always question our certainties." He believed that questioning is how we evolve and can contribute to social transformation. And this requires that we not ever be too sure of our certainties. That's why Paulo never said he was sure; he would, at best, say, "I am *somewhat* sure ..." It's a kind of certain/uncertainty ... a way of rejecting the need to be absolutely certain that something is either right or not. This reflects, again, Paulo's open-mindedness that he believed we needed for dialogue and to not reproduce oppression in schools and in the society.

On class struggle

A/D: Pedagogy of the Oppressed *seems to provide an understanding of class struggle, which is summarily denied in the US. In what ways does this dimension of the book continue to have relevance?*

Nita: Sometimes, in the US, this denial of class struggle makes contending with problems faced by impoverished people more difficult than even in Brazil. It's as if many people in the US don't want to see that class struggle is everywhere. Here, in Brazil, a large segment of the population sees the problem of class; but in the US you cannot readily find people dealing with class struggle … I mean, you do find individuals here and there who think about and challenge this problem, but the collective population, for the most part, seems oblivious and too certain that class is not the problem. Here, in Brazil, with very, very rare exceptions, recognizing class struggle … recognizing that there exist class divisions, antagonism is expected in academic thesis and dissertation work. However, as Paulo would say, "The dominant class truly hates the poor. It's as if the poor were to blame for their poverty." Instead, he said social and material domination is to blame for human oppression in Brazil, North America, and other places in the world.

A/D: *What did Paulo think about neoliberalism, relative to what is happening in education now in Brazil?*

Nita: In *Under the Shade of the Mango Tree* [published in the United States as *Pedagogy of Hope*], a most beautiful book, Paulo precisely makes a condemnation of neoliberalism. He links capitalism to the history of human oppression and refers to neoliberalism as how it exists today. For Paulo, neoliberalism decrees the death of history. It decrees the end of class struggle. That we are all supposedly equals and can move around the world with no borders. However, current conditions are the exact opposite! In fact, class struggle has hardened; the concentration of wealth has increased in all countries of the world, and poverty continues to grow. The impoverished are still more illiterate; illiteracy has grown in some parts of the world; hunger is increasing around the world; unemployment is growing around the world; and all that is taking place as a result of neoliberalism. Paulo used to say that neoliberalism is the antithesis of any possibility for an egalitarian society. Neoliberalism, with its false face as bringer of benefits, in fact brings social and material poverty to the world; so, in many ways, the world is becoming more miserably poor.

In *Pedagogy of Hope*, Paulo deals above all with the manner in which neoliberalism leaves no other way out than the poverty of many; that such is the world and that we must cut jobs for the benefit of the economy, even if it leaves so many in poverty. Paulo would say, "That is so only when it results in gain for the dominant classes." There is a discourse of the inevitability of neoliberalism. But from the standpoint of the rights of workers and the rights of the oppressed, none of that is inevitable. The message of neoliberalism is that "Things cannot change and must indeed be as they are." This implies a double standard that in all circumstances favors the powerful and wealthy. There is no chance for a fairer society with the canvas of neoliberalism, which is what imperialist countries impose on us—the formerly termed "Third World" now called "developing countries."

Brazil is among these nations, so-called in process of becoming developed. Yet, Brazil was until recently the eighth economy in the world. However, it will likely suffer a setback—a lowering of its economic standing in the world—not as a result of our incompetence, but as a preordained consequence of adopting the neoliberal model. The neoliberal discourse camouflages reality; it deceives and seems quite plausible and fair to the unwary. They have hope in what the government we have now, which is becoming more intently neoliberal or something worse, imposing an unfair political economy in the people of Brazil. This is a government geared toward the external economic interests that now dominate the world. I believe we can term it a neoliberal government, which it seems to be; although it presents itself as democratic one, while it closes down democratic possibilities for the participation by the people in the decision-making and management of domestic policy.

This democratic participation by the people is what horrifies the dominant classes in Brazil—a certain autonomy that was being created for policy decision-making by the subordinate classes. This phenomenon stirred the arrogant dominant class into frenzy. Paulo used to often wonder when we would put an end to such injustice in the world. Today, reactionary conservatives find new pretexts to attack progressive state officials. They are trying to find so-called crimes committed by the president [Dilma Rouseff],[5] while the greatest, fairest jurists in Brazil say they have found no responsibility for any crimes on her part. Even so, they have caused the Congress, as it is compromised by neoliberalism, and by their utmost shamelessness, as Paulo called it, to go along, against the popular classes and against a government [Rouseff's] that proposed and carried out important national initiatives for the benefit of the country's dispossessed population. I want to believe that, possibly, the days of neoliberalism are numbered, given the greedy manner that capitalists have moved toward the appropriation of such great wealth by a very few. It seems only a matter of time when neoliberalism will no longer be able to sustain its grip on the world. The danger is that this may usher in a new more authoritarian form of imperialist capitalism capable of massacring the world's population, of violating the human rights of the majority of the world's population.

If we see what has happened over the last thirty years, I would say Paulo was not mistaken to put a great emphasis on class struggle. It is also important to understand that, although many in North America read him, Paulo did not write for Americans. Paulo wrote about the conditions and phenomenon of human oppression, of people oppressed in all sorts of manner—sexism, racism, religion discrimination, sexuality—but above all for Paulo was the issue of class struggle, which he believed affected every other form of oppression. Class struggle is being waged all over the world and encompasses the struggle of women—this morbid and perverse antagonism of men against women. Men who batter and kill women with ease and impunity ... in Brazil it continues to be so. However, the question of class struggle is at work in every form of oppression. This Brazilian coup of 2016 [against Rouseff] must be understood

---

[5]   Dilma Rouseff, a progressive Brazilian economist, was president from 2011 until her impeachment, where she was found guilty of breaking budget laws and was removed from office in August 2016, three months after this interview was conducted. As a socialist activist during the dictatorship, Rouseff was captured, tortured, and jailed from 1970 to 1972. However, some of her political stances (i.e., anti-abortion, anti-gay marriage, neoliberal initiatives) were considered rather contradictory to her constituency, which may have been one of the reason that conservative groups in Brazil found space and opportunity to launch an assault on her presidency.

as a class coup, where other issues were effectively used to camouflage this. It is the upper class, the class that enriches itself from the assets of the state and is allowed to do so, with impunity. Now, if a member of the popular classes were to steal a can of sardines, and that is a fact, they will go to jail! A judge recently convicted a man for stealing a can of sardines! But those who rob the people of their rights to a decent livelihood, their dignity, and at times their lives are allowed free reign.

Paulo's enduring legacy

A/D: *Paulo died almost twenty years ago; what has remained? What is his legacy?*

Nita: The Christian-based communities continue to be vigorously at work today, always seeking out Paulo's praxis as example for their work with the people. In communities focused on health, there is great emphasis placed on the preparation of health educators, who are taking Paulo's words and approach to education and life to the poor, to the popular classes to teach and support the conscientization of mothers, in the most basic aspects of their lives, in the care and education of their children; teaching them how to heal them, with prayer, if they like, but always also through care that is scientific. For example, when treating children with stomach ailments, in the old days, a mother seeing her child going through bouts of diarrhea would stop giving the child water. They thought the child had excess water because they were putting out so much water. In fact, there is a simple formula for rehydrating that combines water with sugar and salt. It is something very simple that anyone can have access to. It came from the work of Zilda Arns, sister of Cardinal Dom Paulo Evaristo Arns [of São Paulo], who put into practice Paulo's ideas in the area of health education with the poor and working classes. That is, we should always start from the concrete realities of communities, from the concrete conditions of their lives. One should not begin by talking about high cost treatments, which cannot be accessed by impoverished populations, or may not be accessed in time. In some instances, a child can die in two days, if there is no intervention.

Starting from what resources are available to them has been the secret. I say this way to thinking about health education in the poor communities of Brazil are an example of how Paulo's pedagogical legacy persists.

Paulo's legacy also continues to have great influence, today, among popular movements, in the Landless Workers Movement (MST).[6] At all their schools, the teachers, generally women, read Paulo's books. I have cleared it with the publisher to give them permission to publish Paulo's writings, but with introductions written by them, as a way of providing the theoretical base for their pedagogical practice among the people. Therefore, this movement, MST as we call it, has all its political educational practice based on Paulo's work. They often honor Paulo; I am often invited. They have debates about the work. I mean he is a name that is not forgotten, in any way. João Pedro Stédile, who is the head of the movement, exercises an effective form of democratic leadership. He is a man who came from the impoverished classes of Rio Grande do Sul, and he is a most capable economist, as well. He is a very intelligent man, and a very good man. He sustains that movement, by maintaining its status as a large organization capable of facing the great inequities that exist in Brazil, the wide gaps in having, knowing, and being able to do. They are always geared to mobilize … the media calls their actions invasions but Paulo used to say that it is not invasions. What they are doing is occupying lands that have been kept unproductive till now.

These days, I see that the reach of Paulo's work is widening to include spaces we would never have imagined. One of Paulo's books was translated last year in Israel, into the Hebrew language. I think this is an important and positive fact. With all the difficulties in the region, it is good to know there are people in Israel who care about building a spirit of tolerance. Also, Paulo's books are

---

[6] Nita is speaking here of the *Movimento dos Trabalhadores Rurais Sem Terra* (MST): a mass social movement, formed by rural workers and those who want to fight for land reform and against injustice and social inequality in rural areas. The MST was born through a process of occupying *latifundios* (large landed estates), becoming a national movement in 1984. The movement has led more than 2,500 land occupations, with about 370,000 families—families that today settled on 7.5 million hectares of land that they won as a result of the occupations. Through their organizing, these families continue to push for schools, credit for agricultural production and cooperatives, and access to health care. Currently, there are approximately 900 encampment holding 150,000 landless families in Brazil. Those camped, as well as those already settled, remain mobilized, ready to exercise their full citizenship, by fighting for the realization of their political, social economic, environmental and cultural rights. See: *Friends of the MST* website for more information: http://www.mstbrazil.org/.

being read in places like Indonesia, Pakistan, Kazakhstan, and India. Educators in these countries are embracing Paulo's ideas. Yes, sometimes only in small areas, but there are groups, even if small ones, that are working to combat the status quo in those national states and they are looking toward Paulo's insights as a starting point for their work in communities, in combination with their own intellectuals. It is good to see that in those countries where citizens still experience repression, there remains an interest in liberation, an interest in social transformation. Brazil in 1997 after Paulo's death, for example, coincided with a very turbulent political period in Brazil. During that time, there was greater demand for Paulo's books. In difficult years, like then and in this period now, from 2012 to now, Paulo' books are again being read more widely in Brazil. And, of course, his books continue to sell around the world.

About Paulo's legacy, what I can say is that there is just one Paulo. The one who started out with *Education as Practice for Freedom*, and already he was asking, "Whose freedom?" Even if not named, it was that of the oppressed. But, above all, starting from the publishing of *Pedagogy of the Oppressed*, Paulo's work is one and the same; it has been consistent in its commitment to the poor; commitment to social transformation … this remained with Paulo to the day of his death. I was able to live that with him with great intensity. Some say I am too in love with him. Yes, I am very much in love with him, but all that subjective passion never got in the way of my objective analysis of Paulo's stance before the world, of what Paulo wrote, and what Paulo practiced. I do not look upon Paulo with benevolent eyes, so as to establish that he was a great man. I indeed knew I had a great man by my side!

It is a great pleasure and honor to have been able to participate in life with Paulo, but I would like readers to see Paulo as a man able to bring light to the darkest and most hidden recesses of human degradation. Paulo's ideas are able to illuminate us, so that we can see the nefarious impact of domination. It is important to see how Paulo thought about and dealt with difficult societal problems, without rancor, without hate, and without meanness. No one can truthfully accuse Paulo of being of bad temperament, of being envious, or of not being a serious intellectual or revolutionary. He lived his politics. He denounced oppression with a great spirit and announced justice with great hope for transformation and change. I would like readers to find this in his writings and to experience, even if only a little, Paulo's enormous capacity for feeling and experiencing the world, which led him to reflection deeply about liberation.

Paulo used to say, "I don't think with my head; I think with my whole body." I think that is what was so fantastic about him! He would say, "I think with my desires, with my frustrations, with my emotions, with my virtues. I think with everything that fits into my body. It is my conscious body that tells me to focus my reflection upon this or that." Again, I think that is fantastic! He would say,

> I don't think with my head. I think with my whole body. How do I think with my whole body? When my hairs go up, it is my body telling me there is something I should look at, to reflect upon. When my heartbeat accelerates to tachycardia, it is because some phenomenon is calling to me, to my attention, but doing so through my body and not only my head. My body is conscious. My whole body, my sensibility, comes before my head. It precedes my ability to engage in reflection. It comes before.

This is why Paulo would say that his intuition never left him on the road. About this, Paulo would say,

> Intuition leads me to experience those symptoms. When I look at something or someone many times, it is because something is being said to me and my body has picked up on it. Once my body realizes that, then, I can tell myself to focus and reflect upon that which is bothering or provoking me, that which is disquieting me. When I get restless, I have to focus my thinking, my reason, never disconnected from my emotions and my feelings.

In so many ways, this embodiment of Paulo is so important to understand him as an intellectual, revolutionary, and a man of the people. One of Paulo's greatest legacies is that he was not afraid to feel, experience, and know life with all of his being. It was also this that he brought to his writing, at every stage of his life. My hope is that readers will discover Paulo, the living, loving, and also indignant man, through his words.

Teaching *Pedagogy of the Oppressed*

Notes from the Field

Through their continuing praxis, men and women simultaneously create his-
tory and become historical-social beings . . . their history, in function of their
own creations, develops as a constant process of transformation . . . Were this
[not] the case, a fundamental condition of history—its continuity—would
disappear.

—Paulo Freire (1970)

In its more than fifty years of circulation, *Pedagogy of the Oppressed* has had one
of the most impressive shelf lives, in comparison to most educational literature.
So much so that Freire, next to John Dewey, is the most cited educational
philosopher of the twentieth century. The book has found itself in the hand
of revolutionary educators on every continent. Whether in classrooms,
workers' unions, prisons, or on the streets, Freire's ideas have provided a
lasting inspiration, a source of new political language, and an introduction
to a living pedagogy of struggle within schools and communities. Whether
in the United States, the Caribbean, South Africa, Europe, Ireland, Turkey,
Palestine, or India, Paulo Freire's ideas have both powerfully fueled a critique
of authoritarian practices within schools and communities and illuminated
new understandings for reinventing an emancipatory educational pedagogy,
inextricably linked to the larger political project of liberation.

The following *notes from the field* can be read as testimonies that not
only speak to the past influence of *Pedagogy of the Oppressed* but also bear
witness to the continuing significance of Paulo Freire's ideas in a world
battered by governmental and institutional policies and practices driven by

the interest of the wealthy and powerful. The contributors featured here are all educators who have consistently engaged the text and are grounded in a commitment to a revolutionary vision and pedagogical practice devoted to the ongoing struggle on the ground against capitalism and its many faces of oppression. These stories of practice and integration of Freire's ideas into their classroom praxis, political activism, and their scholarly commitments signal the lasting salience of Freire ideas not only as a philosophy but also as a way of life.

The underlying intent is that teachers and students will engage these *notes from the field* in ways that will assist them to consider their own personal and collective praxis and further comprehend, through these examples, what Freire meant when he urged educators and activists not to imitate his pedagogy but rather to engage his ideas and reinvent them in ways that are useful, relevant, and applicable to their own cultural, geographic, and generational realities. It is, moreover, the humility of this liberating encouragement that has supported the persistence of *Pedagogy of the Oppressed* for more than five decades.

———————

Paulo Freire: Love, Creation, and Beginning

Walter Kohan
State University of Rio de Janeiro
Brazil

When I began to write this short essay about teaching *Pedagogy of the Oppressed,* I immediately recollected something that Paulo Freire's youngest son, Lutgardes Costa Freire, told me, during a conversation we had a couple of years ago at the Paulo Freire Institute of São Paulo, Brazil. He was sharing stories about his studies in Switzerland when he lived there as a boy. He told me that at the time he wanted to play drums, he really wanted to be a musician. So Lutgardes asked his father what he thought about this, suspecting his father preferred a different path for his son. But Paulo Freire's response surprised him: "It's all right, my son. You can do what you want. But promise me one thing: that whatever you're going to do will be done with love." [1]

Since Freire's response to his son is so inspiring and educative, not only for parents but for educators as well, I thought it could be a sort of gift for those interested in teaching *Pedagogy of the Oppressed*. I can imagine that many teachers of one of the most read educational books of all times might have lots of questions: How should I teach it? Where should I start from? What are the main seminal concepts of the book? What references should I include to make it more understandable and sounder? What must be included when teaching the book? Of course, many readers will find suggestions in this book, but my main response to such questions is one and the same as Paulo Freire's response to his son. Teach *Pedagogy of the Oppressed* in whatever way you prefer; begin where you feel comfortable to begin; choose the concepts you feel closest to; create your own methodology; include the references you believe will provoke a more engaged dialogue, "but promise me one thing: that whatever you're going to do will be done with love."

In fact, I feel this is so important to teaching the book that I would encourage teachers to write this phrase on a board or a paper; have a dialogue with your students of any age to discuss its meaning for them; and, if they agree, write it as a frontispiece at the entrance of your classroom so that you can all read it and remember each time you enter each morning. Of course, "classroom" should not necessarily be taken literally here. It could refer to any educational environment. Can you imagine if whatever we do in our educational practice, no matter who is involved, we do it with love? Can you imagine the pedagogical, aesthetic, and political impact that this "simple" movement might provoke? Isn't it not something that we can all do, and would it not transform us in revolutionary ways? The simple act of doing all things with love.

These also remind me of another quote in *Pedagogy of the Oppressed* that I feel would be meaningful here. Meaning for its content but also in how it speaks to the fact that Freire wrote the book in Portuguese; and, as such, there

---

[1] The entire conversation is reproduced in *Paulo Freire. A philosophical biography* (New York: Bloomsbury, 2021).

are aspects that often are not necessarily exactly translatable when you move from one language and culture to another. The quote, as the one earlier, is also about love and appears as the very last sentence or the grand finale of the original Brazilian edition of the book. Yet, the following words in the English translation are not at the end of the book but extracted from the text and inserted in the preface. In English, the quote reads,

> From these pages I hope at least the following will endure: my trust in the people, and my faith in men and women, and in the creation of a world in which it will be easier to love. (Freire, 2005, p. 40)

This English translation is "slightly" different from the original, at the beginning and at the end of the phrase. Let's begin with the difference at the end: in the English edition it says: "a world in which it will be easier to love," whereas a literal translation of the Brazilian edition would read "a world in which it will be less difficult to love" (Freire, 2018, p. 92). And there is also something missing from the beginning of the English translation that appears in the Brazilian version: "If nothing remains" so that the beginning of the phrase would be: "If nothing remains from these pages."

Let's give a look to what the original phrase might make us imagine. It is the very end of the book. Paulo Freire has already written the whole *Pedagogy of the Oppressed*—his seminal book that contains his life and work, to that moment in his life. He is in Chile, exiled, feeling more than ever the need of an educational revolution. He is entirely confident in his book. But, as the phrase reveals, he is much more confident in the need and power of love. Even if his book can do nothing to transform the world, it would still be faithful in the creation of a world in which it would be less difficult to love. Because he knows with his entire body that this is the worst wickedness of our world: oppression makes it nearly impossible to love. It might never be possible to inhabit a world where it would be easy to love; but if at least it would be less difficult to love, Freire believed, a new world might begin.

For Freire, I would argue, education is principally connected to love and, through love, to new beginnings and ends. Moreover, teaching might be better understood as a regenerative act of beginning and ending, of making it possible for others to begin and end, over and over again. In fact, the ending phrase of *Pedagogy of the Oppressed* seems like an attempt by Paulo Freire to make the ending of the book a kind of beginning, the beginning of a world where it might be less difficult to love.

Paulo Freire was, with no doubt, a person of beginnings. In his lovely conversation with Myles Horton (Horton and Freire, 1990), he unwaveringly declares, "I always am in the beginning, as you" (p. 55). By affirming this idea, he sought to show precisely that education is about beginning: "I am convinced that in order for us to create something, we need to start creating. We cannot wait to create tomorrow, but we have to start creating." (Horton and Freire, 1990, p. 56). Being always at the beginning, our creation is a way of existing in the never-ending dream of a new world. In my estimation, this is what makes Paulo Freire a great educator and all true educators creators of new worlds. And this is also why love is so very necessary to our educational practices because it is the expression of our creative force.

Reaching the end of this short essay, I feel, more than ever, the need to make this end a beginning. Some questions are coming, and I smile because questions are also forms of beginning. What do you think? Any suggestion? It occurs to me that it might be that nothing will remain of this modest text; but if any reader feels inspired by it as a beginning, to begin something in their educational life; if just one reader educationally begins something encouraged by it, then it will be endlessly beginning. Are there any loving educators ready to begin?

The Enduring Influence of *Pedagogy of the Oppressed* in South Africa

Farieda Nazier
University of Johannesburg
South Africa

Growing up in South Africa, my lived experience as a student and educator carries the historical residue of apartheid. Beyond the economic gain and benefits to the apartheid government, the apartheid education system—

based on values of authoritarianism, rote learning, and replete of racism and sexism—was fundamentally used as an "ideological state apparatus to hinder the development of criticality in the black masses" (Dlamini, 1998). Furthermore, apartheid education infused a pervasive sense of cultural and racial inferiority and self-hatred among Black[2] youth. This legislation was but one of the many divisive measures implemented by the apartheid government to deny agency in South Africa's majority Black population.

The late freedom fighter Neville Alexander was arguably one of South Africa's most important public intellectuals. Sentenced in 1963 to ten years on Robben Island Prison and another five years "house arrest" after his release from prison for his role in the armed struggle against the apartheid regime, Alexander was deeply influenced by Paulo Freire's *Pedagogy of the Oppressed*. Alexander, a revolutionary educationist, believed, as did Freire, that it was impossible to wage a successful struggle without a theory to support our actions forward. Throughout his life, Alexander remained committed to using the analytical tools of Marxism to develop this theory. His Marxism was not vulgar; it was enriched by his deep understanding of the South African reality, with its complex intersections of "race," class, and gender. He was a humanist, Pan-Africanist, and internationalist, who keenly followed global developments and struggles. His call for a radical pedagogy, like Freire, advocated a democratic educational process with *praxis* (as the reflective practice of theory) firmly at its core. This radical pedagogy constitutes a people's education that remains cognizant of the pitfalls of ahistorical record and party politics.

The high point of my personal engagement with Freire's *Pedagogy of the Oppressed* was at a two-day annual commemorative conference on Neville Alexander, organized by the Centre for Education Rights and Transformation at the University of Johannesburg on September 7 and 8, 2018. The conference, attended by 300 mostly young Black scholar-activists, involved in student movements, community organizations, and other social movements

---

[2] The Black Consciousness Movement which resisted apartheid education in all its manifestations used the term Black to include all those oppressed by the apartheid regime and rejected the divisive and often arbitrary racial classifications "African," "Colored," and "Indian" nomenclature imposed by the regime.

coincided with the fifty-year celebration of *Pedagogy of the Oppressed.* True to its intent, the conference was titled "50 years of the 'Pedagogy of the Oppressed'—Reflections of the Praxes of Neville Alexander and Paulo Freire." The conference was a platform for dialogue and a much-needed space for reflection on diverse viewpoints and approaches. I was invited by my mentor and conference convener, Salim Vally,[3] who has generously contributed to my developing body of visual and textual research as well as this essay.

The first day of the conference was devoted to Antonia Darder's inspiring keynote address and her dialogue with nine young Black women activists and educators.[4] The dialogical conversation involved Darder's presentation and her book, *The Student Guide to Freire's Pedagogy of the Oppressed.* Her address spoke to the key similarities between Neville Alexander and Paulo Freire and the key lessons they provide for our continuing struggle for liberation. Darder explained how both Freire and Alexander had a keen sense of their social agency and a deliberate political commitment to liberation and why both were dialectical thinkers who were willing to rethink their views in search of the truth—they showed great humility in their way of being. Darder also spoke to the historical materialism that guided their analysis of society and the dialogical methodology central to their pedagogy.

Since its inception, Freire's *Pedagogy of the Oppressed* has proven its deep relevance and applicability globally and has stood the test of time for more than half a century. I refer to both relevance and application, as his theories have inspired, activated, and inspired revolutionary movements the world over. In the South African context, the colonially derived apartheid system permeated and controlled every aspect of the lives of black South Africans. This oppressive system necessitated a commensurate resistance movement.

---

[3] Salim Vally is Professor and Director of CERT, Faculty of Education, at the University of Johannesburg and the National Research Foundation—South African Research Initiative's Chair in Community, Adult and Workers Education. He is a coeditor of *Education, Economy and Society* (2014), *Reflections on Knowledge, Learning and Social Movements: History's Schools* (2018), *The University and Social Justice: Struggles across the Globe* (2020), and a forthcoming coedited book, *Against Racial Capitalism: The Selected Writings of Neville Alexander* (2023).

[4] The discussion was chaired by Leigh Ann Naidoo and included me, Lydia Cairncross, Terri Maggott, Nadeema Jogee, Ntshadi Mofokeng, Sarah Motha, Salma Ismail, and the late Vanessa Merckel.

While many of the anti-apartheid leaders solely focused on the inequalities and economic ramifications of apartheid, Steve Bantu Biko sought to engage and address the consequences of psychological and cultural domination through the Black Consciousness Movement. Reminiscent of Freire's concern with the consciousness of oppression, Biko (1978) argued in his groundbreaking book, *I Write What I Like*, "The most potent weapon in the hands of the oppressor is the mind of the oppressed" (p. 68).

Similarly, Neville Alexander (1988), in *Liberation Pedagogy in the South African Context*,[5] articulated how Freire's radical pedagogy influenced and inspired the development and reinvention of context-specific variants of conscientização. In the South African context, although the apartheid regime banned Freire's works, more than 500 copies of *Pedagogy of the Oppressed* were illegally distributed and studied by the young activists of the Black Consciousness Movement. In Freire's ideas, they found the mirror image of that which they rejected in the apartheid education system as well as possible alternatives. Informal courses in Freire's methods were conducted and soon some of the South African Students' Organization (SASO) students and others begun conducting literacy and other conscientization projects in urban and rural townships.

Hence, both Alexander and Biko, in concert with Freire, believed that liberation had to not only engage the economic and political spheres but had to also contend with the psychosocial realm. True liberation then required freeing our minds, a theme that is well known to reader of Freire's work. As Biko infers, the physical and psychological liberation of blacks in South Africa required a tailored form of critical consciousness (and therefore conscientization) to arouse a sense of self-worth, dignity, and pride to effectively organize the resistance against apartheid. The Black Consciousness philosophy focused in equal measure on structural changes in the policies and laws governing the country as well as the psychological transformation of the oppressed

---

[5] This reference is taken from an amended version of a keynote address, delivered on Wednesday, August 3, 1988, at the Department of Education, University of Natal (Durban), on the theme of "Experiential learning in formal and non-formal education" held on August 3–5, 1988.

(Macdonald, 2010). Neville Alexander's stance too reiterates the sentiments of Freire, in recognizing the role of education and the liberation struggle. Alexander embraced Freire's *Pedagogy of the Oppressed*, which echoed his own commitment to praxis. As such, their lived experience of oppression and impoverishment became the impetus for their decolonizing and anti-capitalist ideas and their commitment to liberation.

As a Black female artist-academic and activist, and descendent of ancestors who were enslaved by Dutch colonizers, I find myself today—thirty years after nominal "democracy"—still seeking modalities and approaches that can be employed to navigate and survive in a neoliberal higher education system. Post the Covid-19 pandemic and in the midst of a climate catastrophe and the global resurgence of right-wing politics, the vision of many South African freedom fighters teeters on the verge of kleptocratic collapse. In addition, ongoing issues with service delivery, power generation, and an ongoing water crisis hamper the daily lives of ordinary citizens and have contributed to violent civil unrest, culminating in the June 2021 riots largely in KwaZulu-Natal. Sadly, even though the internet and social media have provided us with unlimited access to information, without the humanizing praxis suggested by Freire, Biko, and Alexander, theory without criticality and reflection is insufficient for transforming our material and social realities. Drawing on these thinkers, my teaching and artistic practice have sought out ways in which the legacies of oppression are experienced, embodied, and encultured in the present, as we continue to unpack and reconstruct together what it means to be fully human.

A Reflection About Teaching *Pedagogy of the Oppressed*

Peter Mayo
University of Malta
Malta

Pedagogy of the Oppressed is a book that I have taught repeatedly in universities since 1988, after I had returned from Edmonton, Alberta, to take up a part-time lecturing post in Sociology of Education at the University of Malta while working in adult education in the then country's Department of Education in my full-time job. Prior to this, I had been a schoolteacher and could have read the book, to which we were introduced in our initial teacher education course, but with a choice. I would have made a better job of my work in schools soon after had I chosen to read and write my essay on *Pedagogy of the Oppressed*. I had focused instead on Rousseau in that course unit and waited until I was a student in the Sociology of Education at the University of Alberta, six years later, to delve more deeply and enthusiastically into Freire's work. In the interim period between concluding my teacher education degree and starting my master's, I took an external degree in English Literature from the University of London and so literary texts took up most of my time away from my day work as a schoolteacher.

The students I taught at the University of Malta after 1988 responded to *Pedagogy of the Oppressed* warmly and enthusiastically to the point that Freire, like Don Lorenzo Milani, later, became a source of "revelation." Some would tell me that they found in this book the language they were looking for to express their concerns and often frustrations regarding their experiences throughout most of their student lives. "Banking education" was the concept that appealed mostly to them and so was that of dialogue with its connotations of participation and voice. Unlike some graduate students I met when studying in Toronto, few undergraduates, if any, in Malta, would speak of finding Freire's work "oppressive." To the contrary, they felt inspired. Nevertheless, they did pick up what they thought were serious occlusions or, in Dorothy E. Smith's words, signs of "a peculiar eclipsing." Gender occlusions and lack of ecological awareness often featured in critique made by a number of students who were active in "Third World" Environmental and later Fair Trade groups. The danger, however, is reading Freire with a sanitized lens, where historical and geographical contexts are stripped away. Some students, for example, were easily confused by the Latin American context, while others were immediately attracted to it. They felt quite at home, despite the geographical distance, given that the elements of similarity between the Maltese and Mediterranean contexts, especially the Southern European contexts and Latin America, were great.

The last chapter of *Pedagogy of the Oppressed*, heavily influenced by the writing of Frantz Fanon and Albert Memmi, appealed to student teachers, especially prospective teachers of Maltese History and Literature. For students from a former colony of Britain, concepts such as "cultural invasion" and "divide and rule" resonated powerfully. Here one important Freirean point, explained in his later work, *Cartas da Guinea Bissau*, was that of *reinvention*. True to Freire's concept, we worked in the classroom to reinvent *Pedagogy of the Oppressed* within a Maltese context. In this way, Freire's ideas were juxtaposed against those Maltese activists and luminaries who embodied emancipatory ideals, albeit those of the European Enlightenment more than anything else. Two such Maltese key figures were Mikiel Anton Vassalli, who challenged the feudal Hospitaller Order of St. John, and Manwel Dimech, who challenged the British colonizers.

Another aspect of *Pedagogy of the Oppressed* that appealed to many Maltese students was the text's Christian underpinnings and the idea that the Church can be a force for social justice. This makes sense in a nominally Catholic context such as Malta, from where some priests emigrated to Latin America to serve in Brazil and become active in such progressive land reform movements as the Pastoral Land Commission and the Landless Workers' Movement (Movimento dos Trabalhadores Rurais Sem Terra, MST). Moreover, the day of my flying back to Malta from Edmonton, Alberta, in 1988, Frei Betto (Carlos Alberto Libanio Christo), a self-declared Freire disciple, addressed students at our only public university. In my courses, there were students who would connect the book to Betto's emancipatory message in Malta. Here, the strong Marxian and Christian nexus of Liberation Theology, found at the heart of Freire's book, appealed to students. Many considered this an important element, in that it rendered religion more meaningful and palatable to their vision, as it also redefined faith (and pedagogy) as a "liberating praxis" —and this in my non-confessional course units.

In my experience, one of the most challenging concepts to teach from the book is that of *praxis*, to be distinguished from practice or the Italian and Maltese word, prassi. Praxis is often erroneously translated by Maltese and Italians as "prassi," which refers to habitual practice. This is a travesty of the Greek concept of praxis, which, as Freire describes in *Pedagogy of the Oppressed*, is reflection and dialogue for transformative action. This involves reflection and dialogue on the codification of experience into theory to refute, validate, or improve that same theory. I connect this to the well-known Socratic dictum (well known to Maltese students who study this at the sixth form level), from Plato's *Apology*, that the unexamined life is a life not worth living. One must show that this lies at the heart of Paulo Freire's pedagogical political philosophy and the codification/de-codification approach reflects this, though this is no "method" to be generalized: Filosofia Freireana sim, Metodo Freireano não.[6]

One other important feature of Freire's book is the *dialectical* relation. It is a challenge to teach students to think dialectically and, in doing so, to appreciate the way Freire writes the first three chapters of *Pedagogy of the Oppressed*. This task entails getting students to see that what prima facie appear as binary opposites are intimately related; one does not exist without the other. And to go one further, one enables students to appreciate that, in the messy complexity of everyday life, resolving the contradiction of opposites is a critical utopian vision. Therefore, banking and dialogical education exist as ends of a continuum. We strive, as committed progressive educators, to move to one end of the continuum but are buffeted toward the opposite end by the winds of regulation and control in the form of syllabuses, vigilance mechanisms, texts, and all the other forces unleashed on the lifeworld by the "system world." Accepting and engaging with such tensions is tantamount to living and acting critically in the world.

Freire and Education in India

Shivali Tukdeo
Indira Mahindra School of Education (IMSE), Mahindra University
India

Paulo Freire's *Pedagogy of the Oppressed* entered the world of education in India at a time when the long, imposing shadow of colonialism was seemingly fading

---

[6]   Translation: "Freirean Philosophy yes, Freirean Method no."

away, and several new colors with their complications were bursting in. At the time of independence, a sizable population in India had been systematically excluded from formal education (Kumar, 1991; Chopra, Jeffery, and Reifeld, 2005). Adult literacy campaigns and greater expansion of public schooling were two main agendas of the 1950s and 1960s as the newly independent Indian state began to refashion public education. The overall purpose of education as an essential path toward one's own liberation and the shorter, more tangible goals involving skills toward better livelihoods were important in the construction of a national system of education.

Education in the Third World has shouldered an unparallel burden of chaos, instability, and struggle. On the one hand, formal schooling rests on the complicated history of colonialism and violence; and on the other, it pushes to break open the possibilities for democratic thought, participation, and action. As an inherited system, formal education in India continues to remain embroiled in the debates surrounding modernity and tradition; science and religion; and justice and privilege (Nurullah and Naik 1943; Benei, 2008; Tukdeo, 2019). In the midst of such tensions, what possibilities does liberatory education, as Freire proposed, hold within an emergent postcolonial nation? Is it possible to imagine a system of education that could exist outside of the imperialist and feudal logics still embedded within Indian society? What would be the process for the decolonization of education? These and similar questions have been central to our engagement with Freirean thought and its significance to democratizing education in India. Moreover, Freire's attention to the material conditions within which social relations of power get structured and the need to develop a collective political consciousness are crucial to understanding the uneasy transitions India has witnessed.

As the independent Indian state sought to create "a greater India, not a lesser England," several influential paths emerged including Nehru's scientific modernism, Gandhi's local economy, and Phule-Ambedkar's imagination of education as a tool to combat Brahminical order among others. In the midst of this historical shift, Freire's concept of *conscientização* (or conscientization), with respect to the development of political consciousness among students and communities, proved vital to liberatory struggles. Yet, seven decades after independence, as India quietly slides into the aspirational club of developing countries eager to perform its role in the theatre of global capital and educational opportunity and social justice continue to remain important concerns amid a crumbling system of public education, I firmly believe it is useful for us to turn to Freire again.

Since the book was first released, *Pedagogy of the Oppressed* became popular with educators, social movements, students, activists, and theatre groups in India. While there had been impassioned pleas for seeing the layers of exclusion, Freire's text left an impact for its call to humanize us, to keep us from always externalizing the oppressor, and, of course, to dignify the oppressed, their voices, struggles, and politics. The book is still used by aspiring and practicing teachers and artists. I have often wondered about its attraction, considering the changed contexts for teachers in today's India. In the contemporary social life of teaching-learning, with excessive datafication, surveillance, and casualization, what ideas hold ground? In my work with teachers who work in severely underfunded and highly regulated schools, Freirean ideas of fearlessness and humility have guided our practice. Teachers invoke the feeling of family as they care for their students. Through family, the teachers advance a notion of fellow feeling or solidarity with their students and decenter the idea of the distant, authority ideal of a teacher—an idea perpetuated by what Freire describes as a *banking education.*

Paulo Freire's texts and some of the deeper engagements of his texts by scholars such as Darder (2017), hooks (2003), and Giroux (1983b) accompanied me as I began my work as a teacher in a research institution in India. Largely selective by nature, and increasingly being governed by aspirational politics, the institutional space I encountered was small and quaint, without explicit provisions for affirmative action policies. Like several research-focused campuses in India, students came from a wide range of diverse social locations whereas the faculty members were fairly homogenous. The overall academic structure is based on an internalization of the ideology of meritocracy, which was often articulated using different codes such as rigor, scientific practice, and measurable outputs. Observers of Indian higher education are not new to the twin developments in university governance: a growing importance of ranking and similar performative cultures and the erosion of autonomy. In a dehumanizing whirlpool of reforms and regressive practices, I am prompted daily to consider how one can work to enact Freirean concepts such as humility, solidarity, and liberation despite the challenges. As we perform under the enormous weight of structural, historical conditions and strive for small moments of relief and joy, how do we read Freire's insistence on authenticity and humanity? Reflecting on this question, I am always brought back to Freire's words: "At all stages of their liberation, the oppressed must see themselves as women and men engaged in the ontological and historical vocation of becoming more fully human. Reflection and action be-come imperative when one does not erroneously attempt to dichotomize the content of humanity from its historical forms" (Freire, 2005 , p. 66).

Having worked within the context of contentious political and economic conditions in the country and observing a sense of tiredness set in, I have found solace in the patient, wise voice of Freire and other critical scholars who remind us to not let go of the emancipatory purpose of our labor in universities and society. Even when cynicism and failures tell us otherwise, I turn to dialogue, which I believe is Freire's most powerful intellectual contribution to our liberatory understanding. Although we are often cautioned by Freirean scholars against reducing dialogue to a classroom management technique, I must confess that even in its half-done or less experienced execution, I believe dialogic teaching can draw teachers and students toward unexpected turns of clarity, something akin to a tiny blooming flower that pushes through rock, surviving and thriving in its own beauty! My sense is that Freire understood dialogue as an evolving practice and that teachers, just as students, must begin where they are at.

The importance of honoring the lived histories of students has been for me a significant lesson gleaned from Freire's work. Students sit in class, each carrying a unique story. Most of them share a healthy dose of suspicion about education. There is a lot that divides them: unequal backgrounds, schooling, social capital, and what the future may hold. Within the classroom, we begin with our stories and retell those at several points, as the term proceeds. The classroom becomes a space where, for example, uninformed opinions shared by more privileged students are engaged, along with the eruption of anger, hurt, or sharp wit that this can provoke from students from subaltern communities. Here we ask more questions: Can opening up also result in a conversation coming to a screeching halt? How do we understand silence in a dialogic classroom? Or worse, indifference? Why does often the sterilized, sanitized, academic knowledge that promises neutrality and learning outcomes seem so much safer than the unwieldiness of dialogue? Moreover, to grapple with such unruly questions is precisely the underlying purpose of Freire's problem-posing pedagogy, in that its intent is to support teachers and students in breaking the culture of silence.

Freire recognized that this pedagogical process of breaking with the culture of silence is a difficult and complex one. In working with students, classroom dialogues that provide students the space to critically engage stories anchored in their own experience can provoke greater consciousness regarding their own life conditions. In her work tracing changing caste relations in Maharashtra, historian Elenor Zelliot (2013) presents a narrative widely encountered, preserved, and retold. In the late nineteenth century, Kisan Fagoji Bansode enrolled in a school in his village. He was forced to sit outside of class as he was *dalit*—a member of the lowest class in the Hindu social hierarchy. The normalization of exclusion continued, until one day the teacher noticed something. It had started to rain, and Bansode had tried to lean into the classroom, in order to protect himself from rain! Seeing Bansode trying to help himself at that moment profoundly affected his teacher, who told the boy to come inside the classroom. This small cultural narrative, with its power and complexity, swirls around us as we sit in dialogue about its meaning and significance to students' lives.

The power of Freire's *Pedagogy of the Oppressed* is that his ideas and the language he offers us can move us beyond the hesitation, cynicism, and guilt that so many educators and students experience in their everyday lives. Freire provokes to ask the difficult and often unspeakable questions: How do we work to combat structural inequalities? How do we respond to the insurmountable issues that we face in India within the classroom and beyond? How do we even begin to think about genuine transformation? Freire reminds that our past history always bleeds into the present. He argues adamantly that education is the one public sphere remaining where we may still fight collectively for a more just world. Moreover, Freire's uncompromising commitment to literacy and political action reflects a powerful realization: our ability to read and dialogue are essential tools against disabling cynicism and helplessness. And although the path to a genuinely just and transformative world may seem distant, muddled, or unattainable, Paulo Freire's legacy reveals that we can, indeed, begin to take small steps—despite our doubts, fears, and frustrations—and that we can make the impossible possible through our love and solidarity.

Extending Freire through a Critical Feminist Lens

Sheila L. Macrine
University of Massachusetts Dartmouth
United States

Over the past fifty years, Paulo Freire's *Pedagogy of the Oppressed* has inspired educators to renounce "banking" education and to activate *conscientização* or critical consciousness (1970). Freire urges scholars and practitioners to be the "change" they seek in the world, as they teach and learn for democracy, social justice, and the greater good. Freire's (1970) vision of democratic public schooling was not simply about the teaching and learning of content but rather as a transformative process of learning about advocacy (for self and others) and participation in democracy. In his view, democratic public schooling is a seedbed for new knowledge, culture, and the development of a more humane society, marked by a social justice agenda. In his seminal work, he outlined a dialogical method of teaching literacy for empowerment that nurtures *conscientização*—critical consciousness—and encourages active participation in political struggles. So why is this important today? And what does it mean for teachers and students?

Freire's notion of *"conscientização,"* or critical consciousness, epitomizes a different approach to educating and mobilizing the downtrodden masses. He argued that the cultural revolution—education for the "new society"—must begin in the "old society." Noting that a mere change in the power structure without a cultural revolution (i.e., without a heightened awareness by the masses) would again repeat the old hierarchical system of domination. From a critical consciousness perspective, internalized and structural oppression are at the heart of most individual and social (e.g., violence) dysfunction (Chronister and McWhirter, 2006; Mullaly, 2002; Windsor, Jemal, and Benoit , 2014). Therefore, the challenge to educators is to teach empathy and solidarity with the oppressed—who, in many cases, are not in the classroom (Nicholls, 2011).

That said, I teach graduate courses in Special Education. Early in my career as a cognitive psychologist, critical feminist, and activist, I began to see linkages between my advocacy for persons with differences and Freire's philosophy of empowering oppressed populations. I immediately connected with his social justice agenda and the rights of persons with differences who constantly faced bias, prejudice, and discrimination. Therefore, in my classes, we discuss what it means to be a person with differences—whether it be language, race, class, gender, sexuality, cognitive capacity, and so on. During discussions, we explore critical social justice, feminist theory, anti-racism, and anti-discrimination to assist preservice and in-service teachers in developing tools of advocacy and to understand how to teach to combat injustices.

Bringing a Freirean human rights agenda for critical thinking and social justice to my classroom has served as an opportunity to activate *conscientização* for public conversations and critical consciousness-raising about the difficult questions that threaten democracy. Freire's legacy remains pertinent today given our intolerant world and the severe challenges to basic human rights we find everywhere. This is seen in the rise in right-wing politics, prejudice against immigrants and asylum seekers, diminishment of LGBTQ protections, and the deterioration of transexual rights, to name a few. Clearly, the emergence of global social activist's movements such as MeToo, Black Lives Matter, I Can't Breathe, Asia-American Advancing Justice, Gay and Lesbian Rights, Criminal Justice Reform and Latinx Advocacy groups, and others have said enough is enough and have raised the mantel of the early Civil Rights and Anti-Vietnam War movements of the 1960s.

So, once we begin to enter into critical dialogue, Freire proposed, about what multilayered oppression, prejudice, bias, and discrimination is, we soon realize that each of the so-called "protected classes" under federal law state that people cannot be discriminated against on the basis of race, color, national origin, religion, gender, sex, age, or disability. Students soon recognize that the discrimination law is limited, in that it tends to isolate and "compartmentalize categories." As we discuss this law, we realize that these "protected classes" are far from individual silos but rather that discrimination is, in fact, as Freire sought to teach, layered one upon another. For example, racism and sexism combine to shortchange and oppress women of color. Needless to say, if you add disability or age or sexuality, these layers are confounded and hard to tease apart. As such, Freire's notion of critical literacy and *conscientização* shows how courage and determination can create a revolution to help overcome oppressions. In other words, to become an anti-oppressive teacher/ practitioner, educator, and advocate, we need to understand the multiplicity of oppression.

In my teaching, I combine Freirean ideas with a critical feminist lens, which offer students useful ways to engage a critical praxis within a feminist sensibility. For example, the concept of "intersectionality" as an inclusive term for multiple types of layered oppressions has been most helpful. The term, coined by Kimberlé Creshaw (1989), demarginalized the intersections of race and sex within Black Feminist's theoretical critiques. Crenshaw (1989) describes intersectionality with a metaphor of several automobiles (oppression) entering an intersection all at the same time and crashing into one another. As the feminist theory of intersectionality evolved, it is now seen as a synthesis of multiple overlapping oppressions and has proven necessary to understanding a wide range of difference and the connections between gender and sociopolitical categories, such as race, ethnicity, class, gender, sexuality, nationality, (dis) ability, and others—an understanding Freire expressed in his later works.

The late feminist intellectual Iris Marion Young (1988) posits intersectionality as the "five faces of oppression" as: violence, exploitation, marginalization, powerlessness, and cultural imperialism—a wider but yet resonant concept with Freire's *Pedagogy of the Oppressed*. Here, individual, institutional, systemic, and symbolic oppressions create "interlocking systems of oppression" or intersectionalities of oppression. Patricia Hill Collins (2000) uses the concept of intersectionality to analyze how "oppressions [such as 'race and gender' or 'sexuality and nation'] work together in producing injustice" (p. 282) but adds the concept "matrix of dominations," which "refers to how these intersecting oppressions are actually organized. Regardless of the particular intersections involved, structural, disciplinary, hegemonic, and interpersonal domains of power reappear across quite different forms of oppression" (Collins, 2000, p. 18).

Collins and Bilge (2016) argue that today's growing social inequalities foster a rethinking of gender, race, and class as distinct social categories of identity, postulating that systems of social oppression are mutually constituted and work together to produce social inequality. These examples suggest that the "moral positions as survivors of one expression of systemic violence become eroded in the absence of accepting responsibility of other expressions of systemic violence" (Collins, 2000, p. 247). This concept, in particular, echoes Freire's ideas about how the oppressed being fearful for their freedom internalize the image of the *oppressor* and adopt the rules and guidelines of the dominant class.

Hence, I have found in my work that Freire's ideas, when combined with a feminist lens, are important to the preparation of teachers and students. More specifically, a Freirean- inspired pedagogy (1) strengthens the philosophical underpinning of critical practices in education (i.e., his dialogical approach to learning vis-à-vis the banking model of education adds philosophic strength to problem-posing as a primary learning modality); (2) encourages educators to confront directly the tension between teaching for conformity and teaching for liberation—where it is critical to question current assumptions, practices, and knowledge; and (3) encourages expanded thought about approaches to education, for example, in the choice of pedagogical method, defining the role of the educator, and the use of experiences like service learning and advocacy.

Today the legacy of Freire's *Pedagogy of the Oppressed* continues to provide us with comprehensive analyses of issues related to struggles against the forces of prejudice, oppressions, and biases, not just in education but in all of social life for *radical democratization*. Hence, despite reactionary conservative efforts to erase Freire's legacy and history from schools and curriculum, his work remains steadfast as critical Freirean pedagogues continue to stand up, bear witness, and act—with renewed vigor and urgency. True to the liberatory vision of his life, Paulo Freire remains a source of hope and possibility for educators and activists engaged in struggles against oppression within classrooms and beyond.

Cultural Invasion and the Question of Language in Tanzania

Tage Biswalo
University of Tanzania
Tanzania

Teaching *Pedagogy of the Oppressed* is a somewhat challenging experience in the current political atmosphere. There is a lot of hostility toward disseminating ideas that go against the grain (i.e., the neoliberal school of thought). Countries that used to be progressive in educational endeavors have fallen prey to the "new world order thinking." With this in mind, I want to focus this brief essay on Freire's concept of "cultural invasion," specifically regarding the question of language and language of instruction.

Cultural invasion, as Freire describes it in *Pedagogy of the Oppressed*, is inextricably linked to creating a "culture of silence" that often leads to annulling the language and culture of oppressed people. The issue of language has become so critical that it has led many scholars and activists alike to point out that officials/policymakers need to rethink local language policies, as we are in danger of reverting to the old order of linguistic colonization. Over the years, I have had conversations with colleagues in Tanzania on the matter. For example, Elana Shohamy (2006) posits:

Language has become a tool for the manipulation of people and their behaviors,

> as it is used for a variety of political agendas in the battle of power, representation, and voice ... [it has become] a political instrument ... through language . . . group memberships are determined, leading to categories of "us" and "them," inclusion and exclusion, loyalty and "foreign-ness," "haves" and "have-nots" . . . [and] further as a tool for legitimizing people. (22)

Moreover, language usage and language policy generally have reflected progress under the politics of modernity. A nation or society that uses "civilized" or leading languages of the West (i.e., English, French) is considered to possess "superior" civility. As such, individuals too are seen as belonging to a civilized stratum of a particular group or society. Stuart Hall (Hall and du

Guy, 1996) alludes to this process as a "formation of modernity." He identifies four key social processes echoed in Freire's work: political, economic, social, and cultural. These characteristics have played a major role in defining the conditions of modernity, where each is distinct but historically linked in ways that perpetuate inequalities and social exclusions.

Freire's work is useful in helping students to unpack conditions of oppression, in that it highlights the ways in which the dominant culture and language of the colonizer function as levers of cultural invasion within the context of what he referred to banking education. Through Freire's articulations, students can begin to question the way in which the reenforcement of Western "othering" processes renders inferior those seen outside of its historical and epistemological scope. Similarly, Ngugi wa Thiongo (1986) insists that language is culture and culture is language (15). Hence, it is not surprising that for Freire, the connection between culture and language is considered critical to the politics of schooling, particularly in its manifestation of cultural invasion in the education of subaltern populations (Darder, 2012). In reference to this phenomenon, the UNICEF report, *An Unfair Start* (Chzhen et al., 2018), notes:

> Some children do worse at school than others because of circumstances beyond their control, such as where they were born, the language they speak or their parents' occupations. These children enter the education system at a disadvantage and can drop further behind if educational policies and practices reinforce, rather than reduce, the gap between them and their peers.

Many newly independent African countries were blessed with a diversity of languages. However, unlike many other African countries that decided to fully pursue inherited European languages, Tanzania chose to elevate Kiswahili as its lingua franca. This was by design, with the purposes of mass mobilization to realize nation- building efforts. In essence, Tanzania's language choice was tied to the political-state ideology. It was designed to elevate an egalitarian ideology as well as nationalist and Pan-Africanist views. It was an attempt by the government to rid the country of its vestiges of colonialism. More importantly, language was used as a tool to promote the *Ujamaa* socialist policy. However, it seems the revolutionary ideas of the postcolonial government of the 1960s and 1970s have been forgotten to the detriment of the citizenry. The neoliberal machine has betrayed what was envisioned. In short, the neoliberal agenda has managed to obliterate the foundation of what was once a revolutionary project.

It is generally acknowledged that the mastery of language enhances learning across all spheres of knowledge. Language assists the learners to effectively engage their environment. In his work, Kidd and Carel (2016) ask critical questions that resonate with Freire's pedagogical project. These include: Who has voice and who doesn't? Are voices interacting with equal agency and power? In whose terms are they communicating? Who is being understood and who isn't (and at what cost)? Who is being believed? And who is even being acknowledged and engaged with? Working to address such questions with my students is the juncture where Freire's perspective on the culture of silence is most useful. As the language of globalization, English has been the single most powerful "culprit" in perpetuating cultural, economic, and social disruption within colonized societies. About this, Walter Bgoya (2001) argues, "English is the language of globalisation and English serves fundamentally the interests of those for whom it is both an export commodity and a language of conquest and domination" (p. 286).

Freire's efforts to challenge the "culture of silence" points to the role education ought to play in the emancipation of the learners. Freire argues, however, that education can serve as an oppressive or liberating process. It can only be liberating if the means to attainment of education relate directly to the learners' realization of benefits. In my teaching, it has been made very clear that the language of instruction is a key factor to ensure that students reap the benefits of education. This benefit is best realized through dialogue, as Freire explains, that creates the conditions for students' expression of voice and social agency. In contrast, when the possibility of dialogue between the teacher and students is broken in the process of teaching and learning due to a language barrier, student learning is impaired and anticipated learning outcomes cannot be realized. The consequence, of course, is the perpetuation of a culture of silence, carried out, deliberately or otherwise, through a pedagogical process of cultural invasion.

Freire also speaks in *Pedagogy of the Oppressed* about the need to move beyond reformism in our work to enact emancipatory education. Tanzania language policy is a useful example here. Recognizing the importance of the language of instruction, the Policy of Education in Tanzania provides for the use of Kiswahili, the commonly known language of the people, at the primary school level while building a foundation and preparation for the use of the English language at secondary and tertiary levels of education. While this arrangement might appease the public desire for multilingualism and keeping abreast with globalization, its implementation has not been without challenges. Studies have shown that where the preparation has not been successful (in terms of building teachers' and learners' language competence), handling interaction and fruitful engagement has proved difficult.

To ensure effective interaction at secondary and tertiary levels of education, it is imperative for Tanzania to embark on a strategic educational investment to improve the academic linguistic competence—across both Kiswahili and English—of teachers and learners at secondary and tertiary levels. The issue here, as Freire often stated, is not whether one language or another is given primacy but rather language reform that doesn't enact a structural pedagogical commitment to literacy across schools and societies will be limited in its capacity to break with the colonizing dynamics of linguistics oppression, particularly within countries still grappling with the historical impact of colonization.

Through my experience teaching and supervising students in the field when they are conducting their practicals (student-teaching), I have observed a few of the contradictions that Freire unveils in *Pedagogy of the Oppressed*. For example, most teachers are teaching English as a subject (a commodified object) and not a language (a human process). Students in Tanzania, for example, can develop reading, listening, and writing skills in English with little speaking proficiency or actual practice at all. As such, there is negative reinforcement in English acquisition. Students are punished if they fail to use English at school. They are punished in class if they make mistakes. Many teachers teaching at secondary education levels are not proficient in the language of instruction, which makes it a herculean task to motivate learners to speak the language, let alone enter into a critical dialogue about their lived experiences or the larger society.

Finally, echoing Freire's literacy work in Sao Tome, Angola, Mozambique, and Tanzania, research on language use and learning has repeatedly shown that students learn better in their primary language—that is the language they understand best. However, more times than not, children are denied the right to learn in the languages of their communities, which they understand well. As *Pedagogy of the Oppressed* remind us, forcing students to learn in a foreign language far removed from their culture is to perpetuate the "culture of silence." My work as a teacher educator in Tanzania is to challenge notions of cultural invasion within education and seek pedagogical language practices that support the critical literacy development of students and communities. Freire's *Pedagogy of the Oppressed* continues to be an inspiration that fuels my work.

Radical Encounters in University Classrooms: A Freirean Praxis of Dialogue

Tal Dor
CENS— Nantes Université/CNRS
LEGS— Université Paris 8 /CNRS
France

To properly reflect on my experience of teaching Paulo Freire's *Pedagogy of the Oppressed*, I must begin by positioning myself within my feminist formations (and transformations), which enables me to reflect upon my practice as a teacher and educator. This approach bears witness to my multiple positions and positionalities as a constant process "in the making"— in my persistent quest to ask questions as I seek to understand and deconstruct colonial power dynamics that persist in our lives. For example, in my home context, the Israeli matrix of domination and coloniality, I am positioned within what Sara Ahmed (2007) calls "whiteness." I was born into an Anglo-Saxon, South African family. I never lived in South Africa but always wished I could be part of the life that my grandparents left behind. Today I understand that the reason life *"there"* seemed better than life *"here"* was drawn from a common sense of what I call "colonial arrogance."

When I embarked upon my journey of doctoral studies, the epistemological knowledge developed by Paulo Freire and bell hooks on a liberatory consciousness of transformation guided my work. My doctoral research focused on learning what *TransFormation* of political consciousness meant to several Palestinian and Jewish-Israeli political actors, citizens of the State of Israel. Drawing from Freire's ideas, in conversation with feminist epistemologies, I understand TransFormation as an ongoing process through which one perceives the world and one's positions within it. It is a constant task of making knowledge on one hand and an evolving praxis toward profound change on the other. TransFormation is a quest for change that leads to self-realization and the (re)creation of reality. In Freirean terms, the concept echoes conscientização—a critical consciousness for liberation.

However, I must also explain that previous to this, when I was in the field leading actions as an activist, the idea of spending hours alone in front of a computer with books and articles was foreign to my life. My on-the-ground work then comprised of political educational work in "Mahapach," facilitation of Israeli and Palestinian encounter groups, the recognition of the Nakba, and the right of return for all Palestinian refugees, specifically through the work of Zochrot, participation in direct anti-occupation actions and activities against the Israeli army. To all this, I was strongly devoted and engaged since the start of the Second Intifada in 2000.

When I began teaching at a public university in France in 2010, where I have been living for the past fifteen years, I entered the French university classroom with an enthusiasm to finally bring into *praxis* my critical and feminist pedagogical knowledge. I set as a goal to be a teacher who would not "deposit" Knowledge—with a capital K (Freire and Faundez, 1989, p. 45)— within the students but rather to be a teacher who would enter into critical dialogue with them, as Freire advanced in his problem-posing approach. My aim was to cultivate dialogue that would motivate the development of critical consciousness, supporting a dynamic learning process in movement. This is a dialogical process, as Freire described in *Pedagogy of the Oppressed*, which enables students to perceive themselves in the world in complex ways as well

‚as understand the sociopolitical contradictions that shape their commonsense understanding of the world.

Unfortunately, despite my enthusiasm, my eyes were opened when I realized I was alone. There was no critical supervision nor critical dialogue to be found, neither with my colleagues nor with the institution. We were all overwhelmed with the number of students we had to teach, trying to remember their names, while putting faces with their names. At the same time, students often seemed more interested in getting a high grade than in learning. While my curriculum had been set for the year, I now realized that I had to go back and (re)read Freire's *Pedagogy of the Oppressed*, and hooks's *Teaching to Transgress*, in order to find my own creative way to make pedagogical sense with students so that their "education could be the practice of freedom" (hooks, 1994, p. 14).

Revisiting these texts allowed me to *reinvent*, as Freire urged, new ways and methods of critically engaging students on one hand and supporting them to advance in their academic work on the other. This sort of engaged pedagogy, I often remind myself, is hard work and demands creativity and openness by the teacher. It demands seeing students as young adults who have their own interests and are not just numbers or objects to be counted and manipulated. Teachers also have responsibility, as Freire suggested, to accompany students in their learning. In other words, it requires embodying a healthy and empowering process of teaching and learning. So, I made up my mind early on to be in constant dialogue with students, no matter what. A central tenet of *Pedagogy of the Oppressed* is that to challenge and transgress the oppressive system of *banking education*, we must find creative ways to teach and to enter into critical dialogue—radical, reflexive, and meaningful conversations—despite the difficulties we face.

Similarly, *Pedagogy of the Oppressed* inspires educators to confront power dynamics and counter the oppressive system of schooling that shapes students' learning. To carry this out effectively requires engaging students' lived experiences and creating the room for them to critique the institution, as well as their teachers and their classes. In my teaching, encouraging students to question has become my principal aim. Encouraging critical thought among students, of course, can be a challenge, given the culture of silence that often drives the traditional classroom environment. In contrast, liberatory educators must create a platform for students' desire to learn and their curiosity for knowledge to be expressed. But, even in so doing, I realize this still requires me to situate myself critically, by reflecting upon my position and critically observing the power relations that shape my reality. This points to a critically *objective* path (Haraway, 1988) that moves us toward the production of situated feminist knowledge.

The quest for a humanizing pedagogy is ultimately at the heart of Freire's *Pedagogy of the Oppressed*. This asks us to engage with students in ways that consistently express a sense of faith in them and an acceptance for who they are. One of the best ways I have found to accomplish this is to get to know who students are and their fields of interest, as well as what they consider relevant to in their learning. In parallel, I read *Pedagogy of the Oppressed* and *Learning to Transgress* with my students, asking them to reflect on the ways these texts touch their lives. In many instances, students particularly those from minority and racialized communities often express appreciation, in that they feel, for the first time, they can identify, in concrete ways, with their classroom reading.

Today, I enter the classroom each time seeking to enter into what I call a *Radical Encounter* (Dor, 2018) with students—an encounter that thrives to nurture dialogue, that questions the power dynamics at work, that critiques knowledge developed from a dominant *standpoint,* while acknowledging how our own gendered, ethnic/racial, and/or national positions are at work—as both teachers and students.

Today when I enter my classroom, whether I encounter young students in their very first years of university or as graduate and postgraduate students in educational sciences and sociology, I know that teaching and learning cannot be disconnected from either our personal or public lives and that we all exist collectively on this world. But I also enter my classroom with an unfaltering commitment to liberate myself from arrogant patterns so often unjustly acquired within our positions of power (and authority) within schools, universities, or other contexts of coloniality.

Paulo Freire for a Revolutionary Impulse

Alpesh Maisuria
University of the West of England
United Kingdom

In my teaching as a university professor, I have found that many students in Education programs are often apathetic about politics and theory, but they *are* interested in inequality, and this provides an excellent inroad for political education in the classroom. As Freire posits, in *Pedagogy of the Oppressed*, education without engaging politics makes it impotent in making social and material change within schools and societies. Instead, the kind of political education needed, as Freire indicates, is for the development of conscientização, which entails building consciousness about questions of social class and the impact of neoliberalism on students' lives.

In keeping with Freire's insistence that we begin where learners are at, I use the British comedian and activist Russell Brand to connect with students. Brand's docu-film *The Emperor's New Clothes* is a useful pedagogic device to highlight the astronomical level of income inequality between workers and the capitalist class. Many of Freire's concerns become more available for dialogue within the classroom by students watching the film. For instance, in the film Brand starkly shows that it would take 300 years for an average cleaner, cleaning the office of an elite capitalist, to earn the same as that capitalist. This is a powerful explication of inequality and contemporary exploitation. It provokes useful dialogue about a range of issues that explicate the centrality of social class and the need to be conscious of neoliberalism as a real material process that we are forced to embody, internalize, and live out. Only when this consciousness is emergent can we seriously discuss how pedagogy, in all its forms, can be used most efficaciously to realize our innate agency for liberation (see Maisuria, 2016). In this sense, activities that promote students to examine their world more critically assist them to open the way for the development of consciousness and awareness of their positionality as subjects of history.

The experience of facilitating these dialogues that echo Freire's approach also entails critical reflection or internal conversation (Archer, 2003) in learning about the often nuanced and sophisticated realties and struggles of others (Freire, 2005)—struggles that can cause dissonance and discomfort. Knowing how difficult critical dialogue can be for students, I encourage openness by saying to them: "what we are *all* doing is identifying an external and inner-reality, and this can be hard because we will discover our 'chains that shackle us'" (Marx, 1848). I continue my guiding by stating that this is part of the "fear of freedom" that Freire referred to—"who is afraid of freedom, put your hands up!" I put my own hand up but often find that I am the only one! My objective here is about opening up the epistemological field for the development of consciousness and for critical interrogation of reality. This includes problematization of notions of *democracy* and *liberty*, which we discuss as potentially mendacious conceptual devices, designed to mystify reality and justify the prohibition of flourishing of the many.

To address my question in the classroom, "Why the masses acquiesce to the status quo?," Freire's engagement with the concept of *mystification* in *Pedagogy of the Oppressed* is powerful for us. Drawn from Marx, mystification offers students a tool of explanatory critique to better understand a condition in which there is a purposeful negating of deep reality. This creates an exclusion of consciousness that frames capitalism as an exploitative and alienating political economic ideology. We discuss capitalism as destructive and this view as being buffered by capitalists who govern us through their purposeful crafting of the dominant socioculture (see Maisuria, 2016) that informs hegemonic schooling and the larger society.

In his discussion on the schooling of the oppressed, Freire points to the way that the masses are conditioned to believe that it is too much of a difficult terrain to discuss political economy and ideology, and so they should leave it to the experts. Similarly, people are told that politics is about pragmatism and difficult decisions, beyond their understanding. For example, the ruling class often asserts that their policies are about what works and what's "right" not about ideological dogmas (i.e., Tony Blair's case for the invasion of Iraq is used as an exemplar in my teaching). Since most of my students aspire to be school-based practitioners, Freire's ideas encourage them as classroom teachers to critically consider with their pupils why this approach to governance exists and who benefit from a consenting and laissez-faire public. Often in my classroom, the discussion moves on to unveil students' experiences and the utility of an education system that promotes what Freire referred to as banking education—where today, high-stakes testing and league tables function to sustain a system of inequality and alienation.

In *Pedagogy of the Oppressed*, Freire's discussion also signals a concerted attempt by the capitalist ruling class to create a mass belief in the existence of meritocracy and social mobility in direct contradiction with students' life histories. With this in mind, we often discuss openly the success of sociocultural and political narratives that generate justification for mass inequality by, for example, deeming people who are poor as not having tried hard enough nor taking opportunities offered to succeed; and therefore, they *deserve* their lot—the class system has nothing to do with it! Freire's notion of "false generosity" is useful to this analysis, in that it unveils the hypocrisy of a *deserving poor*, which is allied with the idea of a deserving stratum of people who have worked hard to become prosperous, privileged, and powerful (Maisuria, 2021).

Mechanisms of Fatalism

Similarly, Freire's idea of "fatalism" is important here in considering with students how our individual and collective consciousness is purposefully conditioned to accept and acquiesce to unfairness and inequality (Freire, 2005, p. 59). It also points to the *colonized mentality* that internalizes oppression as self-creation (Freire, 2005, pp. 62–3) and emerges through nine identifiable mechanisms that oscillate in degrees of intra-dependency. By critically interrogating the following statements in our dialogues through group work and subsequent role-play, students can more effectively reflect and dialogue on how these are operating in their own lives (see Maisuria, 2016):

1. Neoliberalism best serves the economy through talented individuals being rewarded: self-interest is key for us all to individually prosper.
2. The investment in the concept of *society*, rather than *self*, promotes social loafing and laziness.
3. Selfishness is good because it incentivizes and motivates.

4. *There is no alternative* (TINA) to the status quo.
5. The alternatives to neoliberal capitalism that may/do exist are not feasible because:
    a. They are less desirable since they promote reliance on welfare—those who scrounge from the State or rely on others to be productive, on balance, the status quo is *as good as it gets.*
    b. The problems of inequality are outweighed by the good stuffs (i.e., the availability of commodities).
6. In the end, the communist/socialist alternative is not feasible because it is idealist and utopian, not practically realistic and will end with brutality and barbarism.
7. Inequality is natural. It has always existed in human relations, and always will. It is nature and part of the history of the past and will be the history of the future.
8. We are genetically wired to be competitive and neoliberalism facilitates this most inner urge. Self-interest promoted in political economy and socioculture (i.e., education policy that focuses on personal investment and return in the labor market) aligns with our nature.
9. Neoliberalism advances civilization through advancement in productive technologies.

There is no question that Paulo Freire's *Pedagogy of the Oppressed*, at the time it was written, was focused on the feasibility of revolution. He understood that mechanisms are indeed enmeshed in our social condition (Archer, 2003), and these give rise to oppressive ubiquitous messages that surround us. Two of these include:

-   nothing *needs* to be done,
-   nothing *can* be done for serious change, it's unfeasible.

These messages are effectively symbolized in the popular British cultural slogan: *keep calm and carry on* with suffixes such as *shopping, drinking tea,* which ironically adorns my tea mug while discussing the nine mechanisms and culture (Maisuria, 2016).

Alternatives and Revolutionary Praxis

However, as Freire understood only too well, doing liberatory work with students can potentially cause despairing and may seem counterintuitive, in that there is a real danger that efforts to stimulate awareness and build consciousness about class and neoliberalism may also ignite fatalism, reinforcing the status quo. To negate this, I encourage students to be conscious of the availability of alternatives. As example, I use the Thatcher's maxim of "There is no Alternative" (TINA), commonly heard in English society, to demonstrate the dangers to the ruling class represented by what Freire (2005) posited as a "consciousness of consciousness" among the oppressed (p. 79) and ways in which this can nurture their political formation and what Antonio Gramsci called an optimism of the will.

Further, the act of "naming" (Freire, 2005, p. 86) those mechanisms that create a colonized mentality is pedagogically purposeful for demystification and appetizing *for* feasibility; and this happens best when a mirror is held up to the self and society. The cognitive dissidence that emerges demands making cognizant *how* and *why* these mechanisms appear in our lives and how these affect our consciousness and impact on our practices and agency. Existential questions emerge from engaging in such activity: What nature, power, and capacity do humans possess to remake society (Archer, 2003)?

In Freire's discussion of political leadership, he expressed the significance and necessity of liberatory educators, as cultural workers, to take a lead in revolutionary change through praxis-building dialogue in the world, always open to our larger well-being or eudaimonia (Bhaskar, 2016, p. 164; Freire, 2005, p. 89). However, to do this, we must understand that our labor as educators in the classroom is to learn, create, and engage in the process of revolutionary class struggle (Allman, 1999). Paulo Freire's (2005) invitation for "people [to] carry out a revolution" (p. 162) is the pulse of his pedagogy of the oppressed—a pulse committed to the liberation of our humanity, not our domestication.

Pedagogy of the Oppressed and Trauma-Informed Teaching and Learning

Marcelle Cacciattolo
Victoria University
Australia

I am a teacher educator in an Australian University situated in the west of Melbourne in the state of Victoria. The west of Melbourne is a place and space that has higher rates of unemployment, poverty, homelessness, and social isolation. It also attracts large numbers of newly arrived refugees who have encountered repeated traumatic experiences. Trauma trails made up of forced geographical displacement, racial violence, disability, and genocide are symbolic of many of the families who live in this region.

Many our preservice teachers undertake their practicum in the West. This has meant working alongside children and young people who show emotional and behavioral signs of complex trauma in the classroom. When reflecting on their time in schools, a great proportion of preservice teachers are unaware of what it means to engage in trauma-sensitive teaching and learning approaches. Traditional disciplinary practices such as rewards and punishments often form the basis for discussion around ways of effectively dealing with disobedient students. Pedagogic motivational strategies and/or the threat of disciplinary consequences serve as a dehumanizing tool that seeks to further alienate and silence trauma- affected learners. Moreover, the adoption of a one-size-fits-all approach to addressing disruptive behavior is illustrative of a preservice teacher's inexperience. A safe and culturally inclusive environment is responsive to the nuanced needs of all learners including those from marginalized and disadvantaged backgrounds (L'Estrange and Howard, 2022).

A critique of preservice teacher interactions with school students who have been impacted by trauma, framed through Freire's *Pedagogy of the Oppressed* (1970), provides an analysis of emancipatory learning. As a teacher educator, I have used this text as a starting point for considering pedagogical standpoints that get in the way of emancipatory and liberatory educative spaces. In chapter two, Freire explores the "banking approach" to education and its impact on stifling and annihilating student agency and creativity. This theory of learning positions the role of the teacher as "depositors" of knowledge "which the students patiently receive, memorize, and repeat" (p. 72). In my work with preservice teachers, we read out loud and discuss the ten characteristics of oppressive teacher actions as presented by Freire in chapter two of *Pedagogy of the Oppressed*.

What follows is usually a critical interrogation of the meaning/s behind each of the principles. Conversations on teaching qualities that embody a question-posing approach are encouraged (Freire, 1998b). In my tutorials, preservice teachers are asked to provide examples of their own schooling, or practicum interactions, where teachers or school leaders have enacted some of the principles that Freire lays in his work. This activity always brings with it lengthy discussions and insightful analysis of the impact of didactic teaching approaches that cultivate a pedagogy of oppression.

Over the years, I have come to realize that this activity can be extended as a pedagogical provocation tool for critiquing and considering the lived experiences of children and young people who are trauma survivors. The same questions reframed through a trauma lens draw attention to the impact of fear and anxiety on an individual's ability to fully engage with the learning process. A reinventing of these ten principles, as follows, can be used by teacher educators, teachers, and school leaders to explore pedagogical perspectives that can derail the construction of a trauma-sensitive classroom.

(a) The teacher ignores the signs and symbols of trauma when they teach, and the students are taught while feeling pain, fear, and anxiety.

(b) The teacher knows everything about the impact of trauma on the lives of children and the students' lived experiences of trauma count for nothing.

(c) The teacher thinks about trauma situations that students are faced with and the students are thought about.

(d) The teacher talks to students who have mental, physical, social, and cognitive impairments because of trauma and the students listen.

(e) The teacher disciplines students who display difficulties with self-regulation and concentration—a consequence of trauma and the students are disciplined.

(f) The teacher chooses and enforces their choice on trauma-informed teaching approaches, and the students comply.

(g) The teachers act with the intention of performing through their positionality of what it means to experience trauma and the students have the illusion of acting through the action of the teacher.

(h) The teacher chooses the program content that lacks trauma-sensitive activities and materials, and the students (who were not consulted) adapt to it.

(i) The teacher confuses the knowledge of trauma-informed pedagogies with *his* own professional authority, which *he* sets in opposition to the freedom of students.

(j) The teacher is the Subject of the learning process when managing young people who exhibit signs of trauma, while the pupils are mere objects.

During this activity I consciously engage in a "pedagogy of dialogue" (Freire, 1970). Through the medium of dialogical teaching, there evolves a recognition that all learning and knowing occurs through social connections. Dialogic encounters also privilege states of vulnerability and "uncertainty." Preservice teachers are innately aware of a process of becoming that involves a recognition that they are "unfinished" and "uncompleted beings" (Freire, 1970, p. 65). Throughout the dialogic reflective process, preservice teachers are also "encouraged to engage in the world within its complexity and fullness, in order to reveal the possibilities of new ways of constructing thought and action beyond how it currently exits" (Darder, Baltodano, and Torres, 2017, p. 11). In this way, they come to realize that transformational change requires ongoing dialogue that involves holding the mirror up and asking the question, "what could be otherwise?" Most importantly, there is an understanding that one never becomes an expert in the field of trauma-informed pedagogies, nor do practitioners work in isolation in the development of trauma-informed educative spaces (Howard, 2018). Rather, teaching in liberative and emancipatory ways is a moral and political act. There is also the realization that becoming a trauma-sensitive practitioner is a lifelong commitment that involves working in solidarity with others, including teachers, students, parents, and community.

In the adoption of a praxis inquiry trauma-informed learning space, the teacher educator works alongside his/her/their students to generate new theories of liberatory practice. Preservice teachers create shared understandings of what it means to stand in the shoes of learners from trauma backgrounds (Connell, 1993). This requires a critique of one's positionality and of cultural values that are embodied (either consciously or unconsciously) that oppress marginalized learners even further. There is also a shift in one's ontological gaze and in the way practical questions are asked. Instead of beginning with the starting premise of "what is wrong with you?," trauma-sensitive teachers ask, "what happened to you?" (Van der Kolk, 2015). Similarly, the Freirean-inspired question, "how did you come to be as you are?," is important to this process. Such question presuppose that there are a range of complex forces at play that have led to this moment in time and who each of us is in that moment. McInerney and McKlindon (2014, p. 2) make the point that "by being sensitive to students' past and current experiences with trauma, educators can break the cycle of trauma, prevent re-traumatization, and engage a child in learning and findings success in school." In many ways, this idea of breaking the cycle of trauma—an outcome of disabling relationships—is also at the heart of Freire's *Pedagogy of the Oppressed*, where respect for the humanity and dignity of students are paramount.

Making Another Knowledge and Another Praxis Possible

Maria Alfredo Moreira
Research Centre in Education, University of Minho
Portugal

As a teacher and teacher educator, working in the field of didactics and teacher supervision, I strive to develop a scholarship of teaching and learning that articulates sound technical skills with an awareness of the political and ethical implications of teacher work. To that end, the writings of Paulo Freire and other critical intellectuals have been of paramount importance in this endeavor, given the oppressive context in which we seek to practice liberatory education. The dominant neoliberal ideology espouses educational quality and excellence as value free, as if schools and teacher education take place in egalitarian societies where no profound economic disparities, such as racism, sexism, injustices, or social inequalities, exist (Darder, 2015; Torres Santomé, 2006). In the so-called "neutral space" that is the classroom, student teachers are trained by way of apolitical practices (Freire, 2013, p. 95), a condition that, when they become teachers, they in turn seek to recreate for all students, regardless of who they are, where they come from, or what their aspirations and strengths mat be.

When I hear teachers and student teachers say: "preparing [elementary] students to the tests"[7] or "we have to prepare children to be competitive" or "we have to prepare children for the job market," I realize something is fundamentally wrong with the culture of schooling. Accordingly, there is still the much-needed task of "exercising critical judgement in the resistance to the sly power of ideology" (Freire, 2013, p. 130, transl.). Here, an analysis and critique of *banking education*, as Freire outlined in *Pedagogy of the Oppressed* (1975), continues to be a necessity in our times—over fifty years after the book was published. In my teaching, I have found Freire's seminal work to be significant in assisting students to gain an enhanced consciousness about their own conditions. In three instances, for example, when I invited student teachers to reflect on their schooling experiences, after reading Freire's chapter on banking education (1975, pp. 79–107), their comments help to illustrate some of the shifts they began to experience through their reflection and dialogue about their reading.

> I wasn't used to teachers asking my opinion on anything. As Paulo Freire states, "there is no creativity, there is no transformation, there is no knowledge" in banking education. In my first year at the university, I would react negatively when teachers would ask for my opinion. Banking education is responsible for this reaction as, being used to storing and memorizing

---

[7] All excerpts used in this text are from data collected and then statements translated from the Portuguese.

content and not to exercise critical thinking, students end up being afraid or even disgusted when an opinion is asked of them. (C., April 2021)

When analyzing and comparing the features of banking education with my own experience, there were conservative attitudes that I lived as a student in my relationship with my teachers. . . . Throughout elementary and secondary education, the teaching method would only require that the student memorize content, without dialogue. Students should not question the teacher about what was being taught, because truth would be found only in the teacher's words. (A., April 2021)

During my schooling path, the teacher would be the one who would know about the content and the student would not possess any knowledge whatsoever. The teacher would be in a higher stand and could not be questioned in any manner. . . . However, in secondary education, I was given the opportunity to teach something to my teachers in oral presentations, where dialogue between teacher and learner was possible. This dialogue would bring a collision of ideas, resulting in mutual learning. This was the closest I have ever got to a problematization conception of education, [or a] revolutionary practice, a practice that encourages the learner to question reality and the world he/ she lives in. (N., April 2021)

Along with other critical educators, Freire's *Pedagogy of the Oppressed* has assisted me to unveil the current consequences of the still prevailing banking method of education as well as provided me a language for discussing the impact of this approach on the lives of teachers and students. I strive to critically engage students in ways that strengthen their critical awareness regarding *curriculum epistemicides* (Paraskeva, 2016) in Portuguese schools; the ways the construction of neoliberal, conservative, and neocolonial sensibilities work (Torres Santomé, 2017); and the consequences of conditions that force oppressed groups into a *world of absences* (Santos, 2008). When I hear students or teachers referring to Roma minorities—the ethnic group with the highest rate of school dropout and retention in Portugal[8]—"*she is well behaved even though she is a gypsy*," or "*I have normal students and a few Roma*," or "*we are*

---

[8] See Direção-Geral de Estatísticas da Educação e Ciência (mec.pt).

giving them what is best for them [vocational training]—they have neither the cognitive ability nor the cultural competence to achieve more than this," I am reminded of Freire's (2013) words, "reason is ideological, not grammatical" (48, transl.). Such racializing reasoning and ideologies as those that underly the preceding comments need to be carefully deconstructed in our teaching. By turning these commonsensical beliefs on their head, teachers and students begin to recognize, as Freire (1997b) argues, "school abandonment and dropout are ideological constructs: students do not abandon school willingly—they are abandoned by the school, in several ways prohibited of inhabiting it" (p. 10).

By unveiling the archaeology of teacher work through an understanding of education as either a praxis of domination or liberation, Freire's (1975) *Pedagogy of the Oppressed* has helped me expose the slyness by which the dominant ideology normalizes or makes "natural" structural subalternity for the "usual suspects" in our public schools, prohibiting their democratic participation. Building on my students' lived experience and inviting them into dialogue with the ideas of Paulo has been invaluable to work as a teacher educator. Nurtured by the teachings of *Pedagogy of the Oppressed*, I have worked consistently to facilitate a critical pedagogical praxis with students that seeks to disrupt dominant ideologies and epistemologies that reproduce distorted knowledge and conserve oppressive paradigms of schooling and society. And finally, through a commitment to lovingly expand the horizons of future teachers, we work together to make another world knowledge and another praxis possible.

Beyond "Bread and Circus": Reading and Teaching *Pedagogy of the Oppressed*

Kevin D. Lam
Drake University
United States

I initially read *Pedagogy of the Oppressed* in the first class of my teacher education program. My intent, at the time, was to receive a Multiple Subject

Credential for elementary education. In the course, we were introduced to texts by scholars in critical pedagogy with an emphasis on curriculum theory, including a chapter from Freire's book. I must confess, I remember little from my first reading. I was not sure about what I was looking at or how to go about reading the chapter. However, it was clear to me, even then, that it was an important text that needed to be engaged carefully. Although I had been a sociology major and had read Marx, Weber, Durkheim, and others, I was not able to connect with the texts. I now realize that, as a working-class student, I was never prepared academically to read theory. As I became immersed in critical theory while working on my teaching credential, I felt a great sense of fear and insecurity in the process. Reflecting on that fear, two decades later, I recognize that it was simply part of being immersed in learning how to read theory. I was, as Freire would say, learning *to read the word and the world* (Freire and Macedo, 1987). It was the feeling of this new experience that helped me to know that I had encountered something that spoke to my humanity. Paulo Freire was, for me, a first step into a radically new way of understanding myself and my world.

Many years later, as I began working as a professor at a predominantly white institution, I used Freire's ideas in my efforts to engage issues of culture and difference. Having studied at a working-class institution, where most of the students were of color, reading *Pedagogy of the Oppressed* made sense at the very core of our lived experience. However, as a young faculty at a private university in the Midwest, I found that although the language of diversity was quite prominent, serious engagement with oppression was noticeably missing. The environment posed for me a series of limit situations, as described by Freire, that required me to navigate critically my new context in new ways that stretched my own consciousness as a critical educator.

In my work with students of color from middle-class or more affluent backgrounds, I have noticed that their reading of the world comes from a very particular class location. More often than not, the ways in which students and faculty engage "diversity" are subsumed within a liberal multiculturalist lens. As such, the tendency is to work within the limited structures and logic of the neoliberal university, rather than labor to change the structure itself. I struggled to find my footing in a context that desires to give, as Freire (2018) would say, "bread and circus to the people in order to 'soften them up' and to secure their own tranquility" (p. 140), while keeping relations of power unchanged. To be sure, the common language of diversity, equity, and inclusion (DEI) in the United States has become a legitimating calling card for institutions of higher education and the liberal arm of the university industrial complex.

Such reformist policies, for which Freire expressed much concern, might be seen as the latest form of banking education in a multiculturalism that is a throwback to the past. While there is "diversity" programming, it does not necessarily and substantively disrupt the structures of inequality that inform the neoliberal project of higher education. Suffice it to say, one can be critical but not "too" critical. Radical scholarship (read: political economy-inspired class analysis and racism) is seen, for the most part, to be outside the realm and boundaries of Gramscian "commonsense" thinking and therefore deemed "impractical" or just "theoretical work." The language of "microaggressions" takes precedence within the neoliberal project without any serious account for the superstructure. In *Pedagogy of the Oppressed* it is precisely an understanding of the oppressive nature of the superstructure and its impact on oppressed populations that drove Freire's analysis of education. Hence, through guiding students in the reading of critical texts, they can be encouraged to critically engage the contradictions and inequalities that often lie veiled beneath conservative views of diversity.

Pedagogy of the Oppressed has been a significant tool in my urban education classes, in my efforts to create the conditions for this critical engagement and to encourage culturally democratic life in my classroom (Darder, 2012). I structure the course around engaging intimately with the text over sixteen weeks. I divide the book into two sessions, so the first discussion on Freire falls in the middle of the semester and the second discussion toward the end. Other readings on the "social context of urban schools" are assigned before, in between, and after our readings of Freire, to put these texts in conversation with *Pedagogy of the Oppressed*. The strategic placement of texts begins to make clearer Freire's thesis and liberatory intent.

More specifically, I facilitate Freire's chapters one and four as a way to provide context and wrap up the course, respectively. Students assist in facilitating the dialogue for chapters two and three, in an attempt to decenter the teacher/

professor voice and to better develop the horizontal relationships that Freire considered important to a *problem-posing* pedagogy. I set the parameters for the discussion, but students have the freedom to engage the material as they see fit. As a way to get to know their colleagues and break from the isolation of virtual learning, groups are asked to meet to prepare for their facilitation. During the first session of chapter two, students critically engage the notion of "banking education." Students new to Freire are generally better able to connect with this chapter than others because it tends to be easier for them relate to. However, in teaching *Pedagogy of the Oppressed* it is important that students move beyond the discussion of banking and dialogue in ways that allow them to engage the ideological dimensions related to the development of consciousness. In so doing, they come to understand that Freire's pedagogy is not a method but instead a complex engagement with teaching and learning as praxis.

The second facilitation on Freire's chapter three is generally experienced by students as much heavier or more difficult. Here, we enter into discussions about the meaning and intent of critical dialogue and why it is so challenging to practice, particularly within the context of limit situations that impede our very existence and our ability to work across difference. At this point we unpack the idea of being in dialogue with each other (and the world) *as an act of love*. There tends to be more tension generated among students as our discussions veer more forthrightly toward the question of oppression. Students of color tend to connect the concept of oppression to racism, while white female students make sense of it through their subjectivity vis-à-vis gendered identity. There is more complexity in how students and their teacher make sense of oppression and how we, as a learning community, go about naming it together. This tension is generally informed by the larger institutional logic of "race" and the pervasive "black/white" binary, as well as our lived histories prior to entering the class. That is to say, we already bring all of ourselves to the table, even before we begin to read Freire.

Over the course of reading *Pedagogy of the Oppressed*, I (as the professor) have had to learn to "let go" and have faith in my students. I have had to let go of my own concerns, issues, and questions about the text, which I might inadvertently project onto my students. I have also been reminded, very quickly, that undergraduate students were/are more than capable of engaging Freire's ideas if the space for dialogue is created from the beginning. It was not "too theoretical" for them. When they have struggled, perhaps similar to my own experience many years ago, it might also be their fear taking over. This all points to the need for those teaching *Pedagogy of the Oppressed* to be ever vigilant. Our job is to provide direction or guidance and then move out of the way, so students *can make their way* with the text. This is exciting for me, in that students bring with them a "fresh eye" that is instructive in our collective analysis of the text.

As I conclude here, I am reminded that teaching always entails beginning anew. We begin anew with each reading of the text, with each new group of students, with each time we step into the classroom. True to Freire ideas, there is a certain intimacy with our unfinishedness that is needed, a freedom of creative expression, and a connection with self as a subject of history that must inform our revolutionary dialogue with one another. As such, it seems fitting to conclude with Freire's (2018) words, which remind us of the oppression that can keep us bound and the conditions necessary—beyond bread and circus—for our liberation:

> The oppressed, having internalized the image of the oppressor and adopted [their] guidelines, are fearful of freedom. Freedom would require them to eject this image and replace it with autonomy and responsibility. Freedom is acquired by conquest, not by gift. It must be pursued constantly and responsibly. Freedom is not an ideal located outside of man [or woman]; nor is it an idea which becomes myth. It is rather the indispensable condition for the quest for human completion. (p. 47)

Thoughts on Teaching *Pedagogy of the Oppressed* in Greece

Maria Nikolakaki
University of Peloponnese
Greece

Since the 1970s, Paulo Freire has remained one of the most influential thinkers of education. His work has influenced and transformed the thinking of educators around the globe. His work includes a series of complementary books that together provide readers a comprehensive understanding of emancipatory education. His seminal work *Pedagogy of the Oppressed* is one of the most cited books in education (Green, 2023). Yet often students in teacher education are not introduced to his work. I myself went through my entire educational experience in Greece, prior to my doctoral program, without learning about Paulo's work. My eureka moment was as a young lecturer in 2001 at a conference in the Greek island Syros, where I heard Donaldo Macedo speak of Freire's *Pedagogy of the Oppressed*, in a way that touched my heart. Over the next two decades I became a fierce advocate of Paulo Freire's work and critical pedagogy. As a Greek woman within a Greek tradition, I found in Paulo Freire the wisdom I had known in the writings of my Greek ancestors.

Paulo Freire's work emphasized the importance of quality basic education for everyone, basing itself upon the concept of social justice. "What social justice asks, and let's say even imposes, is that we all become acting subjects of history," clarifies Nita Freire. One of the gravest obstacles to the achievement of liberation is that oppressive reality absorbs those within it and thereby acts "to submerge human beings' consciousness" (Narciso and Neves, 2021 , p. 51). Critical consciousness, what Ancient Greeks called Nous, is the war zone in the new techno-colonial struggle. In the Aristotelian scheme, *nous* is the basic understanding or awareness that allows human beings to think rationally. Paulo Freire assumes that critical consciousness is essential for humanization and liberation. He claims that "our vocation is to be human." As such, we are challenged to fully develop our humanity for voice, participation, and solidarity, through embracing the power of love to transform. This, moreover, entails the exercise of the free will necessary for (re)creating ourselves and transforming the world through our labor. Through recognizing this profound truth, we also begin to better understand why often the practices and politics of those in power attempt to dehumanize us in order to gain control over the will of the masses.

In my teaching in the classroom, I aim to recall what Paulo communicated through his work: to be a critical pedagogue is to exist differently than others in the world. For me, this constitutes one of Freire's most important and accurate observations. A critical pedagogue is instilled with a sense of justice in this world that cannot tolerate exploitation of humans. In many ways, the notion of love that Paulo offers us in *Pedagogy of the Oppressed* echoes Che Guevara, who wrote, "At the risk of seeming ridiculous, let me say that the true revolutionary is guided by a great feeling of love idea." It is this revolutionary love, honest and vibrant in Freire's timeless book, that has also nurtured the praxis of revolutionary teachers and activists in Greece over the many years since the book's release.

Over the last twenty years, my effort to teach Freire's work in Greece has been quite a challenge. This has required cultivating for my students the conditions to support the evolution of their conscientization, so they might not only know *another world is possible* but also *how to exist differently in this world*. This is not about memorizing the contents of *Pedagogy of the Oppressed* but rather coming to understand, through their own experience in the world, the essence of Freire's revolutionary assertions. Two key elements here that students must come to understand before they are ready to teach include: (1) respect for the "otherness" of the "subaltern" and (2) an understanding that inequality restricts the social and material opportunities of students.

As Freire often stressed, the peasants and workers he encountered were not stupid; instead, they were often subjected to a *culture of silence*, which interfered with their learning how to *read the word and the world*. With this in mind, it has been my task over the years to first respect the place that students are at and journey with them from their starting point to a greater fulfillment of their social agency and human potential. Freire proposed in *Pedagogy of the Oppressed* that this requires building a *horizontal* classroom culture of trust and faith in the capacity of students to learn. Moreover, his pedagogy insists that the most rigorous learning takes place when the educator and the students learn from one another. I am also often reminded in my own teaching that in order to accomplish all this, as Freire stressed, requires from us the indispensability of humility. I have found that when my students experience the horizontal classroom culture that Freire proposes, they seem to feel more respected and thus exhibit less defensiveness or resistance to learning and are more open to active participation in a transformative praxis of dialogue.

At the beginning of every semester when I enter into the classroom, I see my students' eyes watching with curiosity to see how they will be taught about Paulo Freire and critical pedagogy. By the end of the semester, I feel that together we have cultivated and planted many seeds of consciousness. Some will plant them and water them to bring forth the fruits of their labor. While others will plant them but not water them now but perhaps later. While still there will be those who keep their seeds in their toolkit and return to them when their social conditions are more conducive. The seeds have been cultivated through our classroom relationships and that is what matters. Not everyone is ready to embrace the life of a critical pedagogue, where they must strive to exist in the world in a different way. However, at the end of the semester, many of my students tell me how different they feel in their humanity. Some have contacted me after a period of time to say that now they understand what I was teaching them. Whatever the case, the challenge to teach *and live* the principles of *Pedagogy of the Oppressed* is an ongoing process, as is our struggle to transform our world, through a humanizing praxis education.

What has been made clear to me in my years as a teacher educator is that teachers who blindly follow the official guidelines seldom enlighten students to become agents of indignation. There is no question that Paulo Freire was firmly committed to a revolutionary pedagogy—one with the collective power to transform our world. This commitment has driven my teaching and my activism in the world. Hence, the purpose of my teaching has been to prepare teachers to participate in the making of a better world. Moreover, keeping with Freirean sensibilities, it is only through *paideia* in the ancient Greek sense, a whole cultivation of mind, soul, and body, that there is hope for humanity in these difficult and trying times, where the abuses of neoliberalism in Greece and other parts of the world continue to plague our lives.

I would argue that the book's value is counted by its transformative timelessness. As long as there is oppression of any sort, the wisdom of *Pedagogy of the Oppressed* will be a needed as we continue the struggle. Moreover, Freire's remarkable and presentient message addresses progressives everywhere, urging us all "to remain active, authentic, democratic, nonsectarian, and unifying. But to do this, he argues, progressives must continuously examine their underlying strategies" (Carnoy, 2000, p. 8). The message of *Pedagogy of the Oppressed* is not about finding a teaching recipe or a method. Paulo Freire never wanted to be replicated, but rather he hoped the power of his ideas would support others in *reinventing* his problem-posing pedagogy into a pedagogy that was relevant to those who draw inspiration from his work. This signals that way in which we must work to find transformative connections between the classroom and community, the society and education, and between the personal and social dimensions of our lives.

———

Looking at Lived Experiences to See Not Only with the Eyes, but with the Mind and the Heart

Ana L. Cruz
St. Louis Community College
United States

Paulo Freire's ideas, as presented in *Pedagogy of the Oppressed,* and the tenets of a Freirean critical pedagogy are infused in all the teacher education courses I teach. To begin, I want to foreground a set of specific remarks to provide a general framework. First, I teach at a community college, which means that students are at the freshman and sophomore level. Second, my students are preservice teachers. For these students to complete a bachelor's degree and receive teaching licensure they will need to transfer to a four-year college/ university, although some commence classroom teaching prior to a bachelor's degree as substitute teachers. Third, and most importantly, the large majority of students are from segments of US society commonly underrepresented within postsecondary education. As examples, they are first-generation students to attend college; low-income students; minority students (based on race, ethnicity, immigration status); military veterans; and "nontraditional" students who have their own family to support and/or whose first priority is work "to make a living" and not college. This also means that the students in my classroom possess a diverse and often astonishing set of lived experiences. In fact, the majority of students can be considered "oppressed" as described by Freire in *Pedagogy of the Oppressed.*

In my classroom, the first engagement with *Pedagogy of the Oppressed* and Freirean critical pedagogy is asking students to conduct some background research on Freire's life. Based on this research, a class discussion contextualizes the important geographic and historical framework fundamental to a comprehensive understanding of Freire's work: What does it mean to be Brazilian and more specifically from the impoverished Northeast? What are issues associated with Freire's book being originally written in Brazilian Portuguese and in English as translation? What was the sociopolitical environment in Brazil at the time Paulo Freire's work originated? Why is *Pedagogy of the Oppressed* still relevant today and not "just for the third world" but for the entire world? Why was *Pedagogy of the Oppressed* first published in English in 1970—translated from the original Brazilian-Portuguese manuscript from 1968 (Freire 2006)—and only later in Brazilian Portuguese (1974)?

Although Paulo Freire's best-known work is *Pedagogy of the Oppressed,* it does not stand isolated as a monolith, in that there were books before and thereafter. We then explore what this may imply regarding the evolving character of Paulo Freire's oeuvre? What does it mean not to limit Freirean critical pedagogy to a "method" and what does this require a teacher to understand with respect to contextualization? Regarding the latter, often students come into the teaching profession with a view of teaching to be primarily about following cookbook-style "teaching recipes." As such, they believe that once these recipes are learned, one is a competent and effective teacher. Even more unsettling is that many teacher education programs seem to share this view of teaching, reflected by their program curricula and how their curricular material is taught. Therefore, it is important to also emphasize that teaching *Pedagogy of the Oppressed* and the concepts of critical pedagogy espoused by Paulo Freire must *not* be relegated to solely an upper-division course or to a graduate-level seminar. Instead, these ideas must permeate the fabric of the teacher education curriculum from beginning to end.

Another aspect about teaching *Pedagogy of the Oppressed* involves initiating a rapport with students, the creation of trust, and the establishment of the classroom as a community where mutual respect is essential. I use the question "Who am I?," which allows both instructor and students to introduce themselves within this respectful environment and to engage in self-reflection and discussion. In this way, students investigate their core values and beliefs, who they are, and their place within society (Cruz, 2013a). This also means that the entire class is aware of (and respects) the diverse lived experiences of fellow students and of the instructor. This approach sets the foundation for *dialogue* and a dialogic and *problem-posing education*—key concepts of Freirean pedagogy introduced and discussed in *Pedagogy of the Oppressed*. Dialogue offers the possibility for a relationship between teacher and students with *everyone* actively engaged in the processes of teaching *and* learning. This approach to teaching is diametrically opposed to a mechanical teaching where prefabricated, packaged, standardized material is transferred along a one-way street from the teacher to the passive students. I practice this dialogic and problem-posing education in my classrooms to ensure that this approach to teaching is exemplified "in real time" with my students and that it is not just taught in an abstract fashion as "curriculum content."

Another important concept that underlies a Freirean pedagogy and that is crucial to his work is ***conscientização*** (conscientization). It "is the active process through which a critical understanding of the socio-political-economic circumstances is gained that enables one to actively change oppressive circumstances" (Cruz, 2013b, p. 173). The concept involves both the process of reaching critical awareness and the acting upon this realization, which leads to a transformation of the conditions that are at the root of oppression. That implies, as Freire made clear in *Pedagogy of the Oppressed*, that teaching is always political and never a "neutral" process. It is through the development of conscientização that a full understanding of lived experiences can lead to agency and transformation. It is, however, important to note that lived experiences are not always perceived as relevant or potentially liberating by students. I vividly recall a discussion with a student problematizing the issue of poverty. The student who experienced poverty, lived on welfare and food stamps, and was able to overcome this socioeconomic status, stated in a very emotional tone, "Can you eliminate poverty? If not, why do we have a discussion in class about it?" She continued by saying that in a college class she did not want to be reminded of the hardships that poverty had caused her and her family. In addition, it was also very important for the student not to be associated anymore with low socioeconomic status because it felt for her as not being perceived as a "human being." Through the process of dialogue, however, the student began to view her lived experiences as fundamentally valuable in teaching others about poverty, making fellow teachers aware of how poverty can affect students' learning, allowing her as a future teacher to deeply understand students and families living in poverty, and being an agent in challenging the reasons for poverty in people's life. Hence, this experience became a transformative moment in her learning as both a student and a future teacher.

Teaching Freirean concepts found in *Pedagogy of the Oppressed* is important not only because students in my classroom are preservice teachers who learn about critical pedagogy and may (hopefully) develop into critical pedagogues but also because many of these students come from a segment of US society that can identify with being part of the oppressed, with their stratum in society being predetermined by the powerful and privileged. In addition, it is also important since these students, as future teachers, will be fundamental to preparing their own students to become engaged citizens in a participatory democracy within a global context. Toward this aim, *Pedagogy of the Oppressed* also provides students with a language to express and make sense of their feelings and lived experiences. By so doing, they are able to understand the social and material conditions that shape their lives, develop transformative action, and come to appreciate their own importance to society more fully, by looking not only with the eyes but also by seeing with the mind and the heart.

The Influence of Paulo Freire's *Pedagogy of the Oppressed* on Our Adult Education Work

Colin Kirkwood
Adult Educator
Scotland

My father was a presbyterian minister of the Church of Scotland. We lived in big houses, called manses, with large gardens, in several different parts of

Scotland, but as a family we were always very badly off. My father used to joke that the managers of the congregation would pray to God, saying: "Lord, you keep him humble, and we'll keep him poor!" We were all familiar with the antagonism felt within Protestantism against Catholicism, which was intense throughout Scotland and had been since the reformation in the sixteenth century. I am glad to say that we did not share it.

I developed an interest in history, moral philosophy, and English and Scottish literature, which I went on to study at the University of Glasgow. Toward the end of my postgraduate studies in objectivist and imagist traditions in poetry, I finally plucked up the courage to speak to a girl I had been attracted to in the fine art library. She was called Gerri Harkin and turned out to be catholic. She agreed to go out with me. A few months later, we got married in a catholic church by a priest called Father Anthony Ross who was later to become head of the Dominican order in Britain. My best man, Bob Tait, was also catholic. He was the first person to publish my poetry and criticism in a very influential magazine called *Scottish International*. This was at a time when the movement for independence, or as I prefer to call it, full self-government, was beginning to flourish in Scotland.

In 1968–9, Gerri and I spent a transformational year in the city of Treviso in northeast Italy, teaching English. We were immersed in the Italian language, the architecture and culture of Catholicism, and the poetry of Dante and Eugenio Montale. And we were caught up in the Europe-wide contestation, or *contestazione*: the movement of student action against authoritarianism and for direct democracy. When we returned to England, we spent three years in the mining, steel, and chemicals town of Staveley in north Derbyshire,[9] where I was Area Principal for Adult Education. I collaborated closely with an inspiring young community worker, Rob Hunter. Together with many ordinary people in the town, we created the newspaper *Staveley Now*, the Staveley Disabled

---

[9] An account of the work done by Robert Hunter and Colin Kirkwood in Staveley, North East Derbyshire, from 1969 to 1972 was published by Brill/Sense in 2020. It has contributions by Colin Kirkwood, Rob Hunter, Linden West, and Sarah Banks. This is based on a text originally written by Colin Kirkwood in 1976. The title is *Community Work and Adult Education in Staveley* (North East Derbyshire, 1969–72).

Group, and the Staveley Festival. Our work[10], in concert with Freire, was not about po-faced institutional reports on "what the churches, and the schools, and the workplaces were doing." No: we encouraged people to speak out in their own voices, to speak for themselves—in poetry, campaigns, community action by housewives, miners, and most dramatically by a group of Hell's Angels, young bikers who I and their youth leader, Joan Turner, interviewed in-depth and published uncensored, against the wishes of the Methodist minister and the Church of England vicar, in the pages of *Staveley Now*. Their words had a significant impact across the country.

Gerri and I wanted to find out more about the lives and experiences of underclass, working-class, and lower- middle-class people. With our small children, we moved back to Glasgow, where we chose to live for five years in Castlemilk, Glasgow's largest peripheral housing scheme. Gerri and I switched roles: she got a job as Reporter to Children's Panels, a radical alternative to the juvenile courts, while I became a house husband. With many other people we started the local newspaper, *Castlemilk Today*. Mary Miller, Carol Cooper, and Irene Graham started the Jeely Piece Club, an after-school club for nursery and primary school- age children, run directly by their own mothers. I played a prominent part in the campaign against the Housing Finance Act, throughout the central belt of Scotland, and was the founding editor of *Scottish Tenant*, the tenants' newspaper. This was also the period of the campaign against the closure of the shipyards on the Upper Clyde, known as the UCS, again an unusual form of radicalism. It was not a strike. It was a work-in, organized by the shop stewards elected by the workers themselves, led by their visionary leader Jimmy Reid and his colleagues. It was a time of great hope, of direct community action: these actions were focused, assertive, and peaceful, in line with the thinking of Martin Luther King and Mahatma Gandhi.

Through the years, Paulo Freire's ideas in *Pedagogy of the Oppressed* and his other publications came to influence our work in adult education. It was between

---

[10] An account of the later development of Colin Kirkwood's thinking and practice is to be found in *The Persons in Relation Perspective: In Counselling, Psychotherapy and Community Adult Learning* (Brill/ Sense, 2012). It includes an analysis of some of the contributions to the 1991 conference held in New York in honor of Paulo Freire's seventieth birthday.

1974 and 1976 that we first encountered the ideas and methods of Paulo Freire. We read and reread these books: *Pedagogy of the Oppressed, Cultural Action for Freedom*, and *Education: The Practice of Freedom*, all by Paulo himself; and *Literacy in 30 Hours: Paulo Freire's Process in North-East Brazil*, by Cynthia Brown. We were astonished. We realized that we were hearing in Paulo Freire's a voice that was in tune with our own. But he was conceptualizing these ideas and practices much better than we could do. Many—probably most—of us had come from Christian backgrounds, both catholic and protestant, but those differences were rapidly dissolving. In any case, our interest lay not in dubious and essentially abstract theological constructs and quarrels but rather in the suffering of people in societies in the here and now and what they and we and we and they could do ourselves by working together.

In the autumn of 1976, Gerri and I and our children moved to Edinburgh, where I had become first Tutor Organizer and later District Secretary of the Workers Educational Association (WEA) in south-east Scotland. Almost immediately I began to teach courses on Freire's ideas and methods, one in our flat, which was really a *Pedagogy of the Oppressed* reading group. The second was a longer WEA course called Community Action and the Pedagogy of the Oppressed, full of community education workers, social workers, area officers, and the odd student and academic. It was in one meeting of that second course when I had given the members a bit of homework to do: to bring forward to the next meeting proposals for how to adapt and apply Freire's ideas and methods in our first world situation of contemporary urban working-class Scotland, that Fraser Patrick and Douglas Shannon brought forward a well-argued proposal, which we all endorsed. Fraser submitted the proposal to the Scottish Office (the then headquarters of the central British government in Scotland. Britain was then and, in many respects, remains a highly centralized hierarchical and bureaucratized system.) Fraser's proposal for an Adult Learning Project (ALP)[11] was accepted. It was launched in the inner-city area

---

[11] The story of ALP can be read in-depth in the carefully researched *Living Adult Education: Freire in Scotland* (Open University Press, 1989). We believe that over 5,000 copies of that first edition have been sold worldwide. A second edition was published in 2011 by Sense/Brill. It updates the story of

of Gorgie Dalry in Edinburgh in the autumn of 1979, ironically at the very same time as Margaret Thatcher's ultra-right- wing Conservative Party came to power in Britain as a whole. For more than forty years, ALP's work, greatly influenced by Paulo Freire's ideas in *Pedagogy of the Oppressed*, has continued to flourish among the people.[12]

Qualities to Possess When Teaching *Pedagogy of the Oppressed*

James D. Kirylo
University of South Carolina
United States

Some years ago, in a conversation I had with Paulo Freire's widow, Nita, she shared that it was important for Paulo to maintain consistency between his private and public life and that he lived what he wrote. Nita further mentioned that Paulo was a man of strength, commanding what she called a pedagogical presence; and that the intention of his work was never for recognition. Rather, the intention was one that worked to dignify the lives of all people. Indeed, Paulo's pedagogical presence was one that radiated an authentic essence of love, particularly through the cultivation of dialogue, which was genuinely grounded in the virtue of humility (Kirylo, 2011). In this light, as one embarks on the journey of teaching Paulo Freire's classic work, *Pedagogy of the Oppressed*, there are three principal qualities one ought to possess to ground that journey. That is, the teacher must emanate a sense of love, work to cultivate dialogical spaces, and realize the value of humility.

ALP's evolution to the middle of the first decade of the twenty-first century. It is worth mentioning the useful glossary of terms used by Paulo Freire or ALP, which is included in both editions.

[12] The Adult Learning Project's brilliant paid workers have included Stan Reeves who has worked for ALP for the whole of his career and has never ceased to innovate and inspire, for example, the Scots Music Group and The Welcoming; Gerri Kirkwood, coauthor of the first and second editions of the ALP book; Fiona McCall, coordinator of the Gorgie Dalry Writers Workshop; and Joan Bree, secretary and administrator. They were followed by Vernon Galloway, Nancy Somerville, and John Player.

Love: Mother Teresa (1910–97), who was a powerful voice for the poor, asserted, "Love cannot remain by itself—it has no meaning" (1983, p. 75). In somewhat an analogous manner, Freire (2005b) declares, "Loving is not enough; one must know how to love" (p. 82). Of course, the implication here is that in order for love to have meaning, it must not only be an authentic emanation from the heart but also—specifically regarding the task of the teacher—it must be demonstrated in meaningful purpose, relationships, and action. In short, love acts; love moves; love is commitment.

Freire love, as an act of commitment, moved through his service to humanity, particularly casting its light on those who have been on the "short end of the historical stick" and "have not found their way into the 'official' story" (Kincheloe, 1992, p. 644). In order to facilitate a process of moving those to participate in the official story, he believed a conversion to the people and solidarity with them is necessary, which "requires a profound rebirth" (Freire, 1990, p. 47). Within the process of exploring what Freire calls our epistemological curiosities while also realizing that we are unfinished beings in an ongoing journey of becoming, the idea of rebirth is one that is rooted in a pedagogical approach that considers the other through dialogical spaces.

Dialogue: A critical aspect of cultivating dialogical spaces is one that enters into what Martin Buber (1958) calls an *I-thou* relationship, as opposed to an *I-it* relationship. For the latter, the relationship is manipulated by the *I*, dictated by a monologue, seeing the other as object, not only subverting the fostering of dialogue, but also represents a deformation of education (Freire, 1994b). For the former, the *I* engages the participant who is viewed as subject in a horizontal (or coexisting) relationship, which realizes that authentic dialogue foundationally rests in love (Freire, 1990).

The idea of the unfolding of an I-thou relationship functions through a teacher's ability to not only be available and present with her students but also suggests attentive listening. The I and the thou imply we are not alone; we coexist; there is a between with one to another, all of which is an encounter of inclusion. In the final analysis, the multidirectional trajectory of the variety of diverse encounters the teacher faces is nourished by recognizing individual identities and mentalities (Gutiérrez, 1990). Realizing such meaningful communication is what fosters an education of truth where "The teacher's thinking is authenticated only by the authenticity of the student's thinking" (Freire, 1990, pp. 63–4). A critical aspect of this coexisting relationship requires the teacher to realize the value of humility, which helps one to stay "close to the ground (*humus*), to people, to everyday life, to what is happening with all its down–to–earthness"(Nouwen, 1983, p. 162).

Humility: Freire (2005b) makes the point, "Humility helps us to understand this obvious truth: No one knows it all; no one is ignorant of everything. We all know something; we are all ignorant of something. . . . Humility helps me avoid being entrenched in the circuit of my own truth" (p. 72). While humility necessitates one to stay close to the ground, to the everydayness of life, and is critical in guiding the certainty–uncertainty tension of our truth, it does not suggest a resignation or a void in strength. To the contrary, humility signals courage, confidence, and respect for oneself and others (Freire, 2005b), leading to clarity in understanding, discernment, empathy, perspectives, tolerance, and acceptance. In short, the virtue of humility, which informs our incompleteness, is a critical component of a progressive teacher, one who embraces the process of becoming, while at the same time realizing that no one is above or superior to anyone else (Horton and Freire, 1990; Freire, 1995, 1998b).

I can't help but think that teachers who desire to teach *Pedagogy of the Oppressed* would take to heart Nita's aforementioned remarks about Paulo and consider the reinvention ramifications in their own lives. In other words, educators—who aim to maintain a consistency between their private and public lives, to realize the power of love through the cultivation of dialogical spaces, and to genuinely possess a disposition of humility—will certainly reflect in their teaching, each in their unique respective ways, that pedagogical presence that is consistent with Paulo Freire's writings and his life.

Questions for Reflection and Dialogue

1. As you have read, the authors of these short essays come from different regional contexts. Where do you note similarities in how they engage

with *Pedagogy of the Oppressed*? Where do you note differences? What do you think accounts for those distinct reading they bring?

2. What are the major ideas that you take away from these narratives? How do they relate to your own experience as a teacher or student? How are these experiences different from your own lived history?

3. As you consider the major themes mentioned in this chapter, which of these seems most relevant to your own teaching? What are other important themes, questions, or issues that you associate with teaching *Pedagogy of the Oppressed*?

4. Culminating with these notes from the field offered in this chapter, how would you describe the overall impact of *Pedagogy of the Oppressed* on your own understanding of inequalities within education?

5. In what ways do the concepts put forth by Paulo Freire inspire or advance your own thinking about educational justice? Have you ever experienced the culture of silence? In what ways has *Pedagogy of the Oppressed* shifted your own understanding of teaching and learning?

6. Where do you find yourself still struggling with Freire's ideas?

Bibliography

Abreu, A. A. (1975), *Nationalisme et action politique au Brésil: une étude sur l'ISEB*. Tese (Doutorado). Paris: Universidade de Paris.

Adorno, T. W. (1973a), *Prisms*. London: Neville Spearman.

Adorno, T. W. (1973b), *Negative Dialectics*. New York: Continuum.

Adorno, T. W. (1991), *The Culture Industry*. London: Routledge.

Ahmed, S. (2007), "A Phenomenology of Whiteness," *Feminist Theory*, 8(2): 149–68.

Alexander, N. (1988), "Liberation Pedagogy in the South African Context." Retrieved from: https://repository.uwc.ac.za/bitstream/handle/10566/2898/Alexander _Liberationpedagogy_1990.pdf?sequence=4&isAllowed=y

Allen Jr., J. L. (2012), "Remembering the Women of Vatican II," *National Catholic Reporter*. Retrieved from: https://www.ncronline.org/blogs/ncr-today/ remembering-women-vatican-ii

Allensandrini, A. C. (2014), *Frantz Fanon and the Future of Cultural Politics*. London: Lexington Books.

Allman, P. (1999), *Revolutionary Social Transformation: Democratic Hopes, Political Possibilities and Critical Education*. Westport, CN: Greenwood Publishing Group.

Almeida, C. Mendes de (1966), *Momentos dos Vivos: A Esquerda Católica no Brasil*. Rio de Janeiro, Brazil: Tempo Brasilero.

Althusser, L. (1967), *Pour Marx*. Le Landreau, France: Editions François Maspero.

Althusser, L. (1969), *For Marx*. New York: Penguin Press.

Althusser, L. (2001), *Lenin and Philosophy and Other Essays*, trans. Ben Brewster. New York: Monthly Review.

Alvarado, Arias M. (2007), "José Martí y Paulo Freire: aproximaciones para una lectura de la pedagogía crítica," *Revista Electrónica de Investigación Educativa*, 9(1): 1–19. Retrieved from: https://redie.uabc.mx/redie/article/view/157

Anzaldúa, G. (1989), *Borderlands: The New Mestiza*. San Francisco: Aunt Lute.

Archer, M. (2003), *Structure, Agency and the Internal Conversation*. Cambridge: Cambridge University Press.

Arrupe, P., SJ (1973), "Men for Others." In C. E. Meirose, SJ (Compiler), *Foundations*, 1–40. Washington, DC: Jesuit Secondary Education Association.

Austin, R. (2003), *The State, Literacy, and Popular Education in Chile, 1964–1990*. London: Lexington Books.

Bakan, M. (1983), "Karel Kosik's Phenomenological Heritage." In W. L. McBride and C. O. Schrag (eds.), *Phenomenology in a Pluralistic Context*, 9. New York: SUNY Press.

Balut, J. M. (1993), *The Colonizer's Model of the World*. New York and London: The Guilford Press.

Beauvoir, S. de (1955), Le Pensée de Droite, *Aujourd'hui*. Paris: Gallimard.

Benade, L. (2015), "Bits, Bytes, and Dinosaurs: Using Levinas and Freire to Address the Concept of 'Twenty-First Century Learning,'" *Educational Philosophy and Theory*, 47(9): 935–48.

Bénéï, V. (2008) *Schooling Passions. Nation, History, and Language in Contemporary Western India*. Stanford: Stanford University Press.

Bergson, H. (1911), *Creative Evolution*. New York: Henry Holt and Co.

Bgoya, W. (2001), "The Effects of Globalization in Africa and the Choice of Language in Publishing," *International Review of Education*, 47(3–4): 283–92.

Bhaskar, R. (2016), *Enlightened Common Sense: The Philosophy of Critical Realism*. Oxford: Routledge.

Bhattacharya, A. (2011), *Paulo Freire: Rousseau of the Twentieth Century*. Berlin, Germany: Springer Science & Business Media.

Biku, S. (1978), *I Write What I Like*. Johannesburg: Heinemann Educational Publishers.

Boff, L. (2011), "The Influence of Freire on Scholars: A Select List." In J. Kirylo (ed.), *Paulo Freire: The Man from Recife*, 235–69. New York: Peter Lang.

Brady, J. (1994), "Critical Literacy, Feminism, and a Politics of Representation." In P. McLaren and C. Lankshear (eds.), *Politics of Liberation*, 142–52. New York: Routledge.

Braidotti, R. (2017), *The Posthuman Condition*. The Netherlands: Presentation at the University of Utrecht.

Braidotti, R. (2023), *The Postman*. Cambridge: Polity.

Bruneau, T. C. (1974), *Catolicismo Brasilero em época de transição*. São Paulo: Loyola.

Buber, M. (1958), *I and Thou*. New York: Free Press.

Burston, D. (1985), *The Legacy of Erich Fromm*. Cambridge, MA: Harvard University.

Cammarota, J. and A. Romero (2014), *Raza Studies: The Public Option for Educational Revolution*. Tucson: University of Arizona Press.

Carnoy, M. (2000), *Foreword in Paulo Freire: Pedagogy of the Heart*. New York: Continuum.

Cassirer, T. and M. Twomey (1973), "Introduction to A. Memmi's The Impossible Life of Frantz Fanon," *The Massachusetts Review*, 14(1): 9–39.

Cesaire, A. (1955), *Discours sur le colonialism*. Paris: Présence Africaine.

Cherki, A. (2006), *Frantz Fanon: A Portrait*. Ithaca and London: Cornell University Press.

Chopra, R., P. Jeffery, and H. Reifeld (2005), *Educational Regimes in Contemporary India*. Thousand Oaks: Sage.

Chronister, K. M. and E. H. McWhirter (2006), "An Experimental Examination of Two Career Interventions for Battered Women," *Journal of Counseling Psychology*, 53(2): 151–64.

Chubbuck, S. (2007), "Socially Just Teaching and the Complementarity of Ignatian Pedagogy and Critical Pedagogy," *Christian Higher Education*, 6(3): 239–65.

Chubbuck, S. M. and R. Lorentz (2006), "Critical Pedagogy and Ignatian Pedagogy: Piecing Together the Why, the What, and the How of Teaching for Social Justice," Paper presented at Commitment to Justice Conference, Marquette University.

Chzhen, Y., A. Gromada, G. Rees, J. Cuesta, and Z. Bruckauf (2018), "An Unfair Start: Inequality in Children's Education in Rich Countries," *Innocenti Report Card*, no. 15, UNICEF Office of Research - Innocenti, Florence.

Clare, R. (2006), "Paulo Freire," La Mirada: Talbot School of Theology, Biola University. Retrieved from: http://www.talbot.edu/ce20/educators/catholic/paulo _freire/

Collins, P. H. (2000), *Black Feminist Thought: Knowledge, Consciousness, and the Politics of Empowerment*. New York: Routledge.

Collins, P. H. and S. Bilge (2016), *Intersectionality*. Malden: Polity Press.

Combahee River Collective Statement (1977; 2015), United States. [Web Archive] Retrieved from the Library of Congress, https://www.loc.gov/item/lcwaN0028151/

Connell, R. W. (1993), *Schools and Social Justice*. Philadelphia: Temple University Press.

Cortesão, L. (2011), "Paulo Freire and Amilcar Cabral: Convergences," *Journal for Critical Education Policy Studies*, 9(2): 260–96.

Counts, G. S. (1932), *Dare the school build a new social order*. Carbondale: Southern Illinois University Press.

Crenshaw, K. (1989), "Demarginalizing the Intersection of Race and Sex: A Black Feminist Critique of Antidiscrimination Doctrine, Feminist Theory and Antiracist Politics," *University of Chicago Legal Forum*, 1989, Article 8.

Cross, W. E. (1978), "The Thomas and Cross Models on Psychological Nigrescence: A Literature Review," *Journal of Black Psychology*, 4: 13–31.

Cruz, A. L. (2013a), "Becoming a Teacher: Fostering a Democratically Conscious Citizenry through Critical Pedagogy." In P. L. Thomas (ed.), *Becoming and Being a*

Teacher: Confronting Traditional Norms to Create New Democratic Realities, 15–25. New York: Peter Lang.

Cruz, A. L. (2013b), "Paulo Freire's concept of conscientização." In R. Lake and T. Kress (eds.), *Paulo Freire's Intellectual Roots - Toward Historicity in Praxis*, 169–82. New York: Bloomsbury.

Darder, A. (2012), *Culture and Power in the Classroom*. Boulder: Paradigm.

Darder, A. (2015a), *Freire and Education*. New York: Routledge.

Darder, A. (2015b), *Cultura e poder na sala de aula. Bases educativas para a escolarização de estudantes biculturais. [Transl. of Culture and power in the classroom. Educational foundations for the schooling of bicultural students]*. Mangualde: Pedago.

Darder, A., R. D. Torres, and M. P. Baltodano (2017), *Critical Pedagogy Reader* (3rd ed.). New York: Routledge.

Davidson, M. (2012), "Albert Memmi and Audre Lorde: Gender, Race, and the Rhetorical Uses of Anger," *Journal of French and Francophone Philosophy—Revue de la philosophie française et de langue française*, 20(1): 87–100.

deAnda D. (1984), "Bicultural Socialization: Factors Affecting the Minority Experience," *Social Work*, 2: 101–7.

Debray, R. (1967), *Revolution in the Revolution? Armed Struggle and Political Struggle in Latin America*. New York: Penguin Books.

Dewey, J. (1916), *Democracy and Education*. New York: The Free Press.

Dewey, J. (1938), *Experience and Education*. New York: Macmillan.

Dixon V. and B. Foster (1971), *Beyond Black or White*. Boston: Little Brown.

Dlamini, S. Nombuso (1998), "Towards an Empowering Education System in South Africa: Youth and the Struggle for Knowledge." In Vincent R. D'Oyley and Carl E. James (eds.), *Re/visioning: Canadian Perspectives of Education of Africans in the Late 20th Century*, 200–24. Ontario: Captus Press Inc.

Dor, T. (2018), "Rencontres radicales : Un positionnement trans/formateur." In M. Altamimi, T. Dor and N. Guénif (eds.), *Rencontres radicales. Pour des dialogues décoloniaux*. Paris: Cambourakis.

Du Bois, W. E. B. (1903), *Souls of Black Folk*. Chicago: A. C. McClurg.

Dufrenne, M. (1953), *Phénoménologie de l'expérience esthétique*. Paris: Presses Universitaires de France.

Dufrenne, M. (1968), *Pour L'Homme*. Paris: Éditions de Seuil.

Dussel, E. (2013), *Ethics of Liberation: In the Age of Globalization and Exclusion*. Durham: Duke University Press.

Elias, J. L. (1994), *Paulo Freire: Pedagogue of Liberation*. Malabar: Krieger Publishing Company.

Elie, P. (2007), "A Man for all Reasons," *The Atlantic* (November). Retrieved from: https://www.theatlantic.com/magazine/archive/2007/11/a-man-for-all-reasons/306337/

Facundo, B. (1984), "Freire-inspired Programs in the United States and Puerto Rico." Retrieved from: http://www.bmartin.cc/dissent/documents/Facundo/Facundo. html

Fanon, F. (1952), *Peau Noire Masques Blancs*. Paris, France: Éditions du Seuil.

Fanon, F. (1963), *Wretched of the Earth*. New York: Grove Press.

Fanon, F. (1965), *A Dying Colonialism*. New York: Grove Press.

Fanon, F. (1967), *Black Skin, White Masks*. New York: Grove Press.

Felluga, D. F. (2015), *Critical Theory: The Key Concepts*. New York: Routledge.

Finlayson, L. (2016), *An Introduction to Feminism*. Cambridge: Cambridge University Press.

Fonseca, M. (2016), *Gramsci's Critique of Civil Society*. New York: Routledge.

Forester, J. (1987), *Critical Theory and Public Life*. Boston: MIT Press.

Foy, R. (1971), "Review of Pedagogy of the Oppressed," *Educational Studies* 2(3/4): 92–92.

Freire, A. M. Araújo (2006), *Paulo Freire: Uma história de Vida*. Indaiatuba: Villa das Letras.

Freire, A. M. Araújo and D. Macedo, eds. (1998), *The Paulo Freire Reader*. New York: Continuum.

Freire, P. (1970a), *Pedagogy of the Oppressed*. New York: Seabury.

Freire, P. (1970b), *Pedagogia do Oprimido*. Rio de Janeiro: Edicões Paz e Terra.

Freire, P. (1975), *Pedagogia do oprimido*. 2ª Ed. [Pedagogy of the oppressed, 2nd Ed.]. Porto: Afrontamento.

Freire, P. (1978), "A Alfabetização de adultos: é ela um quefazer neutro?," *Educação and Sociedade* (Campinas, Brazil), 1(1): 64–70.

Freire, P. (1985), "Caminhos de Paulo Freire. Entrevisita a J. Chasin et al.," *Ensaio: revista da UFPb* (João Pessoa, Brazil), (14).

Freire, P. (1990), *Pedagogy of the Oppressed*. New York: Continuum.

Freire, P. (1991), *Pedagogy of the City*. New York: Continuum.

Freire, P. (1994a), *Pedagogy of Hope: Reliving Pedagogy of the Oppressed*. New York: Continuum.

Freire, P. (1994b), *Education for Critical Consciousness*. New York: Continuum.

Freire, P. (1995), "The Progressive Teacher." In M. de Figueiredo–Cowen and D. Gastaldo, *Paulo Freire at the Institute*, 17–26. London: The 'Brazilian Educators' Lecture Series Institute of Education, University of London.

Freire, P. (1996), *Letters to Christina: Reflections on My Life and Work*. New York: Routledge.

Freire, P. (1997a), *Pedagogy of the Heart.* New York: Continuum.

Freire, P. (1997b), *Professora sim, tia não. Cartas a quem ousa ensinar* [*Letters to those who dare to teach*]. São Paulo: Editora Olho d´Água.

Freire, P. (1998a), *Teachers as Cultural Workers: Letters to Those Who Dare Teach.* Boulder: Westview Press.

Freire, P. (1998b), *Pedagogy of Freedom.* New York: Rowman & Littlefield.

Freire, P. (2002), *Pedagogy of Hope: Reliving Pedagogy of the Oppressed.* New York: Continuum.

Freire, P. (2005a), *Pedagogy of the Oppressed* (30th Anniversary Edition), trans. Myra Bergman Ramos. New York: Continuum.

Freire, P. (2005b), *Teachers as Cultural Workers: Letters to Those Who Dare Teach* (expanded edition). Boulder: Westview Press.

Freire, P. (2013), *Pedagogia da autonomia: Saberes necessários à prática educativa educativa.* 45ª Ed. [*Pedagogy of autonomy: Knowledges needed for educational practice*] (45th ed.). São Paulo: Editora Paz e Terra.

Freire, P. (2018), *Pedagogy of the Oppressed* (50th ed.). London: Bloomsbury Academic.

Freire, P. and A. Faundez (1989), *Learning to Question: A Pedagogy of Liberation.* New York: Continuum.

Freire, P. and S. Guimarães (1987), *Aprendendo com a própria história.* Rio de Janeiro: Editora Paz e Terra.

Freire, P. and D. Macedo (1987), *Literacy: Reading the Word and the World.* New York: Taylor and Francis.

Freud, S. (1949), *The Ego and the Id.* London: The Hogarth Press Ltd.

Freud, S. (2002), *Civilization and Its Discontent.* London: Penguin.

Freud, S. (2010), *The Ego and the Id.* New York: W.W. Norton and Company.

Freyer, H. (1958), *Teoria de la Epoca Actual.* Mexico: Fondo de Cultural Economica.

Friedman, L. J. and A. Schreiber (2014), *The Lives of Erich Fromm: Love's Prophet.* Cambridge: Colombia University Press.

Fromm, E. (1941), *Escape from Freedom.* New York: Henry Holt and Co.

Fromm, E. (1955), *The Sane Society.* New York: Routledge.

Fromm, E. (1956), *The Art of Loving.* New York: Harper and Row.

Fromm, E. (1964), *The Heart of Man.* New York: Harper and Row.

Fromm, E. (1966), *The Heart of Man.* New York: Harper and Row.

Fromm, E. (1973), *The Anatomy of Destructiveness.* New York: Holt, Rinehart, and Winston.

Fromm, E. (2001), *Fear of Freedom.* New York: Routledge.

Furter, P. (1966), *Educacão e Vida.* Rio de Janeiro: Voces.

Gadotti, M. (1994), *Reading Paulo Freire: His Life and Work*. New York: SUNY Press.

Garcia, J. and M. Vargas (2013), "Latin American Philosophy," *Stanford Encyclopedia of Philosophy*. Retrieved from: https://plato.stanford.edu/entries/latin-american-philosophy/

Gerhardt, H. (1993), "Paulo Freire (1921–97)," *Prospects: The Quarterly Review of Comparative Education* (Paris, UNESCO: International Bureau of Education), XXIII(3/4): 439–58.

Gibson, R. (1994), "The Promethean Literacy: Paulo Freire's Pedagogy of Reading, Praxis, and Liberation," Dissertation. Pennsylvania State University. Retrieved from: https://lbsu300s12.wikispaces.com/file/view/Paulo+Freire+(2).pdf

Giroux, H. (1981), *Ideology, Culture, and the Process of Schooling*. Philadelphia: Temple University Press.

Giroux, H. (1983a), *Theory and Resistance in Education*. New York: Bergin and Garvey.

Giroux, H. (1983b), "Paulo Freire and the Politics of Postcolonialism." In P. McLaren and P. Leonard (eds.), *Paulo Freire: A Critical Encounter*, 15–26. London and New York: Routledge.

Giroux, H. A. (2006), "Academic Freedom under Fire: The Case for Critical Pedagogy," *College Literature*, 33(4): 1–42.

Gitlin, T. (1994), "Prime Time Ideology: The Hegemonic Process in Television Entertainment." In H. Newcomb (ed.), *Television: The Critical View—Fifth Edition*, 516–36. New York: Oxford University Press.

Goldmann, L. (1968), "Is There a Marxist Sociology?" *International Socialism*. Retrieved from: https://www.marxists.org/history/etol/newspape/isj/1968/no034/goldmann.htm

Goldmann, L. (1969), *The Human Sciences and Philosophy*. London: Jonathon Cape.

Gomez, M. V. (2009), "Emmanual Levinas and Paulo Freire: The Ethics of Responsibility for the Face-to-Face Interaction in the Virtual World," *International Journal of Instruction*, 2(1): 27–58.

Gorner, P. (2007), *Heidegger's Being and Time*. New York: Cambridge University Press.

Gramsci, A. (1971), *Selections from the Prison Notebooks of Antonio Gramsci*. New York: International Publishers.

Green, E. (2023), "What Are the Most-Cited Publications in the Social Sciences (according to Google Scholar)?" The London School of Economics. Retrieved from: https://blogs.lse.ac.uk/impactofsocialsciences/2016/05/12/what-are-the-most-cited-publications-in-the-social-sciences-according-to-google-scholar/

Grollios, G. (2015), *Paulo Freire and the Curriculum*. New York: Routledge.

Guevara, E. (1969), *Venceremos—The Speeches and Writings of Che Guevara*, ed. J. Gerassi. New York: Ocean Press.

Gunter, P. (1995), "Bergson's Philosophy of Education," *Educational Theory*, 65(3): 379–94.

Gutiérrez, G. (1973), *A Theology of Liberation*. Maryknoll: Orbis.

Gutiérrez, G. (1990), *The Truth Shall Make You Free*, trans. M. O'Connell. New York: Orbis Books.

Habermas, J. (1987), *The Philosophical Discourse of Modernity*, trans. F. G. Lawrence. Cambridge: Polity.

Hall, S. and P. du Guy (1996), *Questions of Cultural Identity*. London: Sage Publications.

Haraway, D. J. (1988), "Situated Knowledge: The Science Question in Feminism and the Privilege of Partial Perspective," *Feminist Studies*, 14, no. 3 (Autumn): 575–99.

Harnett, D. F., SJ (2009), *Transformative Education in the Jesuit Tradition*. Chicago: Loyola University.

Hedges, C. (2017), "Antonio Gramsci and the Battle against Fascism," *Truthout*. Retrieved from: http://www.truthdig.com/report/page2/antonio_gramsci_and _the_battle_against_ fascism_20170604

Hegel, G. W. (1977), *The Phenomenology of Spirit*. Oxford: Oxford University Press.

Heidegger, M. (1962), *Being and Time*. New York: Harper and Row.

Held, D. (1980), *Introduction to Critical Theory*. London: Heinemann.

Heywood, A. (1994), *Political Ideas and Concepts: An Introduction*. London: Macmillan.

Holst, J. (2006), "Paulo Freire in Chile, 1964–1969," *Pedagogy of the Oppressed* in Its Sociopolitical Economic Context, *Harvard Educational Review*, 76(2): 243–70.

hooks, b. (1994), *Teaching to Transgress: Education as the Practice of Freedom*. New York: Routledge.

hooks, b. (2003), *Teaching Community: A Pedagogy of Hope*. New York: Routledge.

Horton, M. and P. Freire (1990), *We Make the Road by Walking*, 55. Philadelphia: Temple University Press.

Horkheimer, M. (1972), *Critical Theory: Selected Essays*. New York: Herder and Herder.

Howard, J. (2018), "Supporting Our Most Vulnerable and Victimised Children," *Every Child*, 24(3): 24–5.

Hsu, F. (1971), *The Challenge of the American Dream: The Chinese in the United States*. Wadsworth: Belmont.

Husserl, E. (1954), *The Crisis of European Sciences and Transcendental Phenomenology: An Introduction to Phenomenological Philosophy*. Evanston: Northwestern University Press.

Husserl, E. (2012), *Ideas: General Introduction to Pure Phenomenology*. New York: Routledge.

Illich, I. (1971), *Deschooling Society*. New York: Harper and Row.

International Commission on the Apostolate of Jesuit Education (1993), "Ignatian Pedagogy: A Practical Approach." In C. E. Meirose, SJ (Compiler), *Foundations*, 237–69. Washington, DC: Jesuit Secondary Education Association.

Irwin, J. (2012), *Paulo Freire's Philosophy of Education*. New York: Continuum.

Jadallah, D. (2012), "The Shibboleths within Albert Memmi's Universalism," *Jadaliyya*, October 8. Retrieved from http://www.jadaliyya.com/pages/index/2829/the-shibboleths-within- albert-memmis-universalism

Jaspers, K. (1953), *The Origin and Goal of History*, trans. Michael Bullock (1st English ed.). London: Routledge and Keegan Paul.

Jaspers, K. (1954), *The Way of Wisdom: An Introduction to Philosophy*. New Haven: Yale University Press.

Jaspers, K. (2010), *Man in the Modern Age*. New York: Routledge.

Jay, M. (1973), *The Dialectical Imagination: A History of the Frankfurt School and the Institute of Social Research, 1923–1950*. Boston: Little Brown.

Jeria, J. (1986), "Vagabond of the Obvious: A Bibliography of Paulo Freire," *Vitae Scholastica*, 5(1): 1–126.

Jessup, B. and S. Ngai-Ling (2001), "Pre-disciplinary and Post-Disciplinary Perspectives," *New Political Economy*, 6(1): 80–101.

Joldersma, C. M. (2001), "The Tension between Justice and Freedom in Paulo Freire's Faith-Full Pedagogy," *Journal of Educational Thought*, 35(2): 129–48.

Kahn, R. (2010), *Critical Pedagogy, Ecoliteracy, and Planetary Crisis*. New York: Peter Lang.

Kahn, R. and G. F. Kellner (2007), "Paulo Freire and Ivan Illich: Technology, Politics and the Reconstruction of Education," *Policy Futures in Education*, 5(4). Retrieved from: http://journals.sagepub.com/doi/abs/10.2304/pfie.2007.5.4.431

Kain, P. J. (2005), *Hegel and the Other: A Study of the Phenomenology of Spirit*. New York: State University of New York Press.

Katsiaficas, G. (2011), "Eros and Revolution," paper delivered for the Critical Refusals Conference of the International Herbert Marcuse Society, Philadelphia. Retrieved from: http://www.eroseffect.com/articles/ErosandRevolution.htm

Kidd, I. J. and H. Carel (2016), "Epistemic Injustice and Illness," *Journal of Applied Philosophy*, 34(2): 172–90. Retrieved from: https://doi.org/10.1111/japp.12172

Kierkegaard, S. (1949), *The Present Age* and *Two Minor Ethico-Religious Treatises*. New York: Oxford University Press.

Kierkegaard, S. (2000), *The Essential Kierkegaard*, ed. H. V. Hong and E. H. Hong. Princeton: Princeton University Press.

Kimmerle, H. (2014), "Hegel's Eurocentric Concept of Philosophy," *Confluence*, 1: 99–117. Retrieved from: https://scholarworks.iu.edu/iupjournals/index.php/confluence/article/view/524

Kincheloe, J. L. (1992, October), "Liberation Theology and the Attempt to Establish an Emancipatory System of Meaning. Paper Presented at the Bergamo Conference on Curriculum Theory and Classroom Practice, Dayton, OH." In W. Pinar, W. Reynolds, P. Slattery, and P. Taubman, *Understanding Curriculum*, 606–60. New York: Peter Lang Publishing.

Kirylo, J. D. (2011), *Paulo Freire: The Man from Recife*. New York: Peter Lang.

Kirylo, J. D. and D. Boyd (2017), *Paulo Freire: His Faith, Spirituality, and Theology*. The Netherlands: Sense Publishers.

Kitano H. (1969), *Japanese-Americans: The Evolution of a Subculture*. Englewood Cliffs: Prentice-Hall.

Kohan, W. O. (2021), *Paulo Freire: A Philosophical Biography*. London: Bloomsbury.

Kosik, K. (1967), *Dialética de lo Concreto*. Mexico: Editorial Crijalbo.

Kosik, K. (1974), *Dialectics of the Concrete*. Holland and Boston: D. Reidel Publishing Co.

Kumar, K. (1991), *Political Agenda of Education. A Study of Colonialist and Nationalist Ideas*. New Delhi: Sage.

Lacan, J. (1977), *Écrits: A Selection*. New York: Norton.

Larraín, J. (2000), *Identity and Modernity in Latin America*. Cambridge: Polity; Malden: Blackwell.

Lawlor, L. and V. M. Leonard (2016), "Henri Bergson," *Stanford Encyclopedia of Philosophy*. Retrieved from: https://plato.stanford.edu/entries/bergson/

Leach, T. (1982), "Paulo Freire," *International Journal of Lifelong Education*, 1(3): 182–201.

Lernoux, P. (1980), *Cry of the People: The Struggle for Human Rights in Latin America*. New York: Penguin Books.

L'Estange, L. and J. Howard (2022), "Trauma-Informed Initial Teacher Education Training: A Necessary Step in a System-Wide Response to Addressing Childhood Trauma." *Frontiers in Education*, 7(1–12). doi: 10.3389/feduc.2022.929582

Lévinas, E. (1979), *Totality and Infinity*. London: Martinus Nijhoff Publishers.

Libano, J. B., trans. F. McDonagh (2017), "St. Ignatius and Liberation." Retrieved from: www.theway.org.uk/Back/s070Libanio.pdf

Lieberman, L. (2007), "Albert Memmi's About-Face," *Michigan Quarterly Review*, 46(3): 1–5.

Lukács, G. (1967), *Reification and the Consciousness of the Proletariat*. London: Merlin Press.

Lukács, G. (1972), *History and Class Consciousness*. Cambridge, MA: MIT Press.

Luxembourg, R. (1905), "The Political Leader of the German Working Classes: Collected Works 2." Retrieved from: http://www.newworldencyclopedia.org/entry /Rosa_ Luxemburg

Luxembourg, R. (1906), "Mass Strike, the Political Party and the Trade Unions." Retrieved from: https://www.marxists.org/archive/luxemburg/1906/mass-strike/

Luxembourg, R. (2006), *Reform or Revolution and Other Writings*. Mineola: Dover Publications.

Luxembourg, R. (2007), *The Essential Rosa Luxemburg: Reform or Revolution and The Mass Strike*, ed. H. Scott. Chicago: Haymarket Books.

Macdonald, T. S. (2010), "Steve Biko and Black Consciousness in Post-Apartheid South African Poetry," Doctor of Philosophy Dissertation presented to the faculty of the College of Fine Arts of Ohio University.

Mackie, R. (1981), *Literacy and Revolution: The Pedagogy of Paulo Freire*. New York: Continuum.

Macrine, S. L. (2020), "Introduction." In *Critical Pedagogy in Uncertain Times: Hope and Possibilities*, 3–15. New York: Palgrave Macmillan. https://doi.org/10.1007/978 -3-030-39808-8_1

Madero, C., SJ (2015), "Theological Dynamics of Paulo Freire's Educational Theory: An Essay to Assist the Work of Catholic Educators," *International Studies in Catholic Education*, 7(2): 122–33.

Mainwaring, S. (1987), "Grassroots Catholic Groups and Politics in Brazil, 1964– 1985," Working Paper #98. Kellogg Institute. Retrieved from: https://www3. nd.ed u/~kellogg/publications/workingpapers/WPS/098.pdf

Maisuria, A. (2016), "Class Struggle in Cultural Formation in Contemporary Times: A Focus on the Theoretical Importance of Antonio Gramsci and the Organic Intellectualism of Russell Brand." In L. McLaren and L. Monzo (2017) (eds.), Revolution and Education Special Issue. *Knowledge Cultures*, 5(1). Addleton Academic Publishers.

Maisuria, A. (2021), "Hegemony." In S. Themelis (ed.), *Critical Reflections on the Language of Neoliberalism: Dangerous Words and Discourses of Possibility*. London: Routledge.

Mandel, M. S. (2014), *Muslim and Jews in France: History of Conflict*. Princeton: Princeton University Press.

Mannheim, K. (1952), "The Problem of Generations." In P. Keeskemeti (ed.), *Karl Mannheim; Essays*, 276–320. New York: Routledge.

Marcel, G. (1949), *The Philosophy of Existence*. New York: Philosophical Library.

Marcuse, H. (1955), *Eros and Civilization*. Boston: Beacon Press.

Marcuse, H. (1964), *One Dimensional Man*. London: Routledge and Kegan Paul.

Mariategui, J. C. (1971), *Seven Interpretive Essays on Peruvian Reality*. Austin: University Texas Press.

Marti, O. (2009), "Early Critics of Positivism." In S. Muccetelli, O. Schutte, and O. Bueno (eds.), *A Companion to Latin American Philosophy*, 68–81. Hoboken: Wiley- Blackwell.

Martínez Gómez, G. I. (2015), "La filosofía de la educación de Paulo Freire," *Revista Internacional de Educación para la Justicia Social (RIEJS)*, 4(1): 55–70.

Marx, K. (1844), "Estranged Labour," *Economic and Philosophical Manuscripts of 1844*. Retrieved from: https://www.marxists.org/archive/marx/works/1844/ manuscripts/ labour.htm

Marx, K. (1848), *Manifesto of the Communist Party*. Marxist Internet Archive. Retrieved from: https://www.marxists.org/archive/marx/works/1848/communist-manifesto/ch04.htm

Marx, K. (1866), "The First Congress of the International in Geneva." Retrieved from: https://www. marxists.org/reference/archive/bakunin/works/1872/karl-marx.htm

Marx, K. (1871), "Resolution of the London Conference on Working Class Political Action," International Workingmen's Association. Retrieved from: https://www. marxists.org/ archive/marx/works/1871/09/politics-resolution.htm

Marx, K. (1933), *Karl Marx: Selected Works*, vol. I. New York: International Publishers.

Marx, K. (1990), *Capital: Volume I*. New York: Penguin.

Marx, K. (1998), *Communist Manifesto*. London: Merlin Press.

Marx, K. and F. Engels (1848), "Manifesto of the Communist Party." Retrieved from: https://www.marxists.org/archive/marx/works/1848/communist-manifesto/ch02 .htm

Marx, K. and F. Engels (1972), *The German Ideology*. New York: International Publishers.

Marx, K. and F. Engels (1996), *Collected Works: Capital*, vol. 1. New York: International Publishers.

Mayo, P. (2010), *Gramsci and Educational Thought*. New York: John Wiley & Sons.

McInerney, M. and A. McKlindon (2014), "Unlocking the Door to Learning: Trauma Informed Classrooms and Transformation Schools." Retrieved from: https://

www.elc-pa.org/resource/unlocking-the-door-to-learning-trauma-informed-classrooms-and-transformational-schools/

McLaren, P. (1989), *Life in Schools: An Introduction to Critical Pedagogy and the Foundations of Education*. New York: Longman.

McLaren, P. (2000), *Che Guevara and Paulo Freire and the Pedagogy of Revolution*. Lanham: Rowman & Littlefield.

McLaren, P. (2002), "A Legacy of Hope and Struggle: Afterword." In A. Darder (ed.), *Reinventing Paulo Freire: A Pedagogy of Love*. Boulder: Westview, 198–200

McLaren, P. and P. Leonard (1993), *Paulo Freire: A Critical Encounter*. New York: Routledge.

McLennan, G. (1989), *Marxism, Pluralism and Beyond: Classic Debates and New Departures*. Cambridge: Polity Press.

Memmi, A. (1957), *The Colonizer and the Colonized*. Boston: Beacon.

Memmi, A. (1973), "The Impossible Life of Frantz Fanon," *The Massachusetts Review*, 14(1): 9–39.

Memmi, A. (2006), *Decolonization and the Decolonized*. Minneapolis: University of Minnesota Press.

Mignolo, W. (2000), "Dussel's Philosophy of Liberation: Ethics and the Geopolitics of Knowledge." In L. M. Alcoff and E. Mendieta (eds.), *Thinking from the Underside of History*, 27–50. Lanham: Rowman and Littlefield.

Mignolo, W. D. (2007), "Delinking: The Rhetoric of Modernity, the Logic of Coloniality and the Grammar of De-coloniality," *Cultural Studies*, 21(2): 449–514.

Moine, A. (1965), *Cristianos y Marxista despues del Concilio*. Buenos Aires, Argentina: Arandu.

Morrow, R. A. and C. A. Torres (2002), *Reading Freire and Habermas: Critical Pedagogy and Transformative Social Change*. New York: Teachers College Press.

Mounier, E. (1970), *O Personalismo*. Lisboa: Moraes.

Mullaly, B. (2002), *Challenging Oppression: A Critical Social Work Approach*, 232. Ontario: Oxford University Press.

Mullarkey, J. C. (1995), "Bergson's Method of Multiplicity," *Metaphilosophy*, 28(3): 230–59.

Mussett, S. M. and W. S. Wilkerson (2012), *Beauvoir and Western Thought from Plato to Butler*. New York: SUNY Press.

Narcisco, F. A. and K. Neves (2021), "Paulo Freire through the Eyes of Nita Freire: A 100-Year Struggle for Equality and Literacy International Cooperation Office." Retrieved from: https://internationaloffice.usp.br/en/index.php/destaques/paulo-freire-through-the-eyes-of-nita-freire-a-100-year-struggle-for-equality-and-literacy/ (accessed September 20, 2022).

Nicholls, T. (2011), "Pedagogy of the Privileged." *The CLR James Journal*, 17(1): 10–36. JSTOR, www.jstor.org/stable/26758832

Nicolaï, A. (1960), *Comportment Économique et Structures Sociales*. Paris: Presses Universitaire France.

Niebuhr, R. (1960), *Moral Man and Immoral Society: A Study in Ethics and Politics*. New York: Scribner.

Nouwen, H. J. M. (1983), *Gracias: A Latin American Journal*. Maryknoll and New York: Orbis Books.

Nowacek, R. S. and S. M. Mountin (2012), "Reflections in Action: A Signature Ignatian Pedagogy for the 21st Century." In N. L. Chick, Aeron Haynie and Regan R. Gurung (eds.), *Exploring More Signature Pedagogies: Approaches to Teaching Disciplinary Habits of the Mind*, 129–42. Sterling: Stylus Publishing.

Nurullah, S. and J. P. Naik (1943), *History of Education in India*. Bombay: Macmillan & Co.

Ohliger, J. (1995), *Critical Views of Paulo Freire's Work*. Madison: Basic Choices.

Oliveira, P. A. Ribeiro (2007), "'*Libertação*': idéia-força da 'Esquerda Católica'." In L. A. Gpmez de Souza (org.), *Relativismo e transcendência*, 31–45. Rio de Janeiro: EDUSC.

Orbe, M. P. (2009), "Phenomenology." In S. Littlejohn and K. Foss (eds.), *Encyclopedia of Communication Theory*, 749–51. Thousand Oaks: Sage Publications.

Paiva, V. P. (1979), "Sobre a Influência de Mannheim na Pedagogia de P. Freire," *Síntese Politica Econômica Social (SPES)*, 14: 43–64. Retrieved from: http://acervo.paulofreire.org:8080/xmlui/handle/7891/1612

Paiva, V. P. (1980), "Estado, Sociedade e Educação no Brasil," *Encontros com a Civilização Brasileira*, No. 22 (abril).

Paraskeva, J. (2011), *Conflicts in Curriculum Theory*. New York: Palgrave.

Paraskeva, J. (2016), *Curriculum Epistemicide: Toward an Itinerant Curriculum Theory*. New York: Routledge.

Patzi-Paco, F. (2004), *Sistema Comunal. Una Propuesta Alternativa al Sistema Liberal*. La Paz, Bolivia: Comunidad de Estudios Alternativos.

Paul, R. (1993), *Critical Thinking* (3rd ed.). Tomales: Foundation for Critical Thinking.

Peterson, C. F. (2007), *Dubois, Fanon, Cabral: The Margins of Elite Anti-colonial Leadership*. Lanham: Lexington Books.

Petrović, G. (1964), "Why Praxis?" In *Praxis*. Retrieved from: https://www.marxists.org/subject/praxis/issue-01/why-praxis.htm

Petruzzi, A. P. (1998), "Between Conventions and Critical Thinking: The Concept of 'Limit-Situations' in Critical Literacy and Pedagogy," *JAC: Journal of Rhetoric, Culture, and Politics*, 18(2): 309–32.

Petruzzi, A. P. (2001), "Kairotic Rhetoric in Freire's Liberatory Pedagogy," *JAC: Journal of Rhetoric, Culture, and Politics*, 21(2): 350–81.

Pinto, A. V. (1960), *Consciencia e Realidade Nacional*. Rio de Janeiro: MEC/ISEB.

Planas, R. (2014), "Why 'Book Ban' is the Right Term for What Arizona did to Mexican American Studies," *Huntington Post*, September 26. Retrieved from: http://www.huffingtonpost.com/2014/ 09/26/arizona-book-ban_n_5887926.html

Postone, M. (1996), *Time, Labor, and Social Domination*. Cambridge: Cambridge University Press.

Prado, J. C. (1969), *The Colonial Background of Modern Brazil*. Berkeley: University of California Press.

Quijano, A. (2000), "Coloniality of Power, Eurocentrism, and Latin America," *Napantla: Views from the South*, 1(3): 533–80. Retrieved from http://iss.sagepub.com/content/15/2/215.short?rss=1andssource=mfr

Ramirez, M. and A. Castañeda (1974), *Cultural Democracy: Bicognitive Development and Education*. New York: Academic Press.

Rashid, H. (1981), "Early Childhood Education as a Cultural Transition for African-American Children," *Educational Research Quarterly*, 6: 55–63.

Red Horse, J. et al. (1981), "Family Behavior of Urban American Indians." In R. Dana (ed.), *Human Services for Cultural Minorities*. Baltimore: University Park Press.

Reynolds, W. (2013), "Liberation Theology and Paulo Freire: On the Side of the Poor." In R. Lake and T. Kress (eds.), *Paulo Freire's Intellectual Roots*, 127–44. New York: Bloomsbury.

Roberts, P. (2000), *Education, Literacy, and Humanization: Exploring the Work of Paulo Freire*. Westport: Bergin and Garvey.

Roberts, P. (2003), "Knowledge, Dialogue and Humanization: Exploring Freire's Philosophy." In M. Peters, C. Lankshear, and M. Olssen (eds.), *Critical Theory and the Human Condition: Founders and Praxis*, 168–83. New York: Peter Lang.

Rooke, M. (1998), "Commodity Fetishism and Reification," *Common Sense*, No. 23. Retrieved from: https://libcom.org/library/commodity-fetishism-and-reification-mike-rooke

Rosiska, D. O. and P. Domonice (1974), *Freire and Illich: The Pedagogical Debate*. Geneva: IDAC Group. Retrieved from: https://archive.org/details/ ThePedagogyOfTheOppressed-FreireAndIllich

Sabastjan, L. and P. McLaren (2010), "Revolutionary Critical Pedagogy: The Struggle against the Oppression of Neoliberalism—A Conversation with Peter McLaren." In S. L. Macrine, P. McLaren, and D. Hill (eds.), *Revolutionizing Pedagogy: Education for Social Justice Within and Beyond Global Neo-Liberalism*, 87–117. London: Palgrave MacMillan.

Sagarin, E. and R. J. Kelly (1970), "Karl Mannheim and the Sociology of Knowledge," *Salmagundi*, 10/11: 292–302.

Santos, B. de Sousa (2007), "Beyond Abyssal Thinking," *Eurozine*. Retrieved from: http://www. eurozine.com/pdf/2007-06-29-santos-en.pdf

Santos, B. de Sousa (2008), "A filosofia à venda, a douta ignorância e a aposta de Pascal" [Philosophy for sale, learned ignorance and Pascal's wager], *Revista Crítica de Ciências Sociais*, 80. Retrieved from: https://portalrevistas.ucb.br/index.php/RCEUCB/article/view/1714

Santos, B. de Sousa (2014), *Epistemologies of the South: Justice Against Epistemicide*. Boulder: Paradigm.

Sartre, J. (1946), *L'Existentialisme est un humanism*. Paris: Éditions Nagel.

Sartre, J. (1970), "Intentionality: A Fundamental Idea of Husserl's Phenomenology," *Journal of British Society for Phenomenology*, 1(2): 4–5.

Sayer, A. (1999), "Long live Postdisciplinary Studies! Sociology and the Curse of Disciplinary Parochialism/Imperialism," Paper presented to the British Sociological Association Conference. Glasgow (April). Published by the Department of Sociology, Lancaster University.

Schugurensky, D. (2014), *Paulo Freire*. London: Bloomsbury.

Sharpley-Whiting, T. D. (1998), *Frantz Fanon: Conflict and Feminisms*. Oxford: Rowman and Littlefield.

Shaull, R. (1970), Foreword for P. Freire's *Pedagogy of the Oppressed*. New York: Seabury.

Shin, J. (2012), "Althusser's Social Theory: In Light of Overdetermination," Daijin University. Retrieved from: https://www.scribd.com/document/243225206/Shin-Jo-Young-Althusser-s-Social-Theory-In-Light-of-Overdetermination-pdf

Shohamy, E. (2006), *Language Policy*. London: Routledge.

Shohat, E. and R. Stam (2014), *Unthinking Eurocentrism*. New York: Routledge.

Shor, I. and P. Freire (1987), *Pedagogy of Liberation: Dialogues on Transforming Education*. Westport: Greenwood Publishing Group.

Smith, A. (2015), "Between Facts and Myth: Karl Jaspers and the Actuality of the Axial Age," *International Journal of Philosophy and Theology*, 76(4): 315–34.

Smith, N. H. (2008), "Levinas, Habermas and Modernity," *Philosophy and Social Criticism*, 34(6): 643–64.

Solis, A. (1980), "Theory of Biculturality," *Calmecac de Aztlan en Los* 1: 7–12.

Stalin, J. V. (2013), *Dialectical and Historical Materialism*. New York: Prism Key Press.

Stehn, A. (2017), "Latin American Philosophy," *Internet of Encyclopedia of Philosophy*. Retrieved from: http://www.iep.utm.edu/latin-am/

Stern, S. (2009), "Pedagogy of the Oppressor: Another Reason Why U.S. Ed Schools Are So Awful: The On-Going Influence of Brazilian Marxist Paulo Freire," *City*

Journal. Retrieved from: http://www.city-°©-journal.org/2009/19_2_freirian-° ©-pedagogy.html

Stevens, R. (2008), *Sigmund Freud: Examining the Essence of His Contributions*. New York: Palgrave.

Stirk, P. (1992), *Max Horkheimer*. New York: Rowman and Littlefield.

Suchocki, M. (1985), "Theological Education as a Theological Problem III," *Proceedings of the Catholic Theological Society of America*, No. 40. Retrieved from: https://ejournals.bc.edu/ojs/index.php/ctsa/article/view/3295/2908

Sue, S. and D. W. Sue (1978), "Chinese-American Personality and Mental Health," *Amerasia Journal*, 1: 36–49.

Taylor, C. (2012), "What was the Axial Revolution?" In R. Bellah and H. Joas (eds.), *The Axial Age and Its Consequences*, 30–46. Cambridge: Belknap Press.

Teilhard de Chardin, P. (1959), *The Phenomenon of Man*. New York: Harper and Brother.

Thiongo, N. (1986), *Decolonizing the Mind: The Politics of Language in African Literature*. Nairobi: East African Publishers.

Thomas, P. (1996), "Locating Freire in Africa Today: Problems and Possibilities," *African Media Review*, 10(1): 21–30.

Thornhill, C. (2022), "Karl Jaspers," *Stanford Encyclopedia of Philosophy*. Retrieved from: https://plato.stanford.edu/entries/jaspers

Tillich, P. (1951), *Systematic Theology, I*. Chicago: University of Chicago Press.

Tillich, P. (1954), *Love, Power, and Justice*. New York: Oxford University Press.

Tlostanova, M. V. and W. Mignolo (2009), "Global Coloniality and the Decolonial Option," *Kult* 6: Special Issue on Epistemologies of Transformation. Department of Culture and Identity. Roskilde University, 130–47.

Tobin, M. L. (1986), "Women in the Church since Vatican II," *America: The Jesuit Review*. Retrieved from: http://www.americamagazine.org/issue/100/women -church-vatican-ii

Torres, C. A. (1993), "From the Pedagogy of the Oppressed to a Luta Continua: The Political Pedagogy of Paulo Freire." In P. McLaren and P. Leonard (eds.), *Paulo Freire: A Critical Encounter*, 119–45. New York: Routledge.

Torres, C. A. (2014), *First Freire: Early Writing in Social Justice*. New York: Teachers College.

Torres Santomé, J. (2006), *A desmotivação dos professores [The Demotivation of Teachers]*. Mangualde: Pedago.

Torres Santomé, J. (2017), *Políticas educativas y construcción de personalidades neoliberales y neocolonialistas [Educational policies and the construction of neoliberal and neocolonial personalities]*. Madrid: Morata.

Tse-Tung, M. (1964), *Little Red Book*. New York: Free Press.

Tse-Tung, M. (1965), *Selected Works of Mao-Tse-Tung*. Peking: Foreign Languages Press.

Tukdeo, S. (2019), *India Goes to School: Education Policy and Cultural Politics*. New Delhi: Springer.

Valentine C. (1971), "Deficit, Difference, and Bicultural Models of Afro-American Behavior," *Harvard Educational Review*, 41: 137–57.

Van der Kolk, B. A. (2015), *The Body Keeps the Score*. New York: Penguin Books.

Walters, M. (2006), *Feminism: A Very Short Introduction*. Oxford: Oxford University Press.

Warren, S. (1984), *The Emergence of Dialectical Theory*. Chicago: University of Chicago Press. Oxford: Oxford University Press.

Watts, R. J., M. A. Diemer, and A. M. Voight (2011), "Critical Consciousness: Current Status and Future Directions," *New Directions for Child and Adolescent Development*, 2011: 43–57. https:/doi.org/10.1002/cd.310

Weiffert, F. (1967), *Politico e Revolução Social no Brasil*. Rio de Janeiro: Paz e Terra.

Wellington, T. S. (2011), "Esquerda Catolica Brasileira," *Revista Nures*, 8(18): 83–96.

Willette, J. (2013), "Post-colonial Theory (Part One: Historical Context)." In *Key Series: Racism, Racist Ideologies and Capitalism*. Heathwood Institute and Press. Retrieved from: http://www.heathwoodpress.com/post-colonial-theory-historical-context/

Williams, P. (2015), *Operation Gladio: The Unholy Alliance between the Vatican, the CIA and the Mafia*. New York: Prometheus Books.

Windsor, L, A. Jemal, and E. Benoit (2014), "Community Wise: Paving the Way for Empowerment in Community Reentry." *International Journal of Law and Psychiatry*, 37(5): 501–11. doi: 10.1016/j.ijlp.2014.02.023.NIHMS576112

Wolin, R. (2017), "Emmanuel Lévinas. Encyclopedia Britannica." Retrieved from: https://www.britannica.com/biography/Emmanuel-Levinas#ref930024

Woodruff, D. (2007), *Husserl*. London: Routledge.

Wright, R. N. (1953), *The Outsider*. New York: Harper & Row.

Young, I. M. (1988), "Five Faces of Oppression," *The Philosophical Forum*, XIX(4): 270–91.

Zelliot, E. (2013), *AMBEDKAR'S WORLD: THE MAKING OF Babasaheb and the Dalit Movement*. Delhi: Navayana Publications.

Index